श्रीदुर्गासप्तशती

FACETS OF SHRI CHANDI-NAVA DURGA

(Mystic Glory of Devi Mahatmya)

Introduction, Commentary and English Translation

CHAMAN LAL RAINA

Foreword

Nathan Katz

Professor and Chair,
Department of Religious Studies
Florida International University
Miami FL33199 (USA)

SHARADA

SHARADA PUBLISHING HOUSE

Delhi-110 035

2004

First Published : 2004

ISBN : 81-88934-00-3

Published by :
B.L. Bansal
SHARADA PUBLISHING HOUSE
(Publishers on India's Past and Present)
40, Anand Nagar, Inder Lok,
Delhi-110035
Ph. : 23657538

Laser Typesetting by
Creative Graphics
Ph. 22195643

Printed at :
Santosh Offset, Delhi

For the New Generation
who are more inclined to
understand the
Mother Tradition of India
through their intellect
and
For my grand children
Vitasta/Bulbul, Vibhasa/Pihu
and
Rajanak Kalhan

In loving memory of
my sister
UMA

Dedicated
to
my preceptors
RAJANAK NIRANJAN
SIBOO JAGANNATH, ZADOO NANDLAL
who taught me the
NAVARANA BIJAMANTRA

ACKNOWLEDGEMENT

With great regard, I acknowledge the letter of appreciation from my revered teacher Dr. R.K. Sharma, who has always been a guiding force for me to work on Indology and the scriptures from the Kashmir Shakta point of view.

With great love and sincerity I acknowledge that Dr. Nathan Katz, Professor and Chair, Deptt. of Religious Studies, Florida International University USA, has been kind enough for going through the manuscript and for writing the foreword inspite of his busy schedule.

Devrshi Kalanath Shastri, Ex. President, Rajasthan Sanskrit Akademi, deserves my gratitude for writing a detailed Critique on my work.

Shri G.S. Raina, Programme Executive (Drama) TV Centre, Delhi and Sr. Research Fellow, Deptt. of Culture, Govt. of India for coordinating, designing, and getting it composed and printed.

Smt. Sarla Ganjoo of Miami, Florida for going through the type script.

Prof. Aalok Sharma for the drawings of Sarswati & Kali paintings.

Thanks are to my friend publisher Shri B.L. Bansal of Sharada Publishing House, Delhi for taking personal pains in getting the sacred text published.

C.L. RAINA

Department of Students Affairs,

Florida International University,

USA

CONTENTS

FOREWORD

Dr. Chaman Lal Raina is a scholar-adept of the Kashmir Shaktivad tradition, and he has brought his outer and inner training to bear on his lovely translation of and introduction to the Sri Durga Saptashati, the "Mystic Glory of Devi Mahatmyam."

It is well-known that India is alone among the world's ancient civilizations to retain its goddess traditions. What is less well-known is that a highly advanced theology accompanies both popular and yogic approaches to Her. We are most grateful to Dr. Raina, then, for his exposition and lucid translation of an important text.

Dr. Raina is most succinct in describing this wonderful text as "philosophic in theme, mystic in language, ritualistic in approach, and yogic in practice." His multidimensional approach to the text reveals Durga as the Life Urge (Shakti) of the Absolute; as the one who brings protection by spreading Her Divine Apron, Kavacham; and Who manifests herself as the Nine Goddesses (Nava Durga), Who end all evil. All phases of the cycles of the universe—creation, maintenance and dissolution—are attributed to the activities of Devi Durga.

Only one initiated into the practices that lead directly to experience Durga, coupled with rigorous academic training in Sanskrit and the Sanantana Dharma, could make this text come alive, as Dr. Raina has done.

December 25, 2002

NATHAN KATZ
Professor and Chair,
Dept. of Religious Studies
Florida International University
Miami FL 33199
USA

राष्ट्रपति-सम्मानित
देवर्षि कलानाथ शास्त्री
(भूतपूर्व अध्यक्ष, राजस्थान संस्कृत अकादमी एवं निदेशक, संस्कृत शिक्षा एवं भाषा विभाग, राजस्थान सरकार)
प्रधान सम्पादक "भारती" संस्कृत मासिक

Devarshi Kalanath Shastri
Ex-Chairman, Rajasthan Sanskrit Academy, Former Director of Sanskrit Education and Bhasha Vibhag, Govt. of Rajasthan
Chairman, Manju Nath Smriti Sansthan and Chief Editor, "Bharati" Sanskrit Monthly

A CRITIQUE

I am delighted to learn that Dr. C.L. Raina who is well-versed in the tradition of Shaivism and the Shakta cult has completed the English translation of the sacred text of the Durga Saptashati along with its accessory texts and directives of performances. It is well known that thirteen chapters of the Markandeya Purana (called Adhyayas) containing the sacred lore of the Shakti assuming the name of Durga have assumed a sacrosanct role as they form the narrative base of the Shakta cult. These chapters have 700 verses which have earned themselves the title of Sapta Shati. Over centuries this Sapta Shati is being chanted by the devout Tantrikas and Shaktas as sacred Mantras in the months of Ashvin and Chaitra of the Hindu Calendar. This has given it an additional significance which obviously has inspired Dr. Raina to take up the translation of this Scripture.

Translating a scripture containing Stotras, Invocation, Mantras and laconic salutations is not everybody's cup of tea. It requires deep understanding of the original and the source language, complete mastership of the target language and a practice of discreet word selection which Dr. Raina possesses very well. And then, the Durga Saptashati while being put into Tantrik Practice requires chanting of the Kavacha, Argala, Keelak and Kunjika, also the Navarna Mantra. In the advanced stages of performance, the Tantrikas Chant three Rahasyas or the mysteries, also the "Aparadha Kshamapana" (apology) composed by the Shankaracharya. It is a known fact that the symbolism underlying the esoteric practices and performances of sacrifices etc. has been kept secret by the devout scholars over the centuries and has by now become characteristic of the oft-quoted phrase "a riddle wrapped in enigma inside a mystery." The symbology of an edifice or a fortress, a well-guarded structure and the words Kavach, Argala, Keelak etc. are expressive of the same mysterious characteristic.

It is gratifying to note that Dr. Raina has translated all these accessory texts (Kavach, Argala, Keelak, three Rahasyas, the Aparadha-Kshamapana Stotra) into English in a lucid style and a language intelligible even to a layman. He has translated and explained vividly the methodology of the Tantrik performances and also the symbolic significance of various Tantrik practices. He has explained the meaning, the symbolism and the objective of various Mantras, Sankalpas, salutations etc. in simple English, thus making the whole corpus of the Sapta Shati and its accessories accessible to the readers in English. It is a pleasure to see that Shri Raina has projected very well the spirit of narrative ease of the Puranic style in the main text and has explained the mysteries of the Tantrik cult according to the tradition of Kashmir Shaivism clearly in the accessory texts, instructional portions, Rahasyas etc.

The introduction in which Dr. Raina explains the background and the objective of the Sapta Shati Patha and the allied Tantrik practices accompanying the Durga Patha is of immense value since he has taken pains to acquaint the reader with the intent and meaning of different practices according to the Kashmir Shaivism and the Shakta cult prevalent in Kashmir. Dr. Raina has a deep erudition of the Tantrik texts and a long experience of Tantrik performances. It goes without saying that with the changing times and cruel turns of circumstances such scholarship and such traditions are disappearing fast and may be extinct soon. It is only such efforts of scholars like Dr. C.L. Raina which can give some understanding of the centuries-long traditions of lauding culture to the uninitiated readers through the medium of English language. Dr. Raina has appended a glossary of technical textual and Tantrik terms in the end with a view to apprising the reader of the meaning and purpose of these terms. I hope this glossary will help the uninitiated reader also to delve deep into the mysteries of Tantrik worship.

I congratulate Dr. Raina for having bequeathed the new generation with the understanding of this Tantrik Tradition by translating into English the Principal text of the Shakta Puranic cult. I have no manner of doubt that with the English translation of the entire text and its accessories and the introduction forming a knowledgeable backdrop to the scriptures and delineating its significance the present work will be received by a large clientele of inquisitive readers and also scholars in India and abroad with wide acclaim and a sense of gratitude to the translater which Dr. C.L. Raina richly deserves.

Devarshi Kalanath Shastri

C/8 Prithvi Raj Road,
Jaipur (Rajasthan)
Pin 302001 (India)
Dated : April 9, 2003

INSPIRATION

With all humility, I express that I was inspired by my saintly mother SHOBHA to recite some of the Argala Mantras for my spiritual awakening. I would do recitation during my evening prayers with her since I started learning the Bija mantra in the year 1946. Later, I started the reading of the Shakta scriptures under the guidance of my traditionalist Shakta teacher who was none-else but my revered father Rajnak Niranjan (Pt. Niranjan Nath Raina). Since we come from the traditional Shakta School of Kashmir of the 'Kadi' vidya, so the atmosphere in which I grew up in our home was the *Patha* and *Homa* of Shri Chandi-Durga Sapta Shati. This took me decades together to understand the procedure of the *Homa* from its philosophic and spiritual point of view. Because of my life-partner Smt. Jaya Siboo, I was inspired to write a detailed philosophic interpretation and literal but lucid translation of the text of Sri Chandi.

I acknowledge that I have been greatly influenced by the discourses listened to by me from my father-in-law Pt. Jagannath Siboo, who performed about a hundred *Homas* for my understanding and for practical knowledge of performing the *Nyasas; Sankalpam* and of *Tarpanam* followed by *Homa* and *Vaishvadevam* and *Prarthana*.

I also acknowledge the guidance which I received form my Vidya Guru Pt. Nandlal Zadoo, who taught me geometry for the graphics of the Chandi Yantra. My father also taught and initiated me in the *Chandi Chakra Pooja Vidhan*, according to the Kashmir School of thought in the later years of his life, from 1990-99 A.D., at Ajmer, during our enforced exodous, due to militancy, from Kashmir.

The tradition has come to our family from Rajanak Siddha Koot followed by Rajnak Divya Koot, Rajanak Bhuvana Koot, Rajanak Raj Koot, Rajanak Amar Koot to Rajanak Niranjan and to me, which I hope will be continued by Abhinav, Rakesh and Rajanak Kalhan.

For writing the philosophic treatise of this scared text, I have gained the treasure of ritualistic knowledge from various books pertaining to the Shakti traditions which my father had learnt from Pt. Lassa Dutta and Pt. Hara Dutta and from her grand-mother Smt. Padman Ded who was born in the Dutta family of Zaindar-Mohalla, Srinagar, Kashmir in 1847 A.D.

I have consulted Sharda manuscript of Durga Sapta Shati written by Pt. Lasa Dutta, Durga Sapta Shati published by the Gita Press Gorakhpur, India and Durga Archana Sratih for comparing the text of Shri Durga Sapta Shati, to arrive at the correct recension of the text.

(C.L.R.)

CHAKRA AND BIJAMANTRA

Shri Chandi is verily, the *Bijam*-primal seed or Primal cause of the Universe of our perception. She is the Mother Creatrix. She is Supreme Sovereign Mother, who controls the Universe through Her triadic nature of Shri Mahakali Mahalakshmi, Mahasarasvati. She holds the Bhava Chakra/ the cycle of transmigration. She is all blessing Mother, who makes the embodied souls to come in Her lap through *Sadhana* and *Bhakti*. She is all infinity. She is in the state of truth, consciousness and bliss She is verily, *Mahamaya*.

Bhakti and *Sadhana* lead us to the *Samvit Shakti* of Mahamaya. She alone exists. She is the uniformity of *Ichcha*, *Jnana* and *Kriya*. It is because of Her continuous flow of eternity that the Divine descent is realised. She is the very nature of Ascent from *Bindu* to the *Ashtadalam*-eight petalled lotus around the circle, in which hexagon finds its formation. This is known as the *Shri Chandi Yantra/Chakra*.

The *Chakra* has to be drawn or written with *kumkum-agru* and *Chandan*. The *Adya-Bijam* or Primal Seeds of the *Navarana Mantra* of **Shri Mahakali-Mahalakshmi-Mahasarasvati** are the seed and sound forms of the universal consciousness. In the *Madhya Bijam*, the Mahalakshmi abides which is verily, the *Hrim*. In the right side abides Mahakali which is the *Klim* and in the left abides Mahasarasvati which is in the form of the *Aim*. The rest of the Bijas/seeds of *Cha, Mun, Dā, Yai, Vi, Chchai* are manifest in this Yantra from the east to west.

The Bija-Mantras are the divine pulsations, frequencies, manifestations to keep the Universe in harmony and equipoise. These are the very sources of Vibrations which make the *Tridevas-Brahma, Vishnu, Maheshvra* assume the Name and Form for creation, sustenance and dissolution along with their Shaktis which are *Brahmi, Vaishnavi* and *Maheshvari.*

Mahamaya is the very innate flux of Durga Sapta Shati, the unified power of *Prakasha* and *Vimarsha;* of *Purusha* and *Prakrati.* The world is to be understood, to be seen and to be realised, the mystry of the world to be known through the *Lila* or play of Mahamaya. It is because of Her Lila that human beings are seen involved in *Bhoga* and the very few blessed are after *Yoga.* Bhoga is to enjoy the world through actions which ultimately become the cause of rebirth like that of king *Suratha.* The Yoga in itself is the love for *Mahamaya.* She is to be realised and seen through inference, perception, verbal testimony and intuition.

Mahamaya declares, "Whenever the *Asuric*-demoniac forces are on the rise and are bent upon harming and destroying the virtuous people, then I assume Forms for Protecting the virtues of sages and for destroying the hostile demoniac forces."

She again affirms with authority : "I alone exist in the universe. None except me excels in the Universe. All are my Vibhutis/manifestations which again merge with me alone."

The same spirit of Mahamaya is to be seen in our lives, so that we may be able to understand the emotive power that drive us to our own source which is Mahamaya herself. She is always and everywhere with us. This attitude will help the readers of the Durga Sapta Shati to understand the religio-philosophic meanings of this great Shakta scripture in respect of Chakra and Bija mantra revered by all.

Om Shantih Santih Santih

Om Peace, Peace, Peace

GHATARGALA YANTRM

घटार्गलयन्त्रम्।।

शारदायां नवमपटले।।

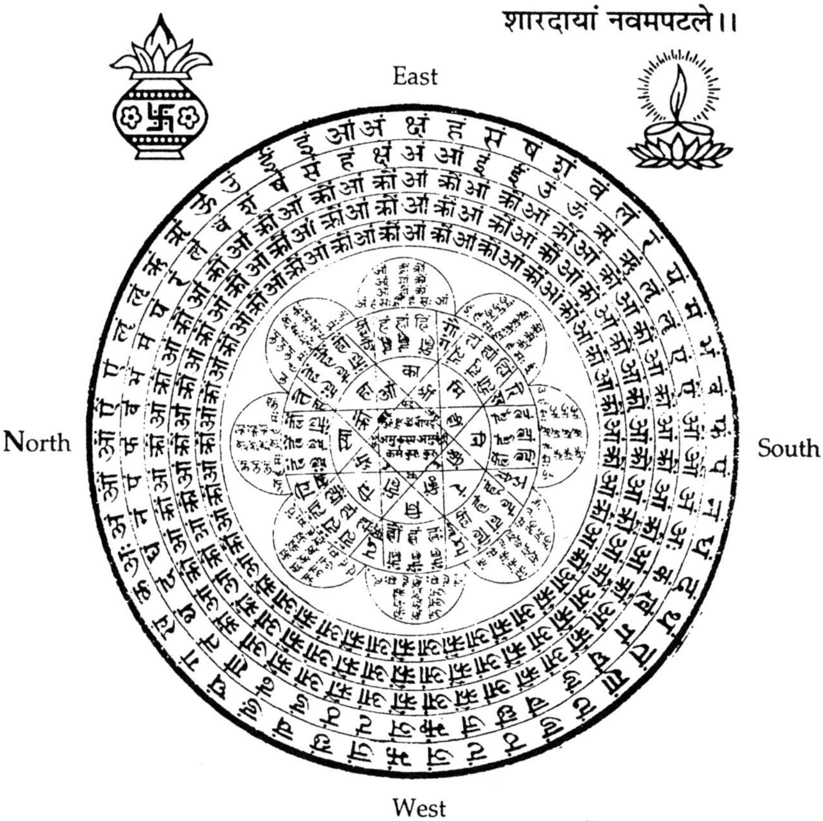

बिन्दु त्रिकोणषट्कोण अष्टदल षड्विंशतिदल भूपुरयुतं यंत्रं विलिख्य

वा

बिन्दु त्रिकोण वृत्त चतुरस्त्रंलिखेत्

Yantra is to be drawn in the design of the dot, triangle, eight petalls, twenty six petalls and Bhupur or to be drawn in the design of dot, triangle, Circle and Squre.

चण्डीयन्त्रम्

CHANDI YANTRAM

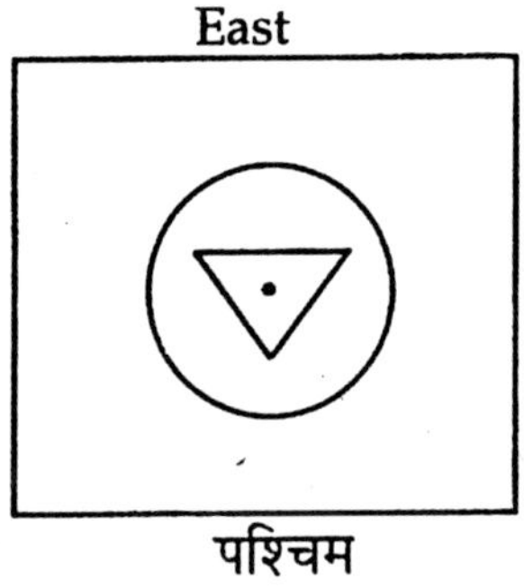

अथ पूजा यन्त्रं

लिखेदष्टदलं पद्मं कुंकुमागुरुचन्दनैः पद्ममध्यै लिखेच्चैव षट्कोणं चण्डिकामयं। षट्कोण चक्र मध्यस्थं आद्य बीजत्रयं न्यसेत् मध्यबीचे महालक्ष्मीः तदक्षिणे महाकाली वामेसरस्वती पूर्वादि षट्कोणेषु बीजान्यऽन्यानि न्यसेत्।

The Eight Petalled Lotus is to be written with *Kumkum-Agru-Chandanam*. The Hexagonal figure of *Chandika* is in the centre of the lotus. Three *Adibijam*—the three Primal seeds ऐं ह्रीं क्लीं/ *Aim-Hrim-Klim* should be written or placed in the central hexagonal Chakra. *Hrim* is *Mahalakshmi* which is in the centre. *Aim* is Mahakali which is on the right side. *Mahasarswati* is klim which occupies the left side. The other Bija mantra चा मुं डा यै वि च्चै/ *Cha Mun Da Yai Vi Chchai* is to be written in the reversed order starting from the eastern direction.

LIST OF ILLUSTRATION

पूजा यन्त्र (Puja Yantra)

ॐ बालार्कमण्लाभासां च्तुर्बाहुं त्रिलोचनाम्।

पाशाङ्कुशवराभीतीर्धायन्तीं शिवां भजे।।

2. श्री महाकाली (Shri Maha Kali)

मुण्डमालाधरां देवीं ललज्जिह्वां दिगम्बराम्।
एवं सञ्चिन्तयेत् काली श्मशानालयवासिनीम्।।

श्री महालक्ष्मी (Shri Maha Lakshmi)

तामग्निवर्णां तपसा ज्वलन्तीं वैरोचनीं कर्म फलेषु जुष्टाम।

दुर्गा देवीं शरणं प्रपद्यामहेऽसुरान्नाशयित्र्यै ते नमः।।

श्री महासरस्वती (Shri Maha Saraswati)

नमो देवि महाविद्ये नमामि चरणौ तव।

सर्वज्ञानप्रकाशं मे देहि सर्वार्थदे शिवे।।

5. कृति (Creativity)

प्रकृष्टवाचकः प्रश्च कृतिश्च सृष्टिवाचकः।

सृष्टौ प्रकृष्टा या देवी प्रकृतिः सा प्रकीर्तिता।।

6. परा प्रकृति (Transcendence/Primordial Nature)

आदित्यो ह वै प्राणो रविरैव चन्द्रमा रयिर्वा।
एतत्सर्वं यन्मूर्त्तञ्च तस्मान्मूर्तिवेव रयिः।।

मण्डलाकार (Mandalakara)

अखण्डमण्डलाकारं व्याप्तं येन चराचरम्।

तत्पदं दर्शितं येन तस्मै श्री गुरुवे नमः।।

शिवशक्ति-एकरूपिणी (Shiv-Shakti in Unison)

हिरण्यगर्भः समवर्त्तताग्रे भूतस्य जातः पतिरेक आसीत्।
स दाधार पृथिवीं द्यामुतेमां कस्मै देवाय हविषा विद्येम।।

9. अष्टदल कमल (Ashtadala / Eight Petalled Lotus)

ह्लादिनी सन्धिनी संवित् त्वय्येका सर्वसंश्रये।
ह्लादतापकरी मिश्रा त्वपि नो गुणवर्जिते।।

10. शक्ति अधिपति (The Energetic Effulgence)

शक्तिशक्तिमदुत्थं हि शाक्तं शैवमिदं जगत्।
नमस्तस्यै नमस्तस्यै नमस्ताभ्यां नमो नमः।।

मूल त्रिकोण (The Primal Triangle)

नभसः शीर्षद्वारा प्रवहन्तीं य इह विग्रहे शक्तिम्।
अनुसन्दधाति नित्यं कृतिनस्तस्येतरैरलं योगैः।।

संवित् शक्ति (Energy of Consciousness)

मायां तु प्रकृतिं विद्यान्मायिनं तु महेश्वरम्।
तस्यावयव भूतैस्तु व्याप्तं सर्वमिदं जगत्।।

13. आरोहण (The Ascent)

मन्त्राणां मातृका देवी शब्दानां ज्ञानरूपिणी।

ज्ञानानां चिन्मयातीता शून्यानां शून्यसाक्षिणी।।

14. अवरोहण (The Descent)

ततः शून्या परारूपा श्रीमहासुन्दरी कला।
सुन्दरी राजराजेशी महाब्रह्माण्ड नायिका।।

अभीप्सा (The Aspiration)

विष्णुशक्तिः परा प्रोक्ता क्षेत्रज्ञाख्या तथा परा।
अविद्या कर्मसंज्ञान्या तृतीया शक्तिरिठ्यते।।

INTRODUCTION

Ancient Indian wisdom is a variegated fabric of many coloured threads of spiritual beauty. It has woven a crown on the forehead of Aryavarta (Bharat). It is that wisdom which has visualised harmony in diverse shades and colours. The spirit of unity which has been inferred from or perceived by the men of spiritual merit was on the analysis, investigations of the bio-physical world. They wanted to see the global unity within the vast expanse of the universe. The analysts and investigators who undertook these investigations were known as Rishis. These Rishis worked hard to realise the Truth about the Supreme reality vis-a-vis man and universe. They studied nature with respect to environment, ecology, atmosphere, time, space, oceanography etc. to arrive at the Truth. These investigations were bio-physical in nature and spiritual in content to know the problem of man, with respect to God and universe.

The **Devi Artharva Shirsha** says—

अहं ब्रह्मस्वरूपिणी। मत: प्रकृति पुरुषात्मकं जगत्।
शून्यं चाशून्यं च।।

These Rishis were the preservers of Indian wisdom in succession, who passed the higher truth from one generation to another in the form of 'Mantras', found in the *Rik, Yajur, Sama* and *Atharva Veda.* They formed their own Ashramas—hermitages under the banner of Tapovanam. It was a place of *Sadhana.* Whatever they realised or achieved after great penances in the *Tapovanas* through intuition is known as *Shruti*—the revealed knowledge. Shruti and the Vedas are synonyms. The word Veda is derived from the root *'vid'* which means to know the truth with sound mind and sound body about the absolute Reality. It is the guidance revealed by a celebrated preceptor who could be a scientist, environmentalist, agronomist, mathematician and above all the knower of 'spirit'. All these were based on intellect but were answered through intuition and *'Sadhana'*. It helped the Rishis to achieve the goal of human life, which is 'Moksha'-the final liberation. Verily, it is a state of bliss, filled with the supreme realisation of the absolute.

The Vedas have been acclaimed as the formost source of knowledge in the library of mankind. This higher revelation has remained a source of inspiration for spiritual and scientific approach to know the truth on the basis of inference, perception, verbal testimony and intuition. The intuition has helped the Rishis to be one with the *Mantra* for higher understanding and realisation of the spirit.

These have been the teachings which were later explained in the *Agamas* particularly in the Shakta literature and Shakta doctrine. They are primarily concerned with fundamental principles of the physical world around the man who is but the particle of the Divine, in this mystic universe. In short, an inquisitive mind endeavours to know about the human creation, involution, evolution, death and life after death.

The *Durga-Sapta-Shati* is a portion but the integral part of the *Markandeya Purana*, known as *Shri Chandi*. In the *'Sapta-Shati'*, we are concerned with life processes of the integration of One and the many, of matter and spirit, of the physical and cosmic world, under the serious investigations of *Medha Rishi* and later explained by him to *Suratha*—the king and *Samadhi*—the Vaishya. They meditated upon the Truth in the Tapovanam for three years, wearing the apron of *'Kavacham'* in their psycho-physical laboratories of their inner beings, i.e., *'Atman'*. They had the perception and intuition both and finally they realised the *'Bijaksharas'*— Immutable seed and sound theory of the Absolute through the theory of the hymns to creation of the universe, which is 'Para-Prakriti'. It is verily, that Primordial energy which is known as *Mahamaya Chandi*. The *'Bija'* as well as *'Shabada'* stand for the clear analysis of being in harmony with the Mother creatrix, in the *Shakti* worship. This is an affirmation that *'Hiranyagarbha'* is the primal cause and effect from which the creation has come into existence. It never dies or decays. It changes for the better shape which is verily, known as *Arohan* or ascent to the higher realms of life. Transformations do take place which create the new worlds, based on the theory of cause and effect.

The Sapta-Shati is an answer to all such questions which evolves us spiritually to know the mystery of this mystic world. It is an interpretation of scientific approach through the *'Kavacham, Argala* and *Kilkam'*. It is the *'Sadhana Shastra'*— scripture of high merit which evolves our inner recesses of heart to know that is within the *'Muladhara Chakra'* which further moves towards the higher realms of the *'Sahasra-ara Chakra'*. The *'Sapta-Shati'* is an integral view of the 'Markandeya Purana' filled with the vibrations of 'Para Shakti', having the phonemes of eternal spirit. This *Shabda-Sharira* which is the immutable sound body of 700 Shlokas, is preceeded by the *'Kavacham, Argala, Kilkam'* — *Nyasas, Ratrisukta,* and *Navarna-mantra* to be undertaken within the parameters of Bhakti—devotional surrender under the instructions of a competent *Guru*/preceptor.

The Sapta-Shati is the vision and the boon which gives us a silence of the 'Void' linked in the grasp of an unspoken joy and bliss. Man is too weak to bear the infinite weight within *annamaya kosha*- the physical sheath for ascending to *Anandmaya-kosha,* the blissful sheath. Verily, the human psyche is so intricate that *Medha Rishi* has to define the Truth about Mahamaya through the genetic symbols and progression systems. This is an anthem of eternal beauty to realise the beatitude within the frame work of *Nava-Durga Puja.*

Nava-Durga is a journey to consciousness from the Divine concept of *Shailaputri* to *Siddhidhatri*, spoken by Lord Brahma for human integration and higher Yoga. Brahma is the *Adi Rishi*, who worshipped the *Yoga Nidra* of Bhagavan Narayana, when *Madhu* and *Kaitabha Asuras*/anti-divine forces sprung up from the ear-wax of Vishnu to kill Brahma, born from the *Nabhi-Kamala* of Vishnu, which is the navel-lotus for creativity. What Lord Brahma spoke while getting frightened is the eternal voice known as the *Ratri-Sukta*. *Mahamaya* is the Supreme energy, which manifests in the various Names and Forms, is the primal realisation of Lord Brahma. Three Devis are *Mahakali, Mahalakshmi* and *Mahasarasvati*, and these are the triple facets of Mahamaya, which give us strength and energy to focus our devotion on *Para-prakriti, Moola-Prakriti* and *Pranava*.

Sri Aurobindo says :

A pure existence safe from thought and mood.
A consciousness of unshared immortal bliss,
It dwelt aloof in its bare infinite,
One and unique, unutterably sole.
A Being formless, featureless and mute
That knew itself by its own timeless self,
Aware for ever in its motionless depths,
Uncreating, uncreated and unborn,
The one by whom all live, who lives by none,
An immeasurable luminous secrecy
Guarded by the veils of the Unmanifest,
Above the changing cosmic interlude
Abode supreme, immutably the same,
A silent Cause occult, impenetrable,
Infinite, eternal, unthinkable, alone.

(Savitri-III.i)

Mahamaya

Mother creatrix is the primordial energy and is revered as Shakti by the followers of Shakti cult. Every object that we see or perceive, understand or recognise around or within ourselves is the great power of Mahamaya. Every *Astika* believes in Shakti as a power of absolute, according to the level of spiritual realization. Shakti is known as *Muda-prakriti*—the dormant nature, *Mula-prakriti*—the primordial nature, *Adya-Shakti*—the primal energy, *Vidya*—the spiritual knowledge and such like attributes and names. The *Shasranamas,* sing the glory of Mahamaya, with thousand attributes and throw light on the *Vimarsha,* which is subjective and inner faculty as the human nature differs according to the tendencies of the *Sattva, rajas* and *tamas,* but *Prakasha* is purely objective, which is Shiva-consciouss. Nature of the Universe can be understood on the basis of *Prakasha* and *Vimarsha.* The *Sahasranamas* which are filled with Prakasha and Vimarsha are studied on the ritualistic pattern of *Homa, Parayanam* and *Japam* or with a philosophic approach to understand the cosmic truth about Mahamaya. *Sahasranamas* are the thousand attributes of Divinity, but the Durga Sapta Shati is the Mantrik composition of 700 Shlokas like that of Shrimad Bhagavadgita.

Para-Shakti in Her infinite attitude has thrown all the doors open to go through *Bhakti,* as She is known as *Bhakti-gamya.* She is attainable through devotion and dedication. She is verily, *Mahakali, Mahalakshmi* and *Mahasarasvati,* as being the triadic power bearing the garland of the *Navarna-mantra.* Mahamaya is agreedly a force behind all human and divine consciousness. This is an aspect of eternity. She is *Vidya-Avidya-Paravidya-Aparavidya* and beyond that. She is the door way of this mystic world. Her spiritual vibrations can be seen through the *Shakta Yoga.* This greatness and sweetness can be attained through her bliss. It is through *Sadhana* and *Tapasya* that Devi comes closer to us and gives us the emotive love of motherhood. She is always present in the recesses of our heart.

It has been said that he who detaches himself from the dualities of name and form associated with the inherent qualities of sense perceptions, acquires a power. It can be in tune and harmony with the *Vidya* aspect of *Mahamaya*. It may be classified as a meditating system in the *Shakta Yoga*. In this system, there is goal of evolution through involution. The triadic face of the absolute gives us ample choice for exercising the free will to know her real nature. Here lies a vast beauty in the Shakti worship, where the Sadhaka can maintain the individuality to chose the path of *Yoga* or *Bhoga*. The experience gained by the Sadhaka is upward looking, and outword seeing. The true realisation lies when he sees his inner being in the lap of Mother-creatrix or at the feet of Supreme sovereign, who is Maheshvari. She regulates the pulsation of cause and effect, to make the cosmic force work according to the law of nature or Primordial energy.

All things which move and change, derive their significance from their relation to the single truth of eternity. Mahamaya says in the Sapta-shati : "*I alone exist.* I am the sole reality". Reality is subjective, objective and abstract in the Shakta tradition. These are but the facets of the Absolute. It is transcendental in spirit and immanent in approach. Shakti is the goal of Sadhaka to see it, touch it, feel it, taste it and above all realise it through the *Annamaya-pranamaya-manomaya-vijnanaya* and *anandmaya Kosha'*. No part of the human anatomy is to be ignored or shunned as She abides in every nerve and cell of human being. It may seem complex to realise the Shakti aspect in every action but Shakti exists as a source of strength and health, both physical and mental. The Ratri-sukta is the source of energy, a power, a strength and above all the psycho-physical capacity to cope with the deadly situation in life. A life process is seen in Shakti, which is immanent and transcendent both.

The grace of Mahamaya is a fateful event in the being of Brahma-born of Vishnu's naval, when he had to cry for the life survival as the death in person was faced by him. It was created by the terror of Madhu and Kaitabha—the two Asuras. The Lord of creation wanted to escape the wrath of two ferrocious Asuras. He prayed the *Yoga nidra* in the mystic sleep of Bhagavan Vishnu to come to his help and kill those two powerful Asuras born from the ear-wax of Bhagavan Vishnu. Mysterious are the ways of Mahamaya, as is clear that Brahma-the creator could not contain the wrath of Madhu and Kaitabha. Why so? Death is no welcome to anyone, from Jiva-the embodied soul to Brahma-the creator. It is a cessation of life. Death is mortality.

Vedic Rishis therefore, pray for immortality :

मृत्योर्माऽमृतं गमय

'Mritur ma-amritam gamaya'/Lead me-from death to immortality.

Why should a living being die? Why he loses his coherence, regularity and orderliness? Why a sense of attachment is found with children, wife and the material wealth? We have the answer of all such types of questions in the Sapta-shati. Every human being is either a Suratha or a Samadhi, who is psychologically depressed, physically oppressed and spiritually lost in this *Samsara*—the bonded world. *Mahamaya* is ever gracious to awaken Her Shakti to one and all who seek Her help and pray for grace. She lifts them up by giving them the company of sages and seers. The men of spiritual understanding come to help and bestow grace to the devotee through the commands of Mahamaya. Medha Rishi is such an elevated Rishi, who analyses the Truth and goes deep into psycho-physical behaviour of Jivas—the embodied souls. He is more concerned about the mental state of human beings, who suffer from depression and torture, stress and strain.

The basic principle of energy lies in the growth of *Jivatman*. It is an instrument to get evolved from the earthly existence to the higher dawn of life alone. Para-shakti is Divine essence in the fundamental principle of energy. 'Her passionate influence is a changeless law'—says the Sapta-shati, 'when She grants the lease of life to *Danvas*—the anti divine forces in the battle field where She plays the role of *Katyayani.*' This world of ours is wonderful planet thrilled with the beauty and charm of senses which make us move towards *Bhogha* or enjoyment. But this world is equally suggested for the realisation of Yoga or supreme perfection. Hence the *Pravratti* and *Nivratti* are the two ways of cling to Her lofty self around our human aspiration. Verily, those are the two opposite directions which reflect the human actions caught in the whirlpool of *Samsara*—the earthly existence.

This world of immanance is the 'Iccha shakti' of Mahamaya. This is not mere static awareness but total consciousness with a force of its own 'Chit shakti'. It is a divine puissance, which is infinite in nature and eternal in substance. The only way to realise the 'Chit shakti' is to identify one's own spirit with eternal consciousness. The devotee makes a prayer in the Sapta-shati :

इन्द्रियाणामधिष्ठात्री भूतानां चाखिलेषु या।
भूतेषु सततं तस्यै व्याप्तिदेव्यै नमो नमः।।
चितिरूपेण या कृत्स्नमेतद् व्याप्य स्थिता जगत्।
नमस्तस्यै।। नमस्तस्यै।। नमस्तस्यै नमो नमः।।

5, 77–80

The *Shloka* says that Mahamaya abides in the form of conciousness. She pervades the entire world. She is to be adored again and again. Through the power of consciousness, Mahamaya dispells ignorance dwelling in all sentient beings through *'Chit shakti'*, which is pure intelligence. *Chit* and *Chetana* are identieal but it is immediate awareness of *Ahami*—consciousness of spiritual existence, which is *Soham* or *Hamsa*. This happens when *Chit* is qualified by *Shakti. Chit* is dominanted by *Chit shakti* but conditioned by mind because it is the small part of that *Chidakash* or gross energy manifest in the embodied soul by *Chit shakti*. It is the subtle energy of the divine. Verily, the role of Mahamaya is inherent in every action. Action binds the *Jivas*—the embodied souls even if a person be a *Jnani* man with knowledge and realisation. Medha Rishi explains to Suratha Raja and Samadhi Vaishya about the influence of Mahamaya, when they both approach him in his hermitage after they were thrown away by their own kith and kin.

Verily, Durga is the **One** and only Mahamaya, who forcibly draws the minds of even Jnanis and throws them in *Moha*-the delusion. Mahamaya is One and only One, who knows that All is She. She is the spirit of universal personality, One with the universal Self and Absolute reality.

Thus Rishi says :

ज्ञानिनामपि चेतांसि देवी भगवती हि सा।
बलादाकृष्य मोहाय महामाया प्रयच्छति।।

The Sapta-Shati makes the stress on the Supreme Will of the divine, as desire is the basis of all actions. The embodied soul cannot avert the force behind action but a man with strong *Iccha shakti* must abandon the fruits of every action. Actions are three-fold viz., *Sattavic-rajasic-tamasic* in this cosmic behaviour. We cannot renounce the actions but a *Sadhaka* has the capacity to abandon the fruits of action. All the *Ashta-siddhis* go before the *Sadhaka* but a true *Sadhaka* does not allow the *Ashta-siddhis* to be dominant in the *Sadhana*. These are but temptations, temporary in nature and fall in the category of small ego or *Ahamakara*.

A true and genuine *Sadhaka* has to be in tune with timelessness and to be in *Sayujya*—one with Mahamaya, one with the great Supreme Mother who is known as *Adya-shakti*. Mahamaya descends to beat out the sparks of *Avidya*, on the psycho-spiritual plane. It is to be dealt with great wisdom, intellect and understanding, while being in the psycho-physical plane of consciousness. The Saptashati says :

या देवी सर्वभूतेषु बुद्धिरूपेण संस्थिता।
नमस्तस्यै।। नमस्तस्यै।। नमस्तस्यै।। नमो नमः।।

5, 20–22

"May we bow to that Supreme Devi who abides in the Jivatman in the form of *Buddhi*—the intellect. All intellectual processes must be surrendered at the feet of Mahamaya. Action if taken in impersonal way, will maintain the law of *Karma* in harmony. Actions done for the personal material gain, will only lead to *Rajas* and *Tamas* state of life. Actions of Trinity are also subservient to the free-will of Mahamaya. The cosmic principle of life is seen in the manifestation of *Brahma* who is associated with *Sarasvati; Vishnu* with *Lakshmi; Rudra* with *Gauri*. Thus *Brahmi Shakti, Vaishnavi Shakti* and *Raudri Shakti* are the integral aspects of the same reality which has created the Trinity to perform their respective roles and functions. Mahamaya has conditioned the Trinity in time and space but the sovereignty lies in Devi's free-will.

The Divine Mother abides in the *Shabda-Brahman*. It is that casual sound, out of which all the triadic function ensue. Mahamaya is verily, the inner consciousness and the whole Universe manifests through Her. Everything lies in Her eternal womb in the form of seed. She is the seed-syllable of the *Brahmanda* with the instrumental cause having spontaneous vibrations. Seed is Her primal substance filled with the universal potency and syllable is thrilled with the power of opening the Yogic channel. Her Bijakshara is the matrix of *Shabda* which is the dynamis of life. Seed syllable is the bliss to be flowered through the process of Sadhana at the feet of the Supreme Mother Mahamaya.

PUJA PADDHATI

Mode of Worship & Rectial

Preliminaries

The Sapta-Shati is the sacred text of *Mahamaya,* known as *Shri Chandi* in the popular language and diction. Some observations are to be strictly adhered to in the worship of *Mahamaya.* One has to go through *Snana*—taking a bath, *Achmana*—taking a sip of fresh water, *Pranayama*—breath control, *Sankalpa*—resolve to perform the worship, *Prarthana*—making an obeisance, *Asana*—sitting at the right place, *Bhutapasarpana*—purifying the five elements, *Bhutashuddhi*—cleaning the objects, *Pranapratishtha*—infusing the vital force, *Dipsthapan*—keeping the *Dipak*—lamp at the proper place, *Shapoddhara*—lifting the curse and *Utkilana*—to remove the nailing through *Mantras.* These are the essentials of the *Sapta Shati Patham/Homa.*

(i) The following four Mantras are to be recited after *Achamana*—the sips of water (taking a bath, sipping the pure water, holding of breath, commitment, worship, sitting posture):

Aum is the *Vedic* and *Aim* is *Shakta Pranava.*

ॐ ऐं आत्मतत्त्वं शोधयामि नमः स्वाहा।

Aum-Aim-Atama tattavam Shodhayami Namah Svaha.

ॐ ह्रीं विद्यातत्त्वं शोधयामि नमः स्वाहा।।

Aum-Hrim-Vidya tattavam Shodhayami Namah Svaha.

ॐ क्लीं शिवतत्त्वं शोधयामि नमः स्वाहा।

Aum-Klim-Shiva tattavam Shodhayami Namah Svaha.

ॐ ऐं ह्रीं क्लीं सर्वतत्त्वं शोधयामि नमः स्वाहा।।

Aum-Aim-Hrim-Klim Sarva tattavam Shodhayami Namah Svaha.

a. *Aum-Aim,* I am purifying and conducting the self constituent of Macro in myself. *Svaha* to it!

b. Aum-Aim, I am purifying and conducting the knowledge constituent in myself. *Svaha* to it!

c. Aum-Aim, I am purifying and conducting the Shiva constituent in myself. *Svaha* to it!

d. Aum-Aim Hrim-Klim. I am purifying and conducting all the constituents in myself. *Svaha* to it!

ii. A Sadhaka has to do *Pranayama* and invoke *Ganesha* and other Devatas.

iii. A *Pavitri* of *Kusha* grass should be put in the ring finger taking red flowers, some grains of rice and water in his/her right hand and must do *Sankalpa,* which is the commitment with definite set of words as prescribed in the scripture.

iv. The Sapta-Shati text is to be put it on *Adhar Shakti Pitha*/wooden stand and worshipped with *Navarana Mantra,* viz., Aum-Aim-Hrim-Klim-Cha-Mun-Da-Yai-Vi-Chchai-Namah.

v. *Shapoddhara* is to be recited seven times with the Mantra of *Aum-Hrim-Klim-Shrim-Kram-Krim-Chandika-Devyai-Shapanashan-Anugraham-Kuru-Kuru-Svaha.*

vi. The *Japam of Utkilana Mantra* is to be recited 21 times with the *Mantra—Aum-Shrim-Klim-Hrim-Sapta-Shati Chandike-Utkilanam-Kuru-Svaha.*

vii. The *Japam of Mrita-Sanjivani-Vidya* is to be recited with Mantra—*Aum-Hrim-Hrim-Vam-Vam-Aim-Aim-Mrita-Sanjivini-Vidye-Mritam-Uthapaya-Uthapaya-Krim-Hrim-Vam-Svaha.*

DEVI KAVACHAM

The Armour

The life source in the embodied soul is highly essential for communication with the Divine. The body has to be guarded essentially for the proper worship during *Homa, Patham* and above all the *Sadhana* for attainng the grace of *Mahamaya*. The *Devi Kavacham* serves as an armour for it, as all the Shaktis abide in the 'Jiva'—the embodied soul by the grace of *Mahamaya*. The *Kavacham* wards off all calamities and accidental deaths, natural upheavals, diseases arising out of cuts and eruptions. It guards from poison, both elemental and compound. The 'Devi Kavacham' seems materialistic in approach, but in its subtle nature, the Sadhaka ascends to the Eternal realm which is the Supreme abode of Mahamaya. She is verily, *Chandi*. She is the Excellent Mother of the Universe. She protects through *Kavacham*. The *Kavacham* is thus an apron in the spiritual laboratory, where Shri Chandi Mahamaya is adored, as worshipped by Brahma.

Brahma is the Rishi of the *'Kavacham'*. *Anushtup* is the metre. *Chamunda* is the *Devata* or subject matter. *Matri* is the seed. The *Tattva*-element is *'Dikbandha*-devata' of the *'Kavacham'*. It serves the *Limba*—an integral part of the Sapta-Shati.

In this context, a nice exposition of devotional philosophy in the Shakti tradition is found in the *Devi-Mahatmayam*, popularly revered as the *Durga Saptashati*. Shakti as a Supreme Mother has found an elaborate position in this highly occult scripture of the *Shaktas*. Devi is adored with the name and form of *Mahakali, Mahalakshmi* and *Mahasaraswati*. This sacred scripture is a section in the *Markandeya Purana*. It is multi-dimentional in spirit and throws sufficient light on 'Jnana-karma-bhakti Yoga'. This is the triadic approach through which a 'Sadhaka' enters in this Divine laboratory, putting on the apron of various moods of Divine mother, around the spiritual atmosphere. Being highly occult in the content, the methodology of *Puja Sadhana/ Anushthanam* is revealed only to the initiated in the Shakti tradition. After proper initiation, Sadhana of a devotee gets evolved in understanding the goal of life, which is *Moksha*—release from the cycle of birth and death.

NAVADURGA

Nine Devis

Nava is nine and Durga is Divine Mother, who wards off all the obstacles of life. The Navadurgas are :

1. Shailaputri

Shaila is the rock of spiritual standing and the whole world gets absorbed in it. This is the Yogic procedure for being in tune with the Divine, where human aspiration is for ascending to the spiritual bliss. Verily, Shailaputri is the *Mooladhara Shakti* to be realised and sought for. This is an experience in the soul-searching of immutable within our existence. Shailaputri is the physical consciousness of the Mother Divine. She is truely *Parvati*—daughter of the King Himvan. She is the manifestation of this earth, which includes what is all apparent on the earth and within the globe. She abides in the *Muladhara Chakra*. The Divine energy is latent in man. Its colour is crimson, the tattva is Earth, with the quality of cohesion, with the sense of smell. Its mantra is *Lam*. *Mula* is root and Adhara is support, where the *Sushumna Nadi* has its point of departure, which runs parallel to the spinal column.

2. Brahmacharini

It is the cosmic vibration to be felt within our Sadhana. This is what the cosmic energy of Brahma is. The whole cosmic phenomenon is to be realised through the grace of *Brahmacharini*, which is vibrant in the Universal circumference. This is a call from the intangible heights to see the pulsation of Sadhana within. She abides in the

Svadhishthan Chakra. A realisation of cosmic consciousness is being experienced by the grace of Brahmacharini. She with Her innate nature assumes the form of pure universal consciousness, which is situated between the base of the pubic. Its nature is related to waters with the sense of taste. Its mantra is *Vam.* It is the period of spiritual planning.

3. Chandraghanta

Chandraghanta is the beauty par-excellence. The cosmic sound is the primal vibration to be felt during our Sadhana and merge with the cosmic bell which gives us an inspiration to understand the absolute. Bijaksharas are the vibrating forces to feel the vibrations of the Eternal within our being, during Sadhana. The 'Bijaksharas' are the sound syllables which create an atmosphere of transcendence. She abides in the *Manipura Chakra.* Fluid energy centre is situated corresponding to the gastric plexus. Its nature relates to the forces of stimulating the sense of form and colour. Its mantra is *Ram.* It is an alarm to see the vibration in and around.

4. Kushmanda

It is the Universal seed which remains ever conscious. This is the *Shudha-Vidya* aspect of Shri Chandi. The physical mind has to transcend to the higher tiers of consciousness. It has to see the measureless in the unseen spirit. There is stable force in the seed, which moves in all the directions to manifest for higher dawn. Harmonious are the ways, which we find during our Sadhana while taking the spirit of Kushmanda within our psycho-physical existence. She abides in the *Anahat Chakra.* It is situated on the Cardiac plexus in the heart region. Its nature is Shiva and Shakti aspect and mantra is *Yam.*

5. Skandamata

Skandamata is the mother of valour. It is the power of existence. It is swift, joyful and perfect in its nature. It is field of creation, sustenance for spiritual beauty in the *Navarana mantra*. She is the mother of Kartikeya/Skanda, who killed the *Tarakasura* for the welfare and protection of the Devas. She abides in the *Vishudha Chakra*. The Skandamata is the force behind that power, which makes the *Sattva* flow in the universe. This is purification for rejecting the impure and admitting only the sacred moments of speech, mind and vital force. She is manifest as power in the warrior, who fights for preserving the harmony of body, mind and soul. It is situated in the throat region the nerve plexus of the pharynx region. It location is the inhalation of breath. It is the Sadashiva aspect represented as the androgynous (Ardhanarishwar aspect) which is half male and half female. Its mantra is Ham, always eager to help the Devatas during their problems. She is all wisdom and effulgence. She helps the devotees for transcending all the aspects of *Avidya*/ignorance. She abides in the *Ajna Chakra*. It is situated between the eyebrows, which is the place of the third eye of Shiva. It is the union of Shiva with Shakti.

6. Katyayani

Katyayani is the daughter of the Katyayana Rishi. She is the mother of excellence, the inner beauty, the inspiration and supreme understanding. She is the Mother of the Arya PPak-the Supreme word which descends through invocation after meditating upon the Supreme energy. *Katyayani* is the inherent faculty within human soul which can be achieved through meditation

7. Kalaratri

Kalaratri is the Time eternal. It is the hour before the Devtas are born. It is auspicious to have her glimpses as She is manifest in all the units of time from moment to eternity. She abides in the *Shasra-ara Chakra*. She is what man wants to achieve for understanding the Benign aspect of night, though it appears to be dark. It is the thousand petalled

Charkra. Three force Channels *Ida, Pingla* and *Sushumna nadis* converge at the Yogic heights.

8. Mahagauri

Mahagauri is having the effulgence of golden hue. She is what the *Hiranya garbha* exists for. Because of Her Spiritual effulgence, She activates the *Kundalini Shakti* to stay in the harmony of *Iccha, jnan* and *kriya*—the triple aspects of Shakti for maintaining the balance of *Satyam* and *Ritam* on the basis of Dharma.

9. Siddhidhatri

Siddhidhatri is all perfection. It is the *Prakasha* and *Vimarsha* woven together in the inner recesses of Yoga and Bhakti. The Divine Shakti is measureless. She structures the whole Universe through Her grace of being in *Brahmarandhra* and passing through the nerve-channels of Yoga. She is indefinable, unageing, unborn but flowing in all the Sadhakas, who seek Her grace in every breath of life.

These are the Nine Durgas, which are being adored by the devotees during the *Nava-Ratra* days of *Chaitra* and *Ashvini* months from *Pratipada* to *Navami*, during the Shukla Paksha i.e. the lunar fortnight.

A Sadhaka needs to be protected in every anatomical structure of his very existence and in every direction. The Devi Kavacham gives a boon of strength to him to overcome any anti-divine tendency, he who wears the *Kavacham* in his Sadhana with devotion. He is expected to live a full span of life, *Brahma* is the *Rishi* of *Chandi Kavacham. Chamunda* is the Devata—deity. *Bija*—the seed has its origin in the deity of *Anga-nyasa.*

Brahma is the force of creativity through the grace of Shri Chandi. Limitless and mysterious are the ways of Mahamaya in uniting *Jiva* with *Jaganmata*. The Devi is *Viratrupa*—the macroself, whose expansion is vast. She links Herself in the anatomical structure of Jiva—the embodied souls which is the homogeneous development of body, mind and spirit.

So great is Her transcendental power that the whole Universe is just a reflection of that glory. The aggregate of Nava Durgas forms the wholesome cosmic function of creation, preservation and dissolution. In Her creative Shakti, Shri Chandi has assumed the form of Divine Mother. She is the Mother of grace removing the sufferings of Jivas and releasing them from the cycle of birth, death and rebirth.

The Matrikas/Personified Energies

Chamunda is the Supreme Mother. The Kavacham describes the Yogic manifestation of *Chamunda, Varahi, Aindri Vaishnavi, Maheshvari, Kaumari, Lakshmi, Ishvari* and *Brahmi.* These are the mothers of Supreme Yogic power. The vehicle of Chamunda is a *Preta*—bereft of life. Chamunda is the most ferrocious form of Shri Chandi. She gets in action at any movement by being on the throne of Eternity. Kali is commissioned by Shri Chandi to slay the Asuras. She gets terribly angry and in anger, She becomes dark like *mashi*—the ink. Out from the surface of Her forehead, Kali appears bearing the garland of skulls, fearful with opening of tongue, having deep sunk reddish eyes, slaughtering the great *Asuras.* Kali needs no vehicle as Time is ever Eternal. Kali is apparent form of Chamunda by killing *Chanda* and *Munda.* Hence the name Chamunda.

Varahi is seated on the 'buffalo'. She is all consuming. She is potential energy of the Universal flux. She is the Shakti of 'Matrikas'—little mothers or phonemes and is revered as the fifth Matrika. Creation has to be digested to make the Universal play in harmony. Real beauty lies wherein the cycle of creation, preservation and destruction is seen in every breath of life. *Varahi* digests whatever She gets without any discrimination between the beautiful and the ugly. Her coach is Mahisha, a buffalo, bearing the symbol of power which is to make the soil of land more cultivable for producing

'Anna'—the food. This is essential for the 'Annamaya-kosha'—the physical sheath of the 'Jiva'. Varahi is the Shakti of *Bhagavan Vishnu* and also the *Prithivi-tattva* or earthly element.

Aindri is the third mother. She is the Shakti of Indra, the Master of weapons and thunder who rides on the elephant. All the existence which we do perceive or infer is a manifestation of the Shakti. Through the merits of our actions, we come closer to Aindri for ascending to Svarga—the transitory heaven. Her vehicle is the elephant which is the symbol of grace, wisdom and beauty.

Vaishnavi is the fourth in the line of Mothers. She is all sustenance, perservation, perfection and performance. Her function is to make the Universal tree alive and giving its vibrations to the cosmic world. She holds conch, club and disc in Her hands giving blessings through Her *Abhaya-mudra*. Her preservative character is highly visualised through the primal seed of sustenance. It is a cosmic play of Vaishnavi through which the real power is executed for creation. Her vehicle of 'Garuda'—the bird of observance and justice. She looks for preservation of every soul from 'Jiva to Brahma' as She is the Mother of all manifestation.

Maheshvari is fifth in the line of Matrikas. She is Supreme ruler with imperial majesty, who is seated on *Mahisha* the buffalo. A cosmic vastness and infinity is executed by Her. In Her tranquil nature, She governs the universe and handles the human fate according to their *Karmas*—action. Being the Sovereign Supreme, She is bound by none but is compassionate of all. Her aim of awarding punishment to Jivas is to tansform them into the spiritual life. Her vehicle is *Vrishbha*—ox, being strong enough to carry out the order of the Divine Mother. She is vigorous in operations of the Mother's will.

Kaumari is the Mother of valour, and sixth in the line of Matrikas. Harmony and beauty of thoughts, actions and feelings are directed by Kaumari, as valour is the capacity to contain the psycho-physical energy. A Jiva can only attain perfection, if he maintains the norms of discipline and Sadhana. Kaumari is the power projected in the cosmos. Her vehicle is *Mayur*—peacock. Peacock is the bird of dance while Kaumari is at work. She dances to maintain the law of authority. She is the Mother supporting the *Chidagni*—the Fire of consciousness and dedication in the *Shakti Homa, Japam* or *Patham*.

Lakshmi is the seventh Mother with the functions of granting auspiciousness, wealth and prosperity. She has sprung from the great ocean deluding the Asuras and crush their evil tendencies. She gives a full base to life and Her grace lies in being the inseparable self of Narayana. Her seat is on the lotus, which is the symbol of Yogic perfection. It is found in the *Sahasrara*—thousand petalled mystic lotus of a Sadhaka. She is adored as a Mother holding lotus in Her hand. The stalk of lotus resembles the *Kundalini Shakti. Kamal* or lotus is the symbol of purity, eternity and sovereignity which blooms for higher dawn.

Ishvari is the eighth Mother, who has assumed the white form resembling Sattva—pure reflections. She accepts no ignorance and no *tamas*—inertia in any form. She is the chaste beauty par-excellence that cools the *tamas* tendency of the 'Jiva'. A 'Jiva' is a candidate of Immorality for blooming at the feet of Ishvari, who holds the authority of Dharma. She does not favour without reason but removes all the obstacles in his candidature for higher bliss. On the basis of devotion, sincerity, unconditioned submission, She grants the boons for evolution. Her vehicle is Ox. Ishvari is the *Ahamta*—universal ego, *Svatantraya*—absolute freedom and *Chitta*—consciousness.

Brahmi is the last in the line of Mothers. She is divine speech. She is the mother of *Akshara*—the immutable sound. The inner sound of Akshara is the process of divine communication with the Bija-mantras with definite ranges known as *varna-atma*—the spirit of phonemes. She abides in

Akshara and gives the book of *Vaikhari.* It is because of consciousness of Akshara that the Matrikas assume the form of vowel and consonants. Brahmi is both *Shabda-Artha* and *Pranava AUM.* She is decorated with all sorts of ornaments in the form of Vedas and allied *Vidya* both *Para*-transcendent and *Apara*-apparent. Her vehicle is *Hamsa*—swan. It is reversed *Soham* which means I am That, I am Truth. Hamsa is for purity and sattva, with a power in realizing the Real.

Devi Kavacham

Devi Kavacham is therefore, the elixir of life, mind and spirit. It is the great saviour. Brahma visualises the Kavacham, as He is the Universal precepter. The Kavacham is not an armour alone, but an assembly of all those Devis, who manifest under the spell of Mahamaya-the Mother of absolute Reality. The *Patham* of this Kavacham is covered in 56 Shalokas, adored with poetic beauty, mystic subtlity and ritualistic depth. The whole *Kavacham* is potential in meaning and gives us divine strength to be in tune with Chandi *Homa/ Patham* and *Japam.*

He who wears this Kavacham assumes identity with Shiva after the Sadhaka leaves the mortal frame, which is apparent death. He is blessed with *Dharma-artha-kama-moksha.* What does the wearing of Kavacham mean? A Sadhaka should realise the spirit of vibration in every nerve and cell, limb and organism of his physical sheath. It is a mystic apron woven with spiritual thread of *Sattva* on the loom of *Sadhana.*

Argala Stotram

The next requisite is the recitation of the *Argala.* It literally means a wooden belt pin or bar for closing/fastening the door. It is bolting. It is a mode of prayer prescribed for attaining the grace of Mahamaya. The Shakti of Argalam are the forces of victory, auspiciousness, time, eternity, consciousness and reverence for manes. Thus its recitation helps a *Sadhaka* to become perfect in life. Every breath of a

Sadhaka is longing for purity, auspiciousness and glory. Whatever may be the nature of enjoyment and pleasures of material world, but all of them are transitory. The *Sadhaka* should not long for the sensual pleasure as it devoids him of the grace of Mahamaya. A *Sadhaka* needs to be disciplined, must have control over his *Jnanendriyas* and *Karmendriyas*—senses of knowledge and action. Divine consciousness leads to victory as it is a promise of eternal grace from Shri Chandi, to the devotee, who take refuge in Her gracious self.

A Sadhaka rises above the physical plane to realise the true nature of Mahamaya. This is to be learnt through devotion and surrender. Thus the Sadhaka goes beyond the mental curtain and finds mysterious visions for the devotee. Shri Chandi is the true support of this world. A supreme grace dawns and Sadhaka finds a *Sankalpa,* a determination for higher Sadhana. His state of mind approaches the Immortal gate.

Argala is a beautiful expression of *Stuti.* Vishnu is the Rishi. Devata is Mahalakshmi. It is recited in the *Anushtup* metre to please the Divine Mother. It is an integral limb of Durga Saptashati, which works for the spiritual bolting for self-awareness.

Markendeya is the seer and his submission is always before Mahamaya, who is presiding over an aggregate of eleven Shaktis. The first Shakti is *Jayanti*—all excellence in victory. The second Shakti is *Mangla*—the bestower of final liberation. The third Shakti is *Kali*—who consumes everything and absorbs the universe in Her lap. The fourth is *Bhadrakali*—who accepts everything for betterment. She is the benign Mother. The fifth is *Kapalini* holding skull in her hand and wearing the garland of skulls. The sixth Shakti is *Durga* who cannot easily be approached, only Her grace can be obtained through great *Sadhana* and *Tapasya.* The seventh Shakti is *Kshma*—the very nature of great mercy and love. The eighth Shakti is *Shiva,* who descends for providing auspiciousness. The ninth Shakti is *Dhatri.* She holds this whole world and is the giver of the best to the Sadhaka. She sustains the Universe. The tenth Shakti is *Svaha,* who accepts the sacrifice for the Devas through *Homa*. The eleventh Shakti is *Svadha* who accepts the oblations for the departed souls.

Shri Chandi is the giver of boon to the *Vidhata* Brahma—the architect of fate by destroying *Madhu* and *Kaitabha*. She is the killer of *Mahishasura* and *Raktabija*. She is Chamunda, the destroyer of '*Chanda*' and '*Munda*'. She is with form and full of activities. She is the destroyer of all the diseases and hostile forces. Verily, She is 'Chandika' with infinite form and characteristics. She cannot be perceived through sense organs. She is attained through Sadhana and removes the sins of the devotees, those who serve Her with submission, devotion and prayer. She grants *Rupa*-form, *Jaya*-victory, *Yasha*-prosperity and kills the enemy and foes. She is the destroyer of '*Shumbha* and *Nishumbha*'.

A Sadhaka pays his obeiance to Mahamaya for welfare, meaningful knowledge, prosperity and health. *Krishna*—incarnation of Vishnu is ever attuned with Her potent 'Mantra'. She is *Parmeshvari*—the sovereign supreme, who has been adored by Rudra. She is *Ambika*—the Emotive Mother. She is All in this Universe and grants unfettered happiness and bestows all the grace, with faculty of good mind, birth in a noble family, a good wife/life partner.

The Sadhaka asks for the best in human birth with physical ability, name and fame. In the concluding Shlokas, the Sadhaka's prayer is for the survival of progeny. This stotram gives us boons to maintain harmony in this bio-physical world for the realisation of the Supreme dawn.

Argala Stotram is filled with the devotional hymns of 25 Shalokas and forms a portion of the Saptashati. The Presiding diety of Argala bestows grace with Supreme knowledge, wealth, health and other merits to the Sadhaka. It is a Stotram of great liberation with spiritual harmony and perfection.

Kilkam

The third step in the process in the *Kilakam*. It is the Divine nail of the hidden secrets of the glory of Mahamaya. Here lies the spiritual process to reach the realm of higher consciousness while being in the process of nailing. It is the pivot fixed by Mahadeva—the Supreme Lord. It is to be freed from constraint, to help a Sadhaka to move on the pathway of Siddhi—perfection. The Siddhas/accomplished devotees realise the oneness of *Navarana mantra* through the pre-requisites.

The cause of Universal consciousness with the effect of manifestation is excellent beauty of the Saptashati. The Vedas are the eyes and Jiva is the spark of the Divine to realise the beauty of Mother creativity in and around the human thought-channel. Motherhood is the feminine embodiment of the Absolute, which keeps the harmony of spirit in the right balance. She is all pervading. She is Chandika and Shiva gave this Stotram for understanding the Mother Divinity in the world and made it an auspicious *Mantra*. It is occult in nature, so Shiva put a restraint on it. The Divine communication is the goal of human birth, which is the quintessence of the '*Kilkam*'.

The Stotram is to be recited with devotion and dedication. It gives the results of high merit. The auspiciousness lies in the motherhood aspect of Mahamaya, which is the Supreme grace of Shri Chandi. The Kilakam is the safe mantra as it has been *unnailed* by Shiva Himself. It has received Shiva's approval as being the most spiritual and mysterious mantra. It covers the whole range of Universal flux of spiritual enlightenment. Markendeya says the japam of the 'Saptashati' alongwith the Kilakam should be performed on the eighth or fourteenth *tithi* of the dark fortnight to obtain the grace of Mahamaya. The procedure is known as *Nishkilan*/unnailing. The knowledge of *Kilan* and *Nishkilan* is highly technical and needs to be learnt under the guidance of a celebrate Guru/preceptor.

Ratri–Suktam (Vedic)

Kushika, Saubhara, Ratri, Bhardwaja are the *Rishis* of the Ratri-Suktam. Ratri is *Devata,* metre is *Gayatri,* and application of the Sukta is for Patham/recitation, in the Devi Mahatmya Patham.

The procedure of Sapta Shati determines that the Ratri-Suktam should be recited after the three essentials of Kavacham-Argala-Kilakam. The Ratri-Suktam is both 'Vedic' and 'Tantric' in nature. The 'Vedic Ratri-Suktam' is highly philosophic and consists of 8 mantras. Ratri is the 'Devi' of Divine Night. She creates *Prakasha*—effulgence by Her own will, is the supreme love of the Divine Mother in this creative world, in which we are but the children of Immortality. It is the *Adi-Suktam.* It surveys manifest world consisting of Mahat-tattva and exercises the Divine power while giving the fruits of every action according to the law of 'Karma'. Ratri is Eternal manifestation. It takes various forms for granting lease of life, development and growth. It dispells darkness of the *'Jiva'* acquired by him through *'Avidya'*. Ratri is the consciousness which creates 'Usha'—dawn. It is 'Brahma Vidya'—the absolute knowledge. Devi abides in the *Saubhagya*—auspiciousness of a Sadhaka. The Sadhaka has to know Ratri Devi. Its essence speaks of *Chaitnya Shakti* :

"May Ratri dawn upon us, be pleased with us, who is vast and present in every place! She repells darkness with Her light. Man takes refuge in her movements as a bird dwells on the tree. Ratri is 'Chit-shakti', which alone keeps the Sadhakas away from unwanted designs of the life."

Ratri-Suktam (Tantrik)

In this *Sukta,* the primal cry of Brahma to avoid death is the basic principle of life. It is a primal worship of Brahma with spontaneous flow of words, come out of fear and emotion and not by intellect. The Sukta invokes *'Nidra Bhagavati'* who has taken Her abode in the form of *Yoga Nidra* of Vishnu. Vishnu is the Lord of preservation and He could not protect Brahma—the Lord of Creation, unless the *Yoga Nidra* was invoked. That moment caused abnormal pulsation in the creative beats of Brahma. Brahma invoked Ratri Devi to make Vishnu awaken from His mystic sleep for destroying *Madhu* and *Kaitabha* born out of the ear-wax of Vishnu. After invoking the Nidra Devi, Lord Vishnu fought for five thousand celestial years and put them in delusion through the influence of Mahamaya. Under the influence of Mahamaya, they asked for a boon from Vishnu. Thus Vishnu could kill them through the grace of Mahamaya, as they were deluded by Mahamaya.

Ratri-Suktam is a *Brahmi* prayer—the primal sound for asking help from the Divine. The Suktam runs from *Svaha*—the mantra of offerings to the Devas, making a spiritual journey through *Svadha*—the oblations to the departed souls, *Vashatakar*—Vedic sacrifice, life principle of sound, which is immutable AUM. It is *Savitri*—solar energy, *Sandhaya*—twilight, creativity, sustenance, termination, great knowledge and illusion. It is verily, intellect, memory and delusion. It is a *Prakriti* of three Gunas—*Sattva, rajas, tamas* which is manifested in the Suktam. It is modesty, nourishment, contentment, tranquility. Ratri is *Hrim* bija of modesty and *Ishvari* is holding the weapon to keep the universe in order. Verily, She is *Parmeshvari.*

The total surrender of Brahma makes him visualise the *Yoga Nidra* manifest in Vishnu. Thus *Yoga Nidra* is *Kalaratri*—*Ratri* of time, *Maharatri* of great existence, *Moharatri* of delusion. It is *Mahavidya*—the ultimate knowledge, *Mahamaya*—great cosmic reality, *Mahamedha*—the great intellect and *Mahasmriti*—the great memory. She holds sword, discus, conch, arrow, club, spear and mace, when Ratri manifests in Vishnu. She is exceedingly beautiful in form. She assumes 'Name and Form' for bestowing grace upon the Sadhakas, who are the true aspirants for realising the 'Truth'. *Karna-mala* of Vishnu is the ear-wax from which Madhu and Kaitabha got their physical existence. This is anti-divine power, which is always fatal and brutal. It brings mortality. It is false ego which institutes the continuance of Samsara—the empirical world through the influence of *Mahamaya*.

Devi is Supreme-matrix, who commands the Universe. She is adored by the Devas to remove the obstacles in their paths created by Mahishasura. Mahalakshmi is the Primal power and Absolute authority, who makes a promise of removing the misfortune and hurdles created by the Asuras. Her words are the bliss rays of authority. Her utterance is precise but conveys the highest Truth of physical, vital, psychic, gnostic and blissful sheath of human existence. She is seated on the Magestic throne of the triple world. She is the Saviour of the Sadhakas, who are subjected to dread, fear, humiliation and all sorts of such other tendencies created by the Asuras, who are the anti-divine forces; bent upon disturbing the global peace, ecology and environment.

Devi with her words teaches the law of *'Dharma'* to learn the Divine wonder and the spiritual bliss. She is Mahasarsvati who prescribed the procedure of her own *'Puja'*, in Her various manifestations. She speaks of 'One in various forms'. All Her powers enter into the Universal cell of Kaushki. She is virgin, holy, pure, auspicious and beautiful. Verily, She is considerate. Her revealation is for *'Yoga'* and *'Bhoga'*. Her word is the wakeful dialect of delight. The fire of Yoga, created by Her, is the purification through the burning force of *'Tapasya'*.

Devi is incomparable but attainable. There is a power of consciousness, ever and always present, which makes us realise that She is 'Time'—the Eternal, the units of which are the life span of *Brahma-Vishnu-Rudra*. Her primordial power is a wonder-house of formless infinity. The 'Sadhakas' realise Her benign presence in the 700 Shalokas of *'Shabda-sharira'*, which is vibrated and woven with the three *'Charitas-*episodes'. The psycho-physical harmony is communicable and understandable through the grace of Shri Chandi. It is possible to understand Her variations in each and every nerve and in every cell of life. She is unborn but is present in every feminine form of the manifestation. Her facets are mysterious and hidden but a Sadhaka realises Her nature in every rhyme of 'Prakrati' within the *Gunas*. She is the playful mood of three qualities of *'Sattva-rajas-tamas'*. Though the qualities are three in essence, yet these are capable of endless modifications on account of Her *'Iccha-shakti'*.

There is a pulsation in every moment of time and the 'cycle of time' is just a dimension of Her universal flux. This is Her *Saguna* aspect of reality. How the formless Absolute assumes form is a mystry for the Yogis, but the Compassionate mother has revealed Her nature through the first utterance of Brahma to teach the human race all about their journey to consciousness. It is an evolution of energy from the stage of *Shailaputri* to *Siddhidhatri*.

SAPTA-SHATI

The *Sapta* means seven and *Shati* is hundred, so Sapta Shati is the scripture of a Divine composition of 700 Shalokas, divided in 13 chapters. Shri Chandi has been mainly styled as Devi having Supreme effulgence with the force of communion in the cosmic scene. Her manifestation is the Universal play and Devatas are intended to participate in governing the cosmic laws of the Universe. When they fail to discharge the functions as prescribed by the Divine law, according to their name and form, they fall under the spell of grief. Mahamaya with Her intrinsic nature assumes the form of multi-faces, multi-hands and multi-feet. She wears the face of Kali, sucks blood, consumes all what is in the Universe. She removes the veil of *Avidya*—ignorance in the form of *Mahakali*, governs as the Supreme Sovereign Mother-Creatrix in the form of Mahalakshmi and determinates knowledge as Mahasaraswati.

Shri Devi Atharva Shirsham says in the 20th Mantra : *Aim* is *Vani*/Speech, *Hrim* is *Maya*/duality, *Klim* is *Kama*/ desire, *Cha* is *Vaktra*/face, *M* is *Surya*/sun, *U* is *Avam shrotra*/ right ear, *Mun* is *anusvar*/consonant, *Da* is *Narayana*, *Y* is *Vayu*/air or *Adhar*/lip with *Yai*, *Vicchai* is the concluding alphabet in this mantric group of letters. The *Siddha-kunjika-stotram* says :

Aim is *Srishti*/creation, *Hrim* is *Pratipalika*/preservation, Sustainer, *Klim* is *Kamarupini*/the form of desire, will and pleasure, which in the All seed. *Chamunda* is *Chandaghati*/ the slayer of *Asura Chanda*, *Yai* is *Varadayini*/the bestower of boons, *Vichhai* is *Abhayada*—the giver of security, freeing from fear. The Devi is *Mantrarupini*—the very self of Eternal word.

Navarana Vidhi

The *Navarana* means the nine-syllabled mantra of Shri Chandi. The Navarana is highly mystical in essence. It consists of the *Mantra-Sharira* of the Devi. The methodology is supremely occult. The nine-syllabled *Bijaksharas*—seed syllables of *Chandi* should be put under practice, through devotion and dedication under the guidance of a Tantric preceptor belonging to the *Chandi* tradition. When Mantra is properly recited, it gives vital vibrations and reveals the omnipresence of *VAK* or *Nada Brahman*, which is always omniscient and omnipotent. It is ever present with Devi's presence filled with Her radiance. It is the Nine fold seed of the Devi as *Aim-Hrim-Klim-Cha-Mun-Dha-Yai-Vi-Chchai.*

'Aim' is the seed, *'Hrim'* is *Shakti*, *'Klim'* is the *Kilkam* of the three episodes of the Devi. *'Brahma-Vishnu-Rudra'* are the Rishis and *'Shri Mahakali-Shri Mahalakshmi-Shri Maha Sarasvati'* are Devatas. The episodes of Chandi are recited in the *Gayatri*, *Ushnik* and *Anushtup Chhandas*/metres. The *'Japam-Patham-Homa'* is dedicated to the Trio of *Mahamaya Chandi*.

Five Nyasas—Placements

The five Nyasas are *Rishi-Kara-Hridaya-Akshara* and *Dik*

etc., *Nyasas*/placements. These are to be performed to realize the presence of Devi on the head, face, heart, excretory organ, feet and navel. *Rishi* is the seer, *Kara* is the hand, *Hridaya* is the heart, *Akshara* is the immutable world, *Dik* (*Din*) is the direction.

Rishi Nyasa

All the fingers and thumbs are to be sanctified with the *Bijaksharas* of *Chandi*. Heart and other parts of the body are to be invoked with the *Navarna-Mantra*. The body has to be sanctified with the *Matrikas* of nine syllables of the sacred *Bijakshara*. The last phase of Nyasa is to sanctify the ten directions, including *Bhumi*—the mother earth.

Rishis are Brahma,*Vishnu* and *Rudra*. *Aim* is the Seed, which abides in the *Guhya*—the secret part of the body *Hrim* is the Shakti in the feet. *Hrim* is the nailing in the navel.

Kara Nyasa

Kara consists of thumb and other fingers including the palm.

Hridayadi Nyasa

Hridayadi Nyasa etc. includes the heart, head, tuft, both the shoulders, the eyes and the mystic sound of *Phat*.

Akshara Nyasa

Akshara consists of the nine limbs of the 'Navarana Mantra', viz., *Aim, Hrim, Klim, Chamm, Mun, Daam, Yai, Vim* and *Chhai*.

'Din' consists of East, South-East, South, South-West, West, North-West, North-East and North, it includes the etheral above and the earth below.

Dhyanam—Contemplative Meditation

The Dhyana Mantras of *Mahakali-Mahalakshmi-Mahasarasvati* are to be recited and the sacred *Mala* is to be worshipped with *Aim Hrim Akshamalikayi Namah*—I pay my obeisance to the Akshamala or a rosary of Rudraksha having 108 beads.

The *Japam* is prescribed in the 108 counts of the *Navarna-Mantra* of Shri Chandi. Whole of the Sapta Shati is to be invoked for the prefection of all the physical and spiritual achievements with the *Sapta Shati Mantras.*

Sapta Shati Nyasa

The hands, heart, head, tuft, shoulders, eyes and the whole physical body is to be invoked with the *Kavacham Mantras* of the Fourth Chapter. The four Mantras are *Shulena Pahi No Devi*..... to .....*Tair asaman raksha sarvatah.*

Snana—taking a bath

The Sadhaka needs to purify himself and be prepared with other purifications for invoking the Divine Mother.

Achamana—sipping of water

The *Sadhaka* has to purify himself with clean pure water as prescribed in the Sandhya. The waves of eternal vibrations create an atmosphere of equipoise in the psycho-physical being of the *Sadhaka.*

Pranayama—holding of breath

It is the regulation of breath. It is to be done with the *Gayatri Mantra/Navarana Mantra.* It is the holding of breath, which is the vital force for sustenance. Mind is controlled and the concentration is fixed on the Divinity or Mahamaya—Shri Chandi.

Sankalpa—determination

It is the resolution, a commitment before the Divine Mother, what the *Sadhaka* is proposed to do during the Sadhana. The act is clearly spelled out with the expression to materialise the *Iccha Shakti* into *Kriya Shaki.*

Prarathana—Prayer

It is submission, a prayer and an invocation to Ganesha and Guru. Ganesha is the Adi Deva with the potential of being the very source of Muladhara-Shakti, who is endowed with *Riddhi* and *Siddhi*. He is invoked as the Supreme Force that creates the atmosphere of purity, eternity and auspiciousness. Guru is great. He is the preceptor, who initiates the disciple with the divine Mantra. Guru is beyond *Nada-Bindu* and *Kala*. He is bestower of *Shaktipata* instilling divine energy in a *Sadhaka*. One recites the *Guru Gita/Guru-paduka Mantra* and pays his obeisence to one's *Guru—Param Guru*—the *Guru* of his *Guru* and *Parameshtti Guru* the *Guru* of his Parama Guru. It is Guru, who can help the Sadhaka to rise above the physical/material senses and transcend to the higher realms of spirituality.

Asana—the sitting postore

The Sadhaka has to seat himself in a particular convenient physical posture to acquire the sustained poise. In the process, the Sadhaka should draw with water the figure of a triangle on the ground, paying his obeisance to *Prithvi Tattva*—the sustained force known as *Adhara Shakti*. A seat/couch should be spread on the Adhara Shakti of woolen cloth/deer skin/tiger skin. The reed like *darbha-kusha* grass is also used as a seat. A Sadhaka should face the east or the north during the Sadhana.

Bhuta Apasarpana—alienation of evil forces

It is a submission that all beings which may cause obstruction be destroyed by the command of Shiva, who may be around the surroundings of *Puja sthala*—the place of worship. All the evil spirits are vanquished. The Sadhaka asks the permission from the terrible *Bhairava* who resembles Fire at the time of the *Kalpa*. The word *Phat* is to be uttered by clapping the fingers round the head. Thus the ten quarters are fenced by striking the earth with the left foot.

Bhuta Shuddhi—elemental purification

It is an important discipline for outer worship and 'Mantra-Sadhana'. Bhuta Shuddhi is the atmospheric and environmental purification around the *Vedi* or sanctum sanctorum of Shri Chandika/Divine Mother. This leads to the '*Antar* and *Bahir Yaga*' or internal and external offerings. All the tamasic forces get neautrilised. *Prana-pratishtha* can only be done after *Bhutashuddhi.* The purification of the various limbs and the mind stuffs need to be purified. Every part of the body is offered to the diety for experiencing the unison with the Divine.

Prana-Pratishtha—Installation/infusing vital breath

This is an act of installing the Life-force during the span of Sadhana. The *Moorti*—image, *Yantra*—diagram are the sacred symbols of the Divine Mother. The *Pranas* as vital breath are infused in the object of worship. Thus the 'Moorti'/diagram becomes vibrant with Her own power and establishes a close link with the Sadhaka.

Dipa Sthapana—positioning of earthen lamp

Dipa is the lamp which lights the surroundings. It is the witness of our actions and its flame is a torch light which gives an atmosphere of *Prakasha*—the absolute reality through *Vimarsha* intellectual reflection. A Dipa is lit till the act of worship is over. The Dipa is the symbol of Devi. It is the sign of auspiciousness and spiritual awakening.

Shapa-Uddhara—deliverance from a curse

Powers of limitations are everywhere. Shapodhara is necessary for progress in this spiritual field. Through the *Shapoddhara* mantra, the Sadhaka prays to the *Rishis* and Devatas to lift the curse and allow him to proceed on the path leading to *Siddhi*—perfection.

Utkilana—unnailing the pivot

Utkilan is the process of unnailing the pivot, on which

the whole realisation of the 'Mantra' is hinged. The *Kilaka* is to be perceived, seen and understood, with the firm resolution of unnailing it. It is verily, an unbolting.

These are the preliminaries for establishing a spiritual link with *Mahamaya* during our *Sadhana, Japam or Homa*. May the Divine Mother be ever pleased, inspite of the errors, which we do commit during our Sadhana!

PRATHAMA CHARITRA

FIRST EPISODE

Viniyoga—Mode of Application for Homa/Patha

The first episode consists of the first Chapter of the text.

Chandi manifests Herself as Mahakali in the form of *Yoga-Nidra* of *Vishnu*. *Mahakali* is the usurper of what has been created by Her *'Iccha Shakti'*. She is the origin of Time. She is Time the eternal, who manifests in Time the serial. She is *Para Shakti*, who at the time of dissolution puts an end to time itself. She is the root of all manifestation. Time does create existence. Time dissolves what has been manifested by *'Ichha Shakti'*. Time is the Supreme witness of all the states viz., *Jagrata-Svapna-Sushupta*. These are the steps of wakefulness, dreaming and sleep.

Chandi as Mahakali is the Sovereignity of time, hence Her manifestation is eternal. Brahma is the creator of this infinite universe, because he has been conditioned to such an eternal act, by the commands of Mahamaya. His act of creation is the supreme will of Mahamaya. He is an embodied Devata with a majestic power in Him. Iccha-Shakti is inherent in him. It is because of the grace of Mahamaya, that Brahma could recite the Ratri-Sukhta. The four faces of Brahma represent the four Vedas, which speaks of Supreme truth of *Mahamaya*.

The 'Rigveda' is open to all. Its study makes us learn that the entire phenomenon can be reduced to 'Nama-Rupa'. It is the name and form of the universe. This process of expansion to the extent of *Nama-Rupa* has been taught by Medha Rishi—the seer of the great intellect and intuition to Suratha Raja—the King and Samadhi Vaishya—the

Merchant. The Rishi reveals the Truth through Mantras, as he communes with the Supreme Power. His teaching is intended to serve the humanity for spiritual enlightenment and for the preparation of higher dawn, with the procedure of Homa-offerings. The aim of human life is to realise Shri Chandi and a Sadhaka must surrender at Her feet and be blissful.

Bhagavan Vishnu is in the blissful state of Yoga-Nidra. The Devi is eternally present in Vishnu—the power behind preservation, sustenance and protection. He is the most vibrant force to encounter the Asuras in the being of Madhu and Kaitabha, born from his own '*Karna-mala*'—ear wax.

Brahma—the Devata with the functions of creativity faces the wrath of *Madhu* and *Kaitabha*. He invokes the Yoga-Nidra through the eternal words of *Svaha, Svadha, Vashatkara* etc., which is the basis of understanding the secrets of Mahamaya. It is spontaneous flow of words known as VAK, by the revered Sadhakas. Thus the *Ratri-Suktam* is a primal prayer of Brahma to see Mahamaya in the *Yoga-Nidra*.

Rishi Markandeya is the seer of this *Puranam* who introduces this episode with the birth of the eighth Manu, who attained the status of being Manu after attaining the grace of Mahamaya. He was dethroned in the previous life. He was the king with royal prestige, who underwent great Sadhana under the guidance of the Medha Rishi. Samadhi Vaishya was a merchant who was insulted and humiliated by his own kith and kins. Hence left the home in despondency and with tense state of mind.

Both of them met Medha Rishi in his Ashram, as they were psychologically depressed, materially deprived and physically humiliated within their surroundings. The sense of sufferings was predominant in them. The king put a submission before Medha Rishi as how he got his misfortune and heavy set backs. He narrated the sufferings of Samadhi Vaishya also to the Rishi. The Rishi explained them the highest truth of psycho-physical existence of the animate beings viz., birds, beasts and animals. All of them cognise, but human-beings are certainly endowed with knowledge. But they suffer because of their attachment. The cause of this attachment is *Moha*—delusion created by Mahamaya by putting them in *Avidya*—ignorance.

The Rishi initiated them in the *Puja* of Mahamaya after explaining them the true nature of Her manifestation. She is always for the protection of the Devas. The first of the Devas was Brahma himself, who was protected and granted the lease of life by Her through Vishnu. Vishnu fought for five thousand divine years and put the two Asuras to death with his Vaishnavi Shakti, which is verily, the Mahakali.

In this episode, we observe the communication of Suratha Raja and Samadhi Vaishya with Medha Rishi. Brahma invokes Shri Bhagvana through his Primal cry, which is the Ratri-Sukta. Markandeya narrates what has been communicated to Suratha and Samadhi by Medha Rishi about the True nature of Mahamaya. Brahma's Ratri-Sukta is the universal prayer. Medha Rishi explains the form of Shri Vishnu holding conch, discus and mace. He took the two Asuras on his loins and severed their heads with Chakra/discus. Thus Mahamaya appeared before Brahma.

This episode is known as *Madhu Kaitabha Vadha*—slaying of Madhu and Kaitabha, consisting of 104 Shlokas. This episode is concluded with *Aim-Aum*, with 14 Uvacha mantra, 24 half Shlokas and 64 Shlokas.

MADHYAM CHARITAM

MIDDLE EPISODE

Middle episode consists of 2nd, 3rd and 4th chapter. The Middle episode is dedicated to *Mahalakshmi*. In this episode, *Vishnu* is *Rishi*—the seer. *Mahalakshmi* is Devata—the deity and the episode is recited in the Ushnika metre.

Shakambari is *Shakti*—the power, *Durga* is *Bijam*—the seed and *Vayu*—the wind is the principal element. The whole episode is the form of *'Yajurveda'*. The application of *Japam* is for 'Artha'—the empirical wealth.

Mahalakshmi is the vanquisher of *Mahishasura*—the Lord of Asuras, who conquered all the Devas including their chief Indra. The 'Devas' became helpless, and were led by *Brahma* to approach *Shiva* and *Vishnu*. Both of them got angry when they listened to the agony and suffering of the *'Devas'*....., then a great effulgence emerged out of *Brahma, Vishnu, Shiva* and other Devas, including *Indra,* which took the form of Devi known as *Mahishasura Mardini*. She was adorned with their weapons and missiles. *Yama* provided Her hair, *Vishnu* gave Her *arms*. By Soma's effulgence Her two breasts came into *force*. By *Indra* effulgence Her waist, by *Varuna* Her shanks and thighs. The effulgence of Earth gave Her lips. Thus Mahalakshmi came into being and emerged from the radiance of the 'Divine' forces. Feet came into formation by the light of *Brahma,* toes by *Surya,* fingers by *Vasus,* nose by *Kubera,* teeth by the radiance of *Prajapati,* the three eyes by *Agni,* eye-brows by the effulgence of two *Sandhyas* and ears by *Vayu*. The radiance of other 'Devas' too contributed to the emergence of Mahisasuramardini. The Chandi in the form of Mahalakshmi came into force as being veryself of all the 'Devas'. She is verily, the aggregate of all Divinity, Effulgence and Radiance. She is revered as Mahishasuramardini. She was provided with various weapons and missiles. Trident was presented by *Shiva,* discus by *Vishnu,* conch by *Varuna,* spear by *Agni,* bow and two quivers by *Maruta,* thunder-bolt and bell by *Indra*. Yama offered a staff of *Death* and *Varuna* a noose, *Brahma* a string of beads and a water pot. *Surya* offered his own rays and *Kala* gave a spotless sword and a shield, as offerings to help in this great fight with Asuras. *Kshir Samudra*—the milk ocean offered a pure necklace and other divine ornaments while *Vishvakarman* gave her a brilliant axe, weapons and impenetrable armour. The *Ocean* offered a garland of lotuses and a lotus for her hand. *Kubera* offered her a drinking cup, *Shesha* a necklace. Thus the *Divine Mother* was the total effulegnce of Divinity for giving a crushing defeat to the Asuras. Thus She roared with a defying laugh.

Devi's existence was touching the ego of the Asuras. So the great war was then evident. Though, She was an aggregate of *Gunas*—the qualities and '*Akaras*', the forms of the multitude of the Devas, yet She was the unifying energy with divine activities and super wit, super consciousness and super power. The individual consciousness of the Devas then merged with the universal consciousness, which helped the 'Devas' to fight with Mahishasura—the gross body of Avidya and Asuri Shakti, with total *Tamas* manifested in him.

Mahishasura's army consisted of cavalry, charioteers, elephants and soldiers led by his Senani—army chief Chikshura, who commanded the different divisions of the Asuric forces. They were fully equipped with and trained in their war missiles and weapons. They were all forceful and it did create a panic in the Universe.

This chapter consists of 69 Shlokas with 1 Uvacha Mantra 68 Shloka Mantras. This Chapter is known as the slaying of Mahishasura's army.

Third Chapter

In the first phase of this great war, *Chikshura* who was the General of the Mahishasura was killed followed by *Chamara, Udgra, Karala, Uddhata, Asiloma, Vashkal, Tamra, Andhaka*. The *Ugrasya, Ugravirya* and *Mahahanu* were followed by *Bidal, Durdhara* and *Durmukh* etc., were all slain by the great *Chandika*. *Mahishasura* got very wrathful to avenge *Chandika*. He also terrified the troops of the 'Devi' who were equally forceful and dreadful. He was filled with great anger who pulled out the surface of the earth with his hooves, causing the earth destroyed into fragments. With his *Asuric Maya*, he turned himself into a lion and instantaneously, She cut off his head. Then he emerged again, with no loss of time as a man and then a big elephant. He transformed himself into a buffalo shape and shook the three worlds. This he did with his Asuric Maya. Enraged at this, the great Chandika took a drink of *Madhu*/elixer of life and said :

"O fool, roar and roar for a brief moment
While I drink Madhu, the honey
You will be slain by Me very soon .....,
The Gods will roar when you will be slain."

Exclaiming with great power, thus, *Chandika* jumped over and climbed up the great Asura, crushing his neck under her foot and hit him with the trident. He tried to emerge again and again but overpowered by the valour of the Chandika. The great Mahishasura was beheaded with her sword and slain. There was joy and delight everywhere and the *Maharishis* sang to the tune of praises for Chandika. *Gandharvas* sang and the *Apsaras* danced, in praise of the *Devi.*

In this Chapter, it is observed that *Vidya* and *Avidya* are the two aspects. Vidya victoriously handled the physical nature of Asuras and annihilitated them. The victory is of the Truth over false ego, inertia and ignorance. It is the fall of physical stregth of the *'Danavas'* before the Divine effulgence.

This chapter is narrated in 44 Shlokas with Uvacha Mantra 3 and Shloka Mantras 41. This chapter is known as *Mahishasura-Vadha.*

Fourth Chapter

There was a potential threat to the Devas from the being of Mahishasura, but he was killed by the great *Chandika*. The 'Devas' heaved a sigh of relief and prayed to the great Chandika under the leadership of *Indra.* All of them bowed down and there was joyous atmosphere and delight. The *Rishi* says that Brahma and Shiva cannot adequately describe the facets of Shri Chandika. "May She be pleased with us and shower Her blessings and destroy the evil forces! She is prosperity, beauty, intelligence and modesty. She cannot be grasped by mind as She is the Primal cause of all the worlds. The whole world is but a portion of Her existence. She is the soul of eternal sound manifest in the 'Vedas'. She is the higher intellect. She is smiling and resembling the orb of the moon. She is the giver of prosperity to those devotees on whom She is gracious. She could have destroyed all the *Asuras* but She purified them by Her weapons so that the *Asuras* would also attain the higher worlds. No body equals Her. May She protect us with spear, sword, ring of bell and twang of the bow-string! May She protect us in all the directions! All of Her auspicious and inauspicious forms may protect us and the earth as well!" This is a Divine prayer sung in praise of Great Chandika. They praised her with celestial flowers that blossomed in *Nandanvana,* the flower garden of *Svarga.* 'Devi' speaks to 'Devas' with caring love of mother, while acknowledging their prayer. They make a request to come to their rescue when they may be put to trouble in future also by the *Asuras.*

The *Rishi* concludes this episode by saying that *Chandi* manifested out of the body of *Gauri* for the protection of the world and for the destruction of *Shumbha* and *Nishumbha.* The fourth Chapter is concluded with *Hrim Aum.* The sound body of the fourth chapter is in 35 Shlokas and is known as *Shakra-Adi-Stuti*—the adoration of the Divine Mother by *Shakra/Indra* and other Devatas.

The last Mantra is concluded with Hrim OM. In this episode 5 are the Uvacha Mantras, 2 are half Shlokas, 35 are full Shlokas.

About Middle Episode

A close relationship is found in maintaining the harmony of 'Devas' and infusing their respective Shaktis in the Supreme effulgence of Mahamaya. The 'Devas' not only require their survival but also the safeguard of the human race as well. As human race is subject to inflictions of *Asuri Shakti* at every step so the 'Devas' are the guardians of immortality and man is a candidate for immortality. Man has the potential to be divine and be a homogenous spirit of Mahamaya. He has to exercise his intellect through unconditional worship, dedication and supreme surrender, before the Divine Mother.

Uttara Charitra—Last Episode

This episode is dedicated to *Mahasarasvati. Rudra* is Rishi—the seer. Mahasarasvati is Devata—the deity and Chhanda meter for recitation is Anushtup. *Bheema* is Shakti—the power and *Brahmi* is Bijam—the seed. *Surya* is Tattva—the principle. The whole episode is in the form of *Samaveda*. The application of Japam is for Kama—the human desire.

Fifth Chapter

In this Chapter the Devas pray *Mahamaya* for help. The two great Asuras—Shumbha and Nishumbha dethroned Indra and other Devas. These Asura brothers dispossessed them of their powers, which vested in them in the capacity of the guardian deities. The Devas thus approached Himavat and invoked Vishnumaya—the Yogic power of Vishnu. Invocation to *Vishnumaya* is termed as the *Tantrik Devi Suktam*. The Shlokas are known as *'Tripanmatras'*. The Devi has been adored as *Mahadevi, Shiva, Prakriti, Bhadra, Raudra, Nitya, Gauri, Dhatri, Jyotsana, Indurupini, Sukha, Kalyani, Vridha, Siddhi, Nairita, Lakshmi, Sharvani.* All these are the forms of *Jagadamba*. She is verily, *Durga, Durgapara, Sara, Sarvakarini, Khyati, Krishna* and *Dhumra*. She is both benign and ferrocious. In Her *Raudra Rupa,* She is to be adored repeatedly. She is *Adharbhuta*—the basis of the universe. Undoubtedly, She is *Vishnumaya,* who is present in consciousness, intellect, sleep, hunger, shadow/reflection, power, thirst, patience, genus, modesty, peace, faith, glowing charm, fortune, activity, existence, memory, mercy, contentment, motherhood and mistake or illusion. She presides over all the senses and consciousness. She is All. What we perceive, infer through emotion and intellect on the basis of verbal testimony and intution, is verily She. She is *Ishvari*—the destroyer of arrogant Asuras with Supreme excellence and sovereignity.

Further, this chapter illustrates a dialogue between *Duta*—a messenger of 'Asura-brothers' and Devi who is all with full effulgence. It is She, who brought forth *'Shiva-Ambika-Kaushiki* and *Kalika'*. Later, *Chanda* and *Munda* came here and got bewitched, when they saw Her effulgence. They narrated about the Supreme effulgence of Devi to their masters. On hearing this, Shumbha asked Daitya Sugriva—his messenger, to go before Devi with the proposal of marriage for him or for his brother Nishumbha. On hearing this, Devi in Her characteristic satire said : "It is true that Shumbha is strong and equally *Nishumbha* is. What can I do? I have made a vow in unthinking moment that whosoever humbles me, can be my Master. Let him do what is proper now, under the present circumstance."

We can understand that Devi gave 'Asura-brothers' an ample opportunity to modify their *Asuric* tendency and nature, but being perverted, they did not humble down as they were the symbols of 'Avidya'—ignorance, malformation and delusion. Devi's treatment with *Duta-Sugriva* is quite examplery, as She spoke in the considerate language when he conveyed the sentiments of Shumbha-Nishumbha of marrying Her. Devi played a dynamic role by involving the Asura brothers into direct conflict and fight with Her, when She promised to marry either of the two brothers, who would show Her down in the battle.

This chapter consists of 129 Shlokas with 9 Uvacha Mantras, 66 Tripan mantras and 54 Shlokas. This is known as Devi-Duta-Samvada/dialogue between the Devi and Duta.

Sixth Chapter

In this chapter *'Dhumralochana'* was slain, after he expressed the desire of dragging Her by hair, so that She could be presented before his lord. 'Dhumralochana' was reduced to ashes, after She pronounced the sound 'Hum'—a mystic syllable, came out of the Devi's speech.

This Chapter is known as *Dhumralochana Vadha*—the slaying of the Commander of the forces of *Shumbha-Nishambha* and is concluded in 24 shlokas with 4 Uvacha Mantras and 20 Shlokas.

Seventh Chapter

In this Chapter a description is given as how Chanda-Munda were slain by the Devi. At the command of 'Shumbha-Nishumbha the two arrogant Asura chiefs Chanda-Munda were commissioned to capture 'Ambika'. From the surface of Devi's forehead with frown, Kali—the most Terrible one, suddenly appeared to counter them. The manifestation of Kali is the most dreadful form of Mahamaya. She wears garland of skulls, clad in a tiger's skin, having gapping mouth, tongue out, deep sunk reddish eyes, roaring loudly to fill the regions of the sky with terrible sound and thus slaughtering the army of Asuras. Then Kali pierced the head of *Chanda* and *Munda*, Kali held the severed heads of *Chanda* and *Munda* and offered it as two great 'animal offerings' to *Chandika* in this sacrifice of battle, with loud laughter.

Accordingly Kali said to Chandika, "You shall yourself slay 'Shumbha and Nishumbha', Mahamaya was henceforth adored as Chamunda Devi.

This Chapter is known as 'Chanda-Munda Vadha'—the slaying of *Chanda-Munda*, narrated in 27 Shloka with 2 Uvacha Mantras and 25 Shlokas.

Eighth Chapter

This chapter pertains to the disturbances caused in the

arrogant and perverted soul of Shumbha, after Chanda-Munda were slain by *Chamunda*. Eighty six generals of the '*Udayudha*' rank, eight four generals of the '*Kambu*' rank, fifty generals of the '*Koti-virya*' rank and one hundred generals of the '*Dhumra-Kula*' rank were commissioned to wage a deciding war against Devi. *Kalka, Daurhrada, Maurya, Kalkeya Asuras* were ordered to feed back their generals in that great war. Himself *Shumbha* came with an infantry of two thousand battalions.

Since it was the war between the Supreme Devi and Shumbha; the Asuric forces surrounded the Devi Chandika, Kali and the forceful lion. At that critical hour, the Shaktis issued forth from *Brahma, Shiva, Kartikeya, Vishnu, Indra* and other Devas came before Chandika along with their names, forms, vehicles and missiles, for receiving the Devi's orders. Mahadeva made a submission to Chandika for destroying all the Asuras. Then *Ugra-Chandika* emerged from Chandika. Chandika was still compassionate and appointed Mahadeva as an ambassador to warn Shumbha-Nishumbha for evading death for himself and of their Asura race, by going to *Patala*—netherworlds and let *Indra* rule the three worlds. "Let Devas enjoy the oblations and sacrifices. Otherwise, be ready to meet the unavoidable genocide and destruction of the Asura-race," said the Devi. Arrogant, unmindful and the very nature of 'Avidya' were the 'Asura-brothers', who were filled with indignation and went the spot where '*Katyayani*' stood.

At the very outset, they poured their missiles on the Devi. The most wrathful *Kali*, pierced the enemies in front of 'Shumbha', followed by *Brahmani, Maheshvari, Aindri, Varahi, Narsimhi*. All these are Mothers, who crushed the Asuras into pieces. It could not be tolerated and seen by the great Asura *Raktabija*. He was the wonder of the Asura race. His killing seemed mysterious. He was the source of all the Asuric malignancy, born of his own blood drops. The entire universe was then pervaded by the unwanted Asuras. Even he was crushed and pierced into pieces, still he fought unto last, creating asuras everywhere. Seeing all this magic by the Devi, the whole of his blood was swallowed by *Kali*, while *Chandika* was in the process of killing him with her missiles.

Physiologically, Raktabija is the malignant cell which multiplies, the more it is cut or crushed, it regenerates and causes endless troubles. Avidya multiplies in numberless ways thus making hinderences, provocations, disturbances, distortions in the normal functioning of life. Chandi sees no alternative but to suck the blood of the Asuras, lest the hostile force should spread in the universe. In this episode, we observe that the Devi appointed *Shiva* as *Duta*—ambassador. She assumed the name of *Shivaduti* as a result of that act, and was worshipped as 'Shivaduti' by the devotees.

This chapter is known as *Raktabija-Vadha*—the slaying of Raktabija, narrated in 63 Shlokas of 1 Uvacha Mantra, 1 half Shloka and 61 Shlokas.

Ninth Chapter

In this chapter Rishi says that Chandika cut *Nishumbha's* superb sword and shield with *Kshupra* arrow, on which eight moons were figured. Asura advanced with more missiles to confront Devi but he was split into two parts by Her discus. With his Asuric force, he also fought a dreadful battle with Devi, issuing forth new Asuras of great strength and valour. The Devi then severed the head of Nishumbha, while *Kaumari, Varahi, Brahmani, Vaishnavi* and *Aindri* destroyed and killed other great Asuras. Some Asuras fled from that great battle, while Kali, Shivaduti and Her lion devoured others.

This chapter consists of 41 shlokas with 2 Uvacha Mantras and 39 Shlokas and refers to 'Nishumbha Vadha'—the slaying of Nishumbha.

Tenth Chapter

This chapter is introduced by showing the grief-stricken

Shumbha while witnessing the massacre, killing, and wholesome destruction, including the killing of his most dear brother Nishumbha. He was too much enraged and waged a war against Durga by saying : 'You are exceedingly naughty, resorting to the strength of others. You are puffed up with pride.'

The Devi's reply to Shumbha is not directed to him alone but is a declaration of the Supreme Truth revealed by Mahamaya Herself: "I alone abide". Her proclamation stands to be 'One without a second'. Thus all the Shaktis headed by Brahmani got absorbed into the being of Ambika. With fierce shout of 'Hum' sound and the like, Parmeshvari playfully reduced his missiles into pieces. Arrows, discus, blow of Her palm were used to pierce him into the chest. The Devi felled him down, without using any support. Both of them rose upto the sky in their fight. Being in close contact, they were fighting fiercely which surprised the *Sidhas* and sages. The Devi threw him down with Her fist and he met the end by the pointed dart of Devi.

Eventually, a long chain of Asuras were slain by Mahamaya, either by her single 'Shakti' or by the merger of various 'Shaktis', as the situation demanded with respect to time and place; matter and energy. Thus with the slaying of 'Shumbha' the Asuric magic could not stand before Mahamaya. There is no one else save Mahamaya, who in the cycle of Savarni-Manu is revered, invoked, adored and meditated upon as Shri Chandi or Nava-Durga, is.

Tenth Chapter consists of 32 Shlokas with 4 Uvacha Mantras, 1 half Shaloka and 27 Shalokas. The chapter refers to 'Shumbha Vadha'—the slaying of Shumbha.

Eleventh chapter

This chapter is all submission. It is prayer and adoration. It is a praise for Mahamaya. Devi grants them boons of their choice to the devotees. It is the divine commitment and the higher aspiration of a Sadhaka which is found in the working of the Devi. It is a call for association and obedience to the Divine mantra of Truth.

Devi is seen as the manifestation of *'Sat-chit-ananda'*, when Shumbha was slain by Her. Indra and other Devas led by Agni, praised Katyayani. Mentally joyous, physically illumining, the Devas were spiritually in communion with Mahamaya, after they offered mass prayer to the Devi.

This prayer is highly mystique in essence and explains that Mahamaya dwells in all and all dwell in Mahamaya. The prayer is for universal welfare, as Mahamaya is the source of all what is moving and unmoving, which constitutes the whole universe. The substratum of the world is seen in the form of earth, water, fire, air and space, with which the universe is filled with Her manifestation. Devi manifests in the *Vaishnavi Shakti* and is therefore, the *Vishva-Bija* or Universal seed of the whole existence. She is *Vidya*—knowledge and *Stri*—womenhood of all nature. She grants *'Svarga'*—heaven and *Mukti*—final liberation. She is *Narayani* in the form of *Kshana*—moment and other units of time. She is *Gauri*—the giver of refuge. Being *Sanatani,* She is eternally conscious of creative process, preservative action and destructive power. As *Brahmani,* She rules the world. As She is *Kaumari* and *Vaishnavi,* She grants the lease of life and harmonious development. In Her *Varahi* nature, She uplifts the earth with Her tusk. In Her *Narasimhi* power, She slays Daityas or anti-divine forces. She took away the life of Vritrasura, when assumed the form of *Aindri.* In Her terrible form of *Shivaduti,* She slew the mighty hosts of Daityas. As *Chamunda,* She is adorned with the garland of heads, who slew *Chanda* and *Munda.* She is *Lakshmi, Lajja, Mahavidya, Shraddha, Pushti, Svadha, Dhruva, Maharatri, Mahamaya* and above all the manifestation of *Narayani.* Devi manifests in good furtunes, modesty, great wisdom, faith, nourishment, oblations for the departed souls, non-movement, great might and great cosmic play. Her manifestation is in *'Medha'*—the intellect. She is verily, *Sarasvati.* She is both prosperity and auspiciousness. She manifests in the dark colour. She is *Sarva Svarupa*—nature of all what exists. With every might, She is *Durga*—the saviour of all psychic problems and physical ailments. She removes the functional difficulties and hardships. She is *Katyayani,* who protects us from all fears. As *Bhadrakali* She holds the flame and Her look is terrible, but She guards the Sadhakas by Her trident.

The prayer of Devas make Her manifest in various forms and holding Divine arms. The ring of Her 'bell' destroys the powers of Asuras. Her sword consumes all the blood, marrow and fat. She is Chandika, gleaming with rays. She is the Supreme physician to cure all ailments and diseases She multiplies in various forms as Ambika. She is the very self of the Vedas and Shastras. She saves the world from Rakshasas, serpents and valcanoes. Surely, She is the universe, the supporter of universe and the refuge of universe.

The only criterion of a Sadhaka is to be away from stupidity, doubts and disbelief. She is ever gracious and serene, with the commitment that She would again reincarnate in the twenty-eighth cycle of Vaivasvat Manu. She would be known as Raktadantika to devour the Asura race descended from '*Viprachitti*'. She would manifest as Shatakshi—the hundred eyed Devi having been born, but not womb begotten. She also would assume the form of Shakambari—the vegetable and botanical life, born out of Her cosmic body. She would again be born as the celebrated *Durga* and *Bhima Devi.* Assuming the form of 'Bees', She would be revered as *Bhramari.*

Her last word of promise is to incarnate again and again to maintain the law of '*Dharma*'. The '*Artha-Kama-Moksha*' would be in tune with complete harmony and spiritual order, under Her divine spell.

In this chapter Devi speaks of the methods and modalaties of Her own *Stuti*—adoration and promises to remove all the obstacles in the spiritual path of a Sadhaka, provided he worships Her regularly with concentration, devotion, faith and unconditional submission.

This chapter is the Stuti—an obeisance to Devi and covers 55 shloka in 4 Uvacha Mantras, 1 half Shloka and 50 Shloka.

Twelfth Chapter

Twelfth Chapter is dedicated for attaining the desires *Phala Stuti*/merits. This chapter deals with the scope of '*Patha, Japa* or *Homa*'. This Mahatmyam-glory of Devi destroys all sins and sufferings both physical and mental, including three fold natural calamities. Mahamaya, though Eternal, incarnates again and again to make the triple world rid of *Asuric Shakti*. The Devi declares that the destruction of *Madhu-Kaitabha*, the salughter of *Mahishasura* and slaying of *Shumbha* and *Nishumbha* should be recited with devotion on the eighth, ninth and the fourteenth days of the fortnights and thus, nothing adverse shall befall upon.

All the chapters should be recited, while performing the Chandi Homa. Verily, *Rakshasha*—demons, *Bhuta*—goblins, *Pishacha*—ogres are destroyed by mere chanting of the glory of Durga. *Pashu*—sacrifice of animal nature, *Pushpa*—flowers, *araghya*—flowers and rinsed rice, *dhupa*—incense, *gandha*—perfumes, *dipa*—lamps are the physical and psychic offerings, very dear to Devi as told by Her.

Medha Rishi concludes this chapter by telling the king Suratha about the Supreme nature of Mahamaya in the following way :

1. Devi is eternal, but incarnates again and again with the purpose of protecting the world from *Asuric Shakti*.
2. The universe is deluded and created by the Devi.
3. Mahakali consumes the whole of cosmic manifestation at the end of cycle.

4. She is unborn, but becomes the cause of creation and sustains the creation.
5. She is Lakshmi as the bestower of prosperity and at the times of misfortune, helps the devotees to rise from dawn to Supreme dawn.
6. She grants all, what is best for a 'Sadhaka', when adored, praised and worshipped with flowers, incense, perfumes etc., and above all, with Shraddha—devotion.

This chapter is the *Phala Stuti*/merits of reciting the Sapta Shati. It covers 41 Mantras of 2 Uvacha Mantras, 2 half Shlokas and 37 Shlokas.

Thirteenth Chapter

This chapter is the concluding chapter and is the perfection state of Suratha and Vaishya, after great penances of three years. After attaining the Siddhi, the Devi gives them *Varapradanam*, with bestowing the merits to Suratha—the king and Samadhi Vaishya—the merchant.

Here Medha Rishi further recaptulates as a true preceptor, what has been taught to Suratha, the king earlier. Rishi's focus is on the Devi, who is *Vishnumaya*. She alone deludes the whole universe, including Samadhi Vaishya and the king. She grants Bhoga—enjoyment, Svarga—heavenly abode and Moksha—final release from the cycle of birth and death, to those who aspire for Her grace. Rejection of *Tamas*/ inertia and surrender before Her cosmic play alone can elevate and evolve the Sadhaka, to reach the supramental consciousness.

Markandeya, the narrator, said that the king who became despondent for the loss of his kingdom prostrated before the illustrious Rishi and immediately performed *Aradhana* of Amba to obtain Devi's vision. The merchant also practised severe penances on the sand-banks of a river. Both of them made *Murti-mahimayim*—the clay image of the Devi and worshipped and invoked Her by chanting the Supreme 'Devi Sukta'. Initially abstained from and then put restrain on the food. Both of them offered sacrifices, sprinkled with blood taken from their own physical being. It took them three long years of their Sadhana to please Chandika, who spoke to them in the visible form : "I am well pleased, with your Sadhana; receive all that you solicit for. I bestow these to you both."

Devi is All liberal and compassionate. She does not thrust Her will, after the creation takes place. She grants what is desired by the aspirant, as She is the Supreme Sovereign Mother—creatrix. Suratha—the king like a worldly person desired to achieve 'Bhoga', while Samadhi—the merchant aspired for the Supreme knowledge and 'Yoga'.

Para-Shakti partly veils and partly unveils Her true knowledge and power. King and Merchant are two different personalities on the same plane of earthly existence. Their methods of 'Sadhana' were same, but their goals were different. Chandika granted the boon to the king of getting back his lost kingdom, and the super-status of Manu on earth by the name *Savarni* in his next birth. Vaishya was granted Supreme knowledge for the realization of self, which is the ultimate aim of human birth.

Markandeya concludes the whole of the Sapta-Shati, by saying that the Devi disappeared forthwith, after Her mission to establish Dharma, was over. Both of them stood firm in their devotion and paved the way for *Shakti-Sadhana*.

Thirteenth chapter is the concluding chapter and known as '*Suratha-Vaishya-Varapradana*'. It is bestowing of merits to Suratha and Samadhi. This chapter is concluded in 29 Shlokas of 6 Uvacha Mantras, 11 half Shlokas and 12 Shlokas.

Epilogue

The following acts are to be performed : The *Viniyoga-Nyasya* are to be performed after the recitation of Shri Chandi is over. A mala of 108 beads should be counted with the japam of 'Navarana Mantra' and dedicated to Mahamaya, for it evolves the mental capacity of a Sadhaka to concentrate on the 'Mantra-Sharira' of Chandi and to identify his own being with the 'Navarana-Mantra.' This act is dedicated for self-evolvement and thus becoming an integral part of Mahamaya through self-realization.

The **Devi-Suktam** is added to the *Patham*. It reveals the Supreme Truth of Mahamaya, as She abides in the consciousness of every *Jivatman*—embodied soul. The Devi-Suktam is both Vedic and Tantrik hymn. In the Vedic-Sukta, *Vagambrini* is Rishi, the 'Devata' is *Sat-Chit-Sukhatmakah-Sarvagatah Parmatma*. 'Vak' is the daughter of the celebrated Maharshi Ambrina.

Vak identifies her spirit with that of Mahamaya who says : "I am truth, consciousness and bliss. I move in the form of *Rudra, Vasu* and *Vishvadeva*. I sustain *Mitra, Varuna, Indra, Agni, Ashvini, Soma, Tvashta, Pusha* and *Bhaga*. I grant the merits of *Yajna* to *Yajamana*. I am the sovereign spirit. I move in the cosmic show. I dwell in the embodied souls. Devas execute their designated functions for my sake. I am the power of digestion, power of vision, power of breathing and power of hearing. I tell you and reveal my absolute nature for your higher consciousness. I alone am worthy of it. Every merit depends on my freewill. I create Brahma, Rishi and Medhavin. I dance on the bow of Rudra for slaying Asuras. I fight with the foes of those who come at my refuge. I create the father sky and mother earth. The seas and water sources are vibrant through my power of consciousness. I manifest in the universe. I touch the heavenly abode with my own body, as I am cause of the Universe. I am the earthly and ethereal existence. I am such because I am the great.

Devi Sukta is the highest philosophic treatise explained in the form of Mantra consisting of 8 *Richas*—hymns. It is the source of all this philosophic thought which we perceive, infer and understand on the evolutionary plane of intuition and verbal testimony. It is immanent, transcendent and beyond physical understanding. It is spiritual essence bearing the love of human touch with great Supreme Mother. It is subtle voice of the Vedas, where the will of Supreme knowledge descends in every nerve and cell of human consciousness. It is the ocean of bliss as the Sapta Shati itself is the composition of the essence of the Vedas. The Devi is all with an abode of ultimate mystry, known through devotion, dedication and submission. Sadhaka recites this Sukta to establish his identity with the Supreme knowledge.

A Sadhaka must recite the Tantrik Ratri-Sukta as a supplement to the Devi Sukta.

(Note : Ratri Sukta has been explained at Shloka No.70 to 87 in the first episode.)

Rahasyam—Subtle Secrets

For the three secrets the Rishis are Brahma, Vishnu and Rudra. The Devatas are Mahakali, Mahalakshmi and Mahasarasvati. The Metre is Anushtup. The Seed is Nav-Durga Mahalakshmi and Shakti—the Power is Shrim.

Pradhanik Rahasyam—the Primal Secret

The secret is disclosed by the Rishi to the king, who is keen to know the primal nature of the incarnation of Chandika and the methodology of Chandi Sadhana. Medha Rishi imparts a practical training regarding the worship of the Devi with dedication. He teaches him the quintessentials of Chandika as desired by the king Suratha. This secret explains that Mahalakshmi is foremost of all.

She pervades in eternity. She holds *Matulunga*/Sweet lime, pomegranate, mace, shield and drinking vessel in Her four hands. She holds the serpent on Her head. The male and female organism of procreation are on Her head.

The world was filled with void. The free will of

'Mahalakshmi' created the surpassingly wonderful woman with name of 'Tamasi Devi', having the dark black colour and four arms, armed with missiles and wearing a garland of skulls. She was named as *'Mahamaya, Mahamari, Kshudha, Trisha, Nidra, Trishna, Ekavira, Kalaratri* and *Duratyaya,'* according to their designate functions. Later, She created a beautiful woman and thus was named as *'Mahavidya'*, *'Mahavani'*, *'Bharati'*, *'Vak'*, *'Sarasvati'*, *'Arya'*, *'Brahmi'*, *'Kamadhenu'*, *'Vedagarbha'* and *'Dhishvari'*. The woman created by the Sattva, held *Vina*—musical instrument, *pustaka*—the *Vedas, Akshamala*—garland of beads and *Ankusha*—goad, in Her hands.

Mahakali and Mahasarasvati were commissioned to create the male and female twin-principles according to their respective nature and functions. Mahalakshmi created a subtle force of Hiranyagarbha—the cosmic womb in the form of male and female characteristics and genetics, who were seated on the lotus and were surprisingly looking most beautiful. The male was named as *'Brahma-Vidhi-Viranchi'* and *'Dhata'* and the female was named as *'Shri-Padma-Kamala* and *Lakshmi'*.

Mahakali brought forth Shiva, with the name of *'Rudra-Shankara-Sthanu-Kapardi* and *Trilochana'*, *Saraswati* with the name of *'Trayi-Vidya-Kamadhenu-Bhasha-Akshara* and *Svara'*.

Mahasarasvati brought forth the female of fair complexion and the male of light-dark complexion. The male was named as *'Vishnu, Krishna, Hrishikesha, Vasudeva* and *Janardana'* and the female was called by the names of *'Uma, Gauri, Sati, Chandi, Sundri, Subhaga* and *Shiva'*.

All these three manifested women got transformed into males. Mahalakshmi offered Sarasvati to Brahma, Gauri to Rudra and Shri to Vasudeva. Brahma and Sarasvati created the Universe jointly, while Rudra and Gauri pierced it into atoms. All the *Panchabhutas*—the five elements came forth from the universe under the Primal 'Maha-tattva' known as the cosmic elements. Vishnu and Lakshmi sustained the Universe and was put to dissolution by Maheshvara and Gauri. The Rishi finally recaptulated that Mahalakshmi is both in form and formless as well. The middle of the cosmos sprang up as a resulted action of Mulaprakrati with mobile and immobile objects composed of great *tattvas*. Vishnu nourished the creation alongwith Lakshmi. The Supreme Mother must be known as Truth, Knowledge, Consciousness and Great play. She is the Primal cause of this universe. She has to be adored with other names and yet by no other name can She be understood. Thus the secrets of primal creation is the evolutionary, genetic and vital in nature with strong philosophical base and evolutionary synthesis which is absorbed in the quintessence of Mahamaya.

Mahalakshmi has been described alongwith the incarnations. Therefore, Mahalakshmi is understood as a primal cause of Universe. All the three *Gunas* are Her facets. She is omnipresent with names of '*Asti-Bhati-Priya Naam* and *Rupa*', which refers to Her primordial existence. Her 'Shri Vigraha' is of the golden hue. She is always present in the realm of 'Sat-Chit-Anand'. She is both *Prakriti* and *Purusha* associated with 'Kala'—the time which is Eternal.

This Pradhanik Rahashyam is described in 31 Shlokas.

Vaikrtikam Rahasyam—The Secret of Modification

Rishi discloses the secret of the 'Modifications' and says : 'Tamasi' and 'Sattviki Devi' is of triple nature. Verily, She is '*Sharva, Chandika, Durga, Bhadra* and *Bhagvati*, Mahakali' is 'Yoga-Nidra'—the mystic sleep of Hari, who killed 'Madhu and Kaitabha'. She is the embodiment of ten faces, ten arms and ten feet and is dark black, having thirty eyes. Her eyes, teeth and gums are glittering. Though looking too terrible in form, yet She is the very source of auspiciousness, good fortune. She holds in Her hands the sword, discus, arrows, bow, club, spear, missile, mace, conch and pierced bleeding head.

Mahalakshmi is of Primordial triple nature and is known as the slayer of Mahishasura. Her face is fair, light dark are Her arms, breast is extremely white, waist and feet are red, thighs and buttocks are blue. She is superbly decorated with ornaments. Though having thousands of arms, yet She should be adored only with having the eighteen arms, holding rosary, axe, mace, arrow, thunderbolt, lotus, bow, pitcher, rod, Shakti, sword, shield, conch, bell, cup of wine, trident, noose and discus in those arms. She is all authority and sovereignity.

Mahasarasvati killed Shumbha and Nishumbha. She came forth from the body of Parvati. She has eight arms and holds bell, trident, plough, conch, mace, discus, bow and arrow.

Rishi further explains the procedure of worship. Here, like a true perceptor, Medha Rishi imparts the practical training to his disciples. The Rahasya says : Mahalakshmi should be placed and worshipped in the middle of sanctum-sanctorum, keeping Mahakali in the right and Mahasarasvati in the left and the three twin Devatas infront of them. Separate 'Puja' of Mahakali, Mahasarasvati is also prescribed to gain specific merits. Mahalakshmi should be worshipped with the *Namo-Devi-Mantra* of the fifth chapter known as Devi-Shukta. The Devi should be adorned with ornaments, perfume, rice, incense, lamp, edibles etc. and with 'Homa'.

Essentially, Mahishasura with pierced head should be worshipped as he alone could identify himself with the Devi amongst Asuras. The lion should be worshipped, who is the symbol of sixfold prosperity.

The whole of *Sapta-Shati* should be recited and not part thereof. Every Mantra of the Sapta-Shati should be chanted for 'Homa' with sesame, ghee and sweet-dish. Always a *Kshma Prarthana*—apology should be tendered for lapses and for misreadings, as a human being is never complete to perform 'Puja' strictly in accordance with the injunctions of the scripture. Man by nature is a finite being and is subjected to commission and omission.

The secret is to explain the practical aspects of Divinity, which enunciates the truth behind the modifications in 'name and form'. Mahalakshmi is the *Mulaprakriti,* primordial nature, who at Her free will creates *Vikratti*—modifications for issuing forth the universe from void.

Mahalakshmi created Mahasarasvati with Sattva and Mahakali with Tamas. Mahakali is adored with ten hands. She is verily, Sarasvati who killed Shumbha and Nishumbha. She is adored and worshipped in the middle of the *Garbhagraha*—Sanctum Sanctorum. In Her left, Mahakali and Mahasarasvati should be worshipped and three Devatas should be adored in the back of Mahalakshmi. In Her right *Gauri* with *Rudra* and *Lakshmi* with *Vishnu* should be adored. When Devi with eight arms is adored as *Ashtha Bhuja,* She should be adored alongwith *Nava Durgas, Rudra* and *Ganesha.* The Nava Durgas here are *Brahmi, Maheshvari, Kaumari, Vaishnavi, Varahi, Narsimhi, Aindri, Shivaduti* and *Chamunda* are all nine Shaktis. With concentration of mind, Devi should be adored and all the three episodes should be recited. After the recitation is over, the devotee must make *Parikrama* and *Namaskars* with *Kshma-prarthana.* The *Ahuti* should be with sesame and ghee. He who recites the Sapta Shati regularly, gets all the desired *Purusharthas* viz., *Dharma, Artha, Kama* and *Moksha.* The Puja must be done according to the strict instructions as described in the Shastras.

The Upasana is two-fold—Samashti/Combined and Vyashti individual are prescribed. The Samashti Upasana is as under :

i. Rudra-Gauri, Brahma-Sarasvati, Vishnu-Lakshmi

ii. Chaturbhujas-Mahakali, Mahalakshmi, Mahasarasvati

iii. Dashanana Dashabhuja, Ashtadashabhuja, Ashtabhuja.

Vyashti Upasana is as under—

i. Ashtadashbhuja Puja :

Kala,	Ashtadasbhuja Devi	
	Simha Mahisha	Mrityu

ii. Dashanana Puja :

Kala,	Dashanana Devi	Mrityu

iii. Ashtabhuja Puja :

Kala	Ashtabhuja Devi	Mrityu
Rudra	Navashakti	Vinayàka

All this Puja should be learnt carefully and put in practice as described in the scriptures. The Upasanas are based on the devotion which leads the Sadhaka to perfection.

The *Vaikriti Rahasya* is the modifications which brings forth the whole universe and beyond in complete harmony.

Murti Rahasyam—The Secret of Image

Rishi says in this 'Rahasyam'—secret of image that '*Nanda, Raktadantika, Shakambhari, Durga, Bhima* and *Bhramari* are the six Devis issued forth from Para-Shakti. Nanda is of the golden complexion and wears the garments of the same colour and is called by the names of *Indira, Kamla, Lakshmi, Shri* and *Rukma-ambuja-asana*—being seated on the golden lotus.

Raktadantika is of red complexion and is dressed in the same colour. Her weapons and missiles, hair of head, nails and teeth are all in red colours and look is too terrific. She is known as '*Raktachamunda* and *Yogeshvari*'. '*Shakambari*' is all green, full of all kinds of flowers, fruits, roots and leaves. She presides over the botanical life. Verily, She is '*Shatakshi, Durga, Uma, Gauri, Sati, Chandi, Kalika* and *Parvati*. Bhimadevi is also green. She is adored as *Ekavira, Kalaratri* and *Kamada*. Bhramari is of multicolours. Her garments and ornaments are of different colours. A combination of various colours is seen in Her being. She is known with the names of 'Chitra-Bhramara-pani' and 'Mahamari'.

All these are the manifestation of Chandika. Rishi says that the Murti Rahasyam is of top secret. He, therefore, always bows to Vishvarupa—the Universal form of Devi. She is none else but *Parmeshvari*—Supreme Sovereign Mother Creatrix. With this triple secret, the Sapta-Shati popularly known as Shri Chandi is completed.

The whole universe is the manifestation of the Devi as She is *Sarvarupamayi* and the whole universe is absorbed in the Devi. The devotee makes an obeisance during Puja to Devi alone, who is the quintessence of Mahamaya in triple facets of Mahakali, Mahalakshmi and Mahasarasvati.

Aparadha Kshamapana Stotram

Apart from the secret knowledge, the 'Sadhaka' is desired to have an attitude of total surrender, at the feet of Mahamaya. A 'Sadhaka' is a finite being with limited resources, capacities, potentials and intellect, but his heart should be too much filled with extreme emotion. 'Apradha Kshama' is the bilateral process to receive the grace and supreme knowledge from Mahamaya—the Great Mother which comes from above and aspiration from a 'Sadhaka', which begins from below. Divine grace can transform a 'Sadhaka'. The Unfashionable divine is fashioned in his heart, mind and being for higher self. 'Apradha Kshama' means that the Sadhaka submits before the Mother with folded hands for the mistakes committed by him wittingly or unwittingly, during the Puja/Homa.

"Whatever is finite is almost subject to error, forgetfulness and faults. Thus, the absolute surrender before the Absolute is the path to reach to the highest, the Supreme goal of human life," says Shri Chandi, for merging with the Supreme.

The *Kshama-Stotram* is to get pardon from misdeeds done unwittingly by the devotee. It is concluded by saying

'*Mantra-Kriya* and *Bhakti*' I know not, it alone can be your grace, if You acknowledge me as your own, then grant me the Supreme knowledge. For I surrender at Your feet. I donot know '*Avahavanam*'—invitation, '*Puja*'—worship, '*Dhyanam*'—meditation, '*Mantra*'—mystic syllables, '*Kriya*'—action, '*Bhakti*'—devotion. Whatsoever has been committed, right or wrong, is surrendered at Your feet. Now, I do not know, how to perform '*Visarajanam*'—the modalities of bidding farewell! You are '*Kameshvari, Jaganmata, Sat-chitananda*', so accept my floral offerings as a token of submission. May You grant Your benign grace to me!

Philosophical Basis of Shri Chandi

Shri Chandi is the sacred scripture with spiritual vibrations, dealing with human relationship with the Divinity. It is popularly known as the Durga-Sapta-Shati and is highly occult. Each Shloka is potent with Shakti-bija of Mahamaya. She is verily, the *Shabdamayi Shakti,* who is identical with Absolute Reality or *Brahmi.*

Mahamaya is the Primal Deity, who did not utter a single syllable in the manifestations of *Mahakali,* because She never assumed any form She is all witness, path and perfection in 'Yoga'. She is both 'Sadhaka' and 'Sadhana', therefore, no oral communication is needed from either side, She is nameless, unborn but is the Supreme mystic truth. For the convenience of *Sadhaka,* She assumes the feminine role of Mother Creatrix. She is the quintessense of Supreme 'Yoga' or 'Absolute Yoga'. She is the conscious force or '*Chitti*' or *Cit-Shakti,* identity of *Jiva* with *Shakti.* Her nature is to function in the cosmic wheel, where speech does not work, but Her mere Will is ever present. Her *Atman* or self and *Vidya*—knowledge vibrates in the cosmic world. She is manifestation of Prakasha—light, where there is no trace of ignorance but brilliance alone exists. She need not have any medium to manifest, to create, to communicate, as She is eternal force and strength. Her wrath is an expression seen in physical decay and death. She swallows death and brings closer the 'Sadhana' and 'Sadhaka'. She listens to every vibration of a Sadhaka. Every nerve, tissue and cell of the manifested world is but a glimpse of Her *'Iccha-Shakti'*. Though She does not speak, but She reveals herself to every 'Sadhaka'. *Mahakali* is the very self of *Shri Bhagvan Hari*. She is *Jagan-Murti*—the cosmic self.

Mahamaya speaks but a few words in the manifestation of *Mahalakshmi*. Her words to Mahishasura speaks of Her Supreme warning to desist from doing *'Adharma'*—by usurping powers of Devas. She is the Supreme Sovereign, who controls over the universe and maintains the law of *Dharma* and supreme justice. With all her Magestic glances, She asks the *Devas* to seek the boons. This is the only speech that She made, after She listened to their *Stuti*—the Divine praises. Her voice is to be heard with the conscious mind. Her single word is an indication of rhythm and balance, therefore, She speaks the word of command. She only acts as a true liberal Mother, who fulfills every need of the aspirants. She is helping them to exercise their functions without fear or favour. Verily, Her speech speaks of Her mystry beyond the reach of intellect. She speaks a little but reveals to all, the Supreme Truth.

Mahamaya speaks a lot when assumes the form of *Mahasarasvati*. She speaks to the *Duta* in the most dignified manner. Her words are both polite and diplomatic, and assures him of Her being wedded to Shumbha and Nishumbha, provided they win Her over in the battle. What She speaks of Herself as being a woman of lesser knowledge is Her super-wit. She utilises the wit in that diplomatic discussion. Her behaviour is all provoking, when She speaks to *Duta-Sugriva*.

She again speaks to *Dhumralochana Asura*, who was not a *Duta*, but arrogant, embodiment of pride, deceit, wrath and possessor of the false notion that he could lift her away, if Devi does not make compromise with the directives of the

Asura-brothers. Her speech put him in great illusion and his action was the reflection of Her words. She consented to be lifted away and it resulted into his disaster and death, including his masters. This was Her Divine strategy.

She speaks to 'Shumbha' after listening to his Asuric insults and tells him the highest Truth of Her 'Shakti' which is *One* and only one. While speaking, She exhibits all her majestic 'Shaktis' merging in her being. Her tone is that of a true teacher, who wants to bring the ignorant on the path of knowledge, but She does not force to accept it. Again, Her approach is most skillful in executing the force of Divine order. She gives him the full breathing time to get ready for war. This is really a great wisdom in Her speech.

She speaks to 'Devas' after listening to their *Narayani* prayers, when She had already slain 'Shumbha and Nishumbha.' Practically there was nowhere any potential threat seen to them. She asks them to ask for a boon, but lays the condition that the boon would be utilized for the welfare of this empirical world. This is what a genuine master does. Her speech is soothing and helping the world to go from darkness to light, from unreal to real, from confusion to clarity and from death to immorality.

She again speaks to them after they insisted upon to save them from the forthcoming dangers. 'Devas' are more dependent on Mahamaya, as they feel their incompetence to face the '*Danvas*' / *Asuras*—anti-divine forces in future also. Her speech is a divine declaration of Her future incarnation and methods of worship. Her speech is highly spiritual on the plane of physical consciousness.

She speaks to 'Suratha'—the king and 'Samadhi'—the merchant, after they took to severe penances. She gives them the free choice to determine their merits of Sadhana. She blesses them with Her own physical appearance and grants back the kingdom and the 'Manu' status to Suratha. To Samadhi, She graces him with the declaration of his Eternal merger with Her. Her speech is Supremely proficient, excellent and realistic. Her appearance is superb.

Chandi is the wrath of Para-Shakti. She is impetuosly fierce towards the 'Daityas'—anti-divine forces, having unbalanced body and egoistic mind. They are the incarnations of *'tamas, avidya* and *ajnana'*. They uphold falsehood and inertia. Their single aim in life is to defeat, humiliate and usurp their status of being 'Devas'. No doubt, their *Asuric Shakti* is more powerful and the 'Devas' cannot beat them individually. It is only the Devi, who manifests in the various forms of Chandi to counter their 'Avidya' for the sake of 'Devas'. The root of 'Chandi' signifies anger. Consequently, Her manifestation is to exhibit anger with multiforms, multifaces and multiple weapons and missiles. Her embodiment is all terrific and Her ways are mysterious. She descends into the world, which She makes with Her *'Iccha-Shakti'*—free will but She always lives in the glory of infinite.

She is the *'Shrira* of *Devi-Mahatamya'*—the glory of Supreme Mother, consisting of three episodes, the manifestation in the most subtle mantra of *Navarna*. She is inseparable from the manifestation of the *'Nava-Durga'*. In the Sapta-Shati, She is said to be *Mahamaya*—the Absolute reality. In this Mahatamyam, She has been realized as *'Nishkala'* unmanifest and *Sakala*—manifest. In the beginning, the 'Nishkala' aspect of Mahamaya alone existed. It became *Muda Prakrati*—dormant force of nature and got split in 'Sattva-rajas and tamas'. It assumed the forms of variety in relation to time, sound and space. Liberally, She exists in Supreme Eternity, but it creates both 'Vidya' and 'Avidya'. 'Chit' is Her nature and through its power, it brings forth 'Name and Form', and assumes the name of *Shri Mata*—Mother Creatrix.

She guides 'Jiva'— the individual being to realise the *'Chaitanya Rupini Devi'*—divinity of consciousness. It is the highest perfection for a man bound by time and space. Devi is path and the goal, the cause and effect and even beyond that. She transcends all the limitations, mutations and modifications. 'Jiva' complaints of 'death and fate' which is the crux of the 'Sapta-Shati', Devi erases the dust of fate and makes him move towards the realm of higher consciousness.

She is unfathomable in the process of continuity and also in conditioning the psycho-physical and spiritual tendencies of '*Manvas*—the humans—*Siddhas*—the Perfect Sages and *Devas*', the brilliant ones. She sees the clash of forces, strange meetings and companionship of twins to form the world of creation. She is the prayer of Brahma, prayer of Devas and the prayer of 'Samadhi and Suratha'—the human representatives of Yoga and Bhoga. She is the illusion of Asuras. She veils consciousness with 'tamas'. She commands 'Rajas', when reveals Herself to 'Devas' and Asuras like Mahishasura. She is pure 'Sattva' of Yoga, the limbs of Yoga and the quitessence of Yoga.

In human nature, we observe a symbolic fight between pure consciousness and false ego, between creativity and destruction. Though the Sapta-Shati is a highly mystic scripture, yet it is a devotional text as revealed by Mahamaya Herself, in the Rahasyam—secrets of the concluding Chapters of Sapta-Shati.

Prayoga—Procedure

The Sapta-Shati is the Sadhana Shastra—a practical manual to dive deep in the niceties ot the spiritual ocean. The great masters of this treatise have laid *Prayoga* or procedure to undertake the occult Sadhana of Shri Chandi. We witness, a multitude of Devas and Devis around the Supreme Shakti coming forth from Her effulgence and thus merging in the same effulgence. So the Prayoga is an imperative factor for any *Karya-Siddhi*—the accomplishment of purpose. It is the disciplinary aspect of the Sadhana. One must observe *Brahmacharya*—the celibacy in thought, deed and word and devote oneself in understanding the true import of the Mother. Homa offerings with *Payasam-tilam-sarshipam* in the sacred fire is done by reciting each mantra of the text. The 'Sapta-Shati' is the integration of statis with dynamis of *Shabda Brahman*. The ever curious mind is bound to reflect upon human existence in a differentiated manner but it is the Shakti-Yoga which brings him close and closer to higher consciousness. The mind has the potential of bringing perceiver and perceived in the context of '*Chetna*'—doctrine of recognition.

The set up and composition of the Sapta-Shati is in seven hundred mantras—Shlokas in the following manner :

Bhagvan Vishnu utters	...	3	mantras
Brahma utters	...	16	mantras
Markandeya Rishi utters	...	38	mantras
Medha Rishi utters	...	445	mantras
Surath Raja utters	...	13	mantras
Samadhi Vaishya utters	...	12	mantras
Sugriva Duta utters	...	15	mantras
Devi utters	...	76	mantras
Devas utter	...	82	mantras
Total	...	700	mantras

Devi Kavacham consists of	56	mantras
Argala Stotram	25	mantras
Kilkam	14	mantras
Vedic Ratri Suktam	8	mantras
Tantrik Ratri Suktam	15	mantras
Vedic Devi Suktam	8	mantras
Tantrik Devi Suktam	30	mantras
Pradhanik Rahasyam	31	mantras

Vayakritik Rahasyam	39	mantras
Murti Rahasyam	25	mantras
Kshama Prarthana	8	mantras
Total	259	mantras

नवदुर्गाध्यानम्।

Nava Durga-Dhyanam

प्रथमं शैलपुत्री च द्वितीयं ब्रह्मचारिणी।
तृतीयं चन्द्रघण्टेति कूष्माण्डेति चतुर्थकम्।।

पञ्चमं स्कन्दमातेति षष्ठं कात्यायनीति च।
सप्तमं कालरात्रीति महागौरीति चाष्टमम्।।

नवमं सिद्धिदात्री च नवदुर्गाः प्रकीर्तिताः।
उक्तान्येतानि नामानि ब्रह्मणैव महात्मना।।

1. Shailaputri 2. Brahmacharini 3. Chandraghanta 4. Kushmanda 5. Skandamata 6. Katyayyaini 7. Kalaratri 8. Mahagauri 9. Siddhidhatri are the Nava Durgas in succession. All these Devis are celebrated/glorified Durgas. These names have been told by the highly gifted Great Seer Brahma.

शैलपुत्री

वन्दे वाञ्छितलाभाय चन्द्रार्धकृतशेखराम्।
वृषारुढां शूलधरां शैलपुत्रीं यशस्विनीम्।।

Shailaputri is first in the line of Navadurga. I pay my Vandana—obeisance to the Divine Mother Shailaputri, Who bestows upon the choicest boons to the devotees. The moon crescent is adorned on Her forehead. She is mounted on the bullock and holding a lance in Her hand. She is Yashasvini—the celebrated glorious Mother Durga.

ब्रह्मचारिणी

दधाना करपद्माभ्यामक्षमालाकमण्डलू।
देवी प्रसीदतु मयि ब्रह्मचारिण्यनुत्तमा।।

Brahmacharini is second in the line of Navadurga. May the Divine Mother Brahmacharini—the Effulgent Mother be pleased, Who holds a rosary of *Akshamala* in the right hand and *Kamandalu*/a celestial pot in the left hand! She is the most Auspicious Mother of the Universe.

चन्द्रघण्टा

पिण्डजप्रवरारूढा चण्डकोपास्त्रकैर्युता।
प्रसादं तनुते मह्यं चन्द्रघण्टेति विश्रुता।।

Chandraghanta is third in the line of Navadurga. She bestows upon Her gracious blessings, Who is mounted on the shoulders of lion. She holds the sophisticated, deadly missiles in her hand. May She be auspicious to me!

कूष्माण्डा

सुरासम्पूर्णकलशं रुधिराप्लुतमेव च।
दधाना हस्तपद्माभ्यां कूष्माण्डा शुभदास्तु मे।।

Kushmanda is fourth in the line of Navadurga. May the Divine Mother Kushmanda be pleased with me and be gracious enough! She holds *Amrit*/ambrosia, as well as blood in her *Kalasham*—the carry pot in her hands.

स्कन्दमाता

सिंहासनगता नित्यं पद्माश्रितकरद्वया।
शुभदास्तु सदा देवी स्कन्दमाता यशस्विनी।।

Skandamata is the fifth in the line of Navadurga. May the Gracious Mother Skandamata be pleased with us! Her coach is on the line. She is the Eternal Mother, holding a lotus in Her hands. She is for all prosperity/glory.

कात्यायनी

चन्द्रहासोज्जवलकरा शार्दूलवरवाहना।
कात्यायनी शुभं दद्याद्देवी दानवघातिनी।।

Katyayini is the sixth in line of Navadurga. She holds *Chandrahasa,* the Sword which creates illumination/lustre in the Universe. She is mounted on the leopard. She is the Auspicious Mother who annihilets the Rakshasas/anti-divine forces. She is verily, *Yashasivini*—the Glorious Mother.

कालरात्रि

एकवेणी जपाकर्णपूरा नग्ना खरास्थिता।
लम्बोष्ठी कर्णिकाकर्णी तैलाभ्यक्तशरीरिणी।।

वामपादोल्लसल्लोहलताकण्टकभूषणा।
वर्धन्मूर्धध्वजा कृष्णा कालरात्रिर्भयंकरी।।

Kalaratri is seventh in the line of Navadurga. The hue of Kalaratri is of dark black. Her hair is dishevelled. She is putting on the ear-rings of *Japa Kusuma* flower. She remains always naked/uncovered. Her Vehicle is an ass, lips are very long to Her. *Karnika* missiles, which She holds is of arrow like ore. Her left feet is always in unrythemic movement for making hit to the *Danavas.* Her ornaments are like that of thorny cactus. She is Jet Black. Her flag is upright hoisted. Verily, She is ferrocious and furious in form.

महागौरी

श्वेते वृषे समारूढा श्वेताम्बरधरा शुचिः।
महागौरी शुभं दद्यान्महादेवप्रमोददा।।

Mahagauri is eighth in the line of Navadurgas. The complexion of Mahagauri is crystal white. She is mounted on the white bullock. Her robes are spotless White and ever auspicous. She gives excitement to Her consort *Mahadeva.*

सिद्धिदात्री

सिद्धगन्धर्वयक्षाद्यैरसुरैरमरैरपि ।
सेव्यमाना सदा भूयात् सिद्धिदा सिद्धिदायिनी ।।

Siddhidatri is ninth and the last in the line of Navadurgas. She is adored by *Siddha*/Perfect sages, *Gandharvas*/Celestial musicians, *Yakshas*/Celestial custodians of the treasuries. She is always adored by the Immortal Devatas. May She be ever auspicious to grant Siddhi in our existence!

Navadurgas are the Yoginis.

1. On the first day of Navaratra, Yogis keep their mind concentrated on the Muladhara Chakra.
2. On the second day of Navaratra, Yogis move upward in the Swadhisthana Chakra.
3. On the third day of Navaratra, Yogis move upward and enters into the Manipura Chakra.
4. On the fourth day of Navaratra, Yogis move upward in the Anahata Chakra.
5. On the fifth day of Navaratra, Yogis move upward in the Visuddha Chakra.
6. On the sixth day of Navaratra, Yogis move upward in the Ajna Chakra.
7. On the seventh day of Navaratra, Yogis move upward in the Sahasrara Chakra.
8. On the eighth day of Navaratra, Yogis move upward and transcend beyond. They get the Divine Siddhis.
9. On the ninth day of Navaratra, the Sadhaka acquires the unique Siddhis of Absolute perfections.

पाठविधिः

Procedure of Recitation

A devotee must take a bath and sit down on some purified/sanctified *Asanam*/cushion, keeping pure water, *Puja* material and sacred text of Shri Durga Sapta Shati in the Puja room/place of Sadhana.

The text book of Shri Chandi must be placed on the wooden desk while facing towards the east. This place is known as the *Adhara-Shakti*.

The devotee must apply Tilakam of his/her own choice on the forehead and sip the water while reading the following four Mantras for *Tattva-Shuddhi* (purification of the self).

ॐ ऐं आत्मतत्त्वं शोधयामि नमः स्वाहा।
ॐ ह्रीं विद्यातत्त्वं शोधयामि नमः स्वाहा।
ॐ क्लीं शिवतत्त्वं शोधयामि नमः स्वाहा।
ॐ ऐं ह्रीं क्लीं सर्वतत्त्वं शोधयामि नमः स्वाहा।।

OM-Aim-Namah Svaha, I purify Atmatattva—the quintessence of self.

OM-Hrim Namah Svaha, I purify Vidyatattva—the quintessence of knowledge.

OM-Klim Namah Svaha, I purify Shivatattva—the quintessence of Shiva consciousness.

OM-Aim-Hrim-Klim-Namah-Svaha, I purify all the quintessentials of the cosmic life.

After reciting the Mantras for purification, a devotee is required to pay his/her obeisance to *Shri Ganesha,* the *Guru*/preceptor and put on *Pavitri* of *Kusha* grass in the ring finger and recite the *Sankalpa Mantra* while pouring water alongwith red flowers and rice in some copper pot.

Sankalpa Mantra

ॐ श्रीगणेशायनमः। ॐ विष्णुर्विष्णुर्विष्णुः। ॐ नमः परमात्मने, श्रीपुराणपुरुषोत्तमस्य श्रीविष्णोराज्ञया प्रवर्तमानस्याद्य श्रीब्रह्मणो द्वितीयपरार्द्धे श्रीश्वेतवाराहकल्पे वैवस्वतमन्वन्तरेऽष्टाविंशतितमे कलियुगे प्रथमचरणे जम्बूद्वीपे भारतवर्षे भरतखण्डे महामांगल्यप्रदे मासानाम् उत्तमे....... अमुकमासे...... अमुकपक्षे...... अमुकतिथौ..... अमुकवासरान्वि-तायाम्........ अमुकनक्षत्रे....... अमुकराशिस्थिते...... सूर्ये अमुकामुकराशिस्थितेषु.......... चन्द्रभौमबुधगुरुशुक्रशनिषु सत्सु शुभे योगे शुभकरणे एवं गुणविशेषणविशिष्टायां शुभपुण्यतिथौं सकलशास्त्रश्रुतिस्मृतिपुराणोक्तफलप्राप्तिकामः अमुकगोत्रोत्पन्नः अहं ममात्मनः सपुत्रस्त्रीबान्धवस्य श्रीनवदुर्गानुग्रहतो सकलकामनासिद्ध्यर्थं श्रीनवदुर्गाप्रसादेन सर्वापन्निवृत्तिसर्वाभीष्टफलावाप्तिधर्मार्थकाममोक्ष-चतुर्विधपुरुषार्थसिद्धिद्वारा श्रीमहाकालीमहालक्ष्मीमहासरस्वतीदेवता-प्रीत्यर्थं शापोद्धारपुरस्सरं कवचार्गलाकीलकपाठवेदतन्त्रोक्तरात्रि-सूक्तन्यासविधिसहितनवार्णजपसप्तशतीन्यासध्यानसहितचरित्रसम्बन्धि-विनियोगन्यासध्यानपूर्वकं च 'मार्कण्डेय उवाच।। सावर्णिः सूर्यतनयो यो मनुः कथ्यतेऽष्टमः। इत्याद्यारभ्य 'सावर्णिर्भविता मनुः' इत्यन्तं दुर्गासप्त-शतीपाठं तदन्ते न्यासविधिसहितनवार्णमन्त्रजपं वेदतन्त्रोक्तदेवीसूक्तपाठं रहस्यत्रयपठनं शापोद्धारादिकं च करिष्ये।

OM SHRI GANESHAYA NAMAH

OM Vishnu, Vishnu, Vishnu. I pay my obeisance to Parmatman-the Absolute reality who is Shri Purana Purushottama. With His command, I make this resolve during the second aeon of the Shri Shveta Varaha Kalpa falling in the twenty eighth Manvantara. It is the first portion of the Kaliyuga and I perform the Sankalpa in the Jambhu Dvipa—Bharatavarsha and at the time of ..... month, ... fortnight ..... tithi for attaining the merits of Dharma-Artha-Kama-Moksha by propitiating the blessings of Shri Nava

Durga, who is Mother creatrix in the manifestation of Shri Mahakali-Mahalakshmi-Mahasarasvati. I also resolve to recite Kavacham-Argala-Kilkam-Vedic and Tantrik Ratri Suktam and all the three episodes of Shri Durga Sapta Shati from "Markandeya Uvacha/said to Savarni-Bhavitah Manu" and Vedic-Tantrik Devi Suktam with all the Nyasas and the Shapa-uddahara Mantras, to be followed by the Triple Rahasyas of Shri Chandi. The devotees are supposed to recite the name of month, fortnight, day, constellation etc. during Sankalpa at the.... places.

अथ पुस्तकपूजा

Pustaka Puja

(Adoration of the Durga Sapta Shati text)

ॐ नमो देव्यै महादेव्यै शिवायै सततं नमः।
नमः प्रकृत्यै भद्रायै नियताः प्रणताः स्म ताम्।।

(वाराहीतन्त्र तथा चिदम्बरसंहिता)

OM. My obeisance ever and always be to the *Devi, Mahadevi, Shiva*! My obeisance to *Prakrati*, to *Bhadra* and I always surrender to the Divine Mother!

ध्यात्वा देवीं पञ्चपूजां कृत्वा योन्या प्रणम्य च।
आधारं स्थाप्य मूलेन स्थापयेत्तत्र पुस्तकम्।।

After meditating upon the Divine Mother and offering *Pancha Puja* and paying obeisance to Her, the *Adhara*/ basement should be installed and the Sapta Shati text to be kept on that *Adhara*.

The devotee must recite seven times the Shapoddhara Mantra in the beginning and at the end of Patham.

अथ शापोद्धारः

Shapoddhara Mantra

(Mantra for Lifting of the Curse)

ॐ ह्रीं क्लीं श्रीं क्रां क्रीं चण्डिकादेव्यै शापनाशानुग्रहं कुरु कुरु स्वाहा।

After Shapoddhara Mantra, the devotee is required to recite the Utkilana Mantra.

अथ उत्कीलन मन्त्रः

Utkilana Mantra

Mantra for opening of the Nailing

ॐ श्रीं क्लीं ह्रीं सप्तशति चण्डिके उत्कीलनं कुरु कुरु स्वाहा।

After Utkilana Mantra Mritasanjivani Vidya Japam should be performed seven times.

अथ मृतसंजीवनी विद्या जपः

Mritsanjivani Vidya Japam

(Recitation for bringing back the life)

ॐ ह्रीं ह्रीं वं वं ऐं ऐं मृतसंजीवनि विद्ये मृतमुत्थापयोत्थापय क्रीं ह्रीं ह्रीं वं स्वाहा।

Note : The Scripture says : The *Kavacham, Argala, Kilkam* alongwith the three Rahasyas are the six limbs of Durga Sapta Shati. The Yoga-Ratnavali, affirms :

कवचं बीजमादिष्टमर्गला शक्तिरुच्यते।
कीलकं कीलकं प्राहुः सप्तशत्या महामनोः।।

Seed is the *Kavacham,* Shakti is *Argala, Kilkam* is nailing—which is the mode of the Sapta Shati Recitation.

अथ देव्याः कवचम्

DEVI KAVACHAM (ARMOUR OF DEVI)

ॐ अस्य श्रीचण्डीकवचस्य ब्रह्मा ऋषिः, अनुष्टुप् छन्दः, चामुण्डा देवता, अङ्गन्यासोक्तमातरो बीजम्, दिग्बन्धदेवतास्तत्त्वम्, श्रीजगदम्बा-प्रीत्यर्थे सप्तशतीपाठाङ्गत्वेन जपे विनियोगः।

Brahma is the *Rishi*, metre is *Anushtup*, Devata is *Chamunda*, the seed is *Anga-nyasa-ukhta-matra*, the *Tattvam* element is *Dik-Bandha—Devata* of *Shri Chandi Kavacham*. The *Viniyoga*/ application stands for keeping the *japam* as the limb of the Sapta Shati Patham.

ॐ नमश्चण्डिकायै ।।

Om Namaskar to Chandika

मार्कण्डेय उवाच

Markandeya Said :

ॐ यद्गुह्यं परमं लोके सर्वरक्षाकरं नृणाम्।
यन्न कस्यचिदाख्यातं तन्मे ब्रूहि पितामह।।1।।

O Grandsire! Please tell me the secret of secrets, which would protect the human beings from all the quarters and which has not been explored by any body.

ब्रह्मोवाच

Brahma Said :

अस्ति गुह्यतमं विप्र सर्वभूतोपकारकम्।
देव्यास्तु कवचं पुण्यं तच्छृणुष्व महामुने।। 2।।

"Such a means/resource is the Devi Kavacham, which is the quintessence of all the secrets, sacred and giving beneficence to all the human race." O great Muni! listen to that.

प्रथमं शैलपुत्री च द्वितीयं ब्रह्मचारिणी।
तृतीयं चन्द्रघण्टेति कूष्माण्डेति चतुर्थकम्।। 3।।

Shailaputri is the first, Brahmacharini is the second, the third is the Chandraghanta, Kushmanda is the fourth.

पञ्चमं स्कन्दमातेति षष्ठं कात्यायनीति च।
सप्तमं कालरात्रीति महागौरीति चाष्टमम्।। 4।।

Skandamata is the fifth; Katyayani is the sixth, Kalaratri is the seventh, Mahagauri is the eighth......,

नवमं सिद्धिदात्री च नवदुर्गाः प्रकीर्तिताः।
उक्तान्येतानि नामानि ब्रह्मणैव महात्मना।। 5।।

.....Siddhidhatri is the ninth. These are said to be the Nava Durgas of great excellence. These have been said by the Mahatma—the great seer Brahma himself.

अग्निना दह्यमानस्तु शत्रुमध्ये गतो रणे।
विषमे दुर्गमे चैव भयार्ताः शरणं गताः।। 6।।

Any person caught in highly flames of fire; encircled by the enemies in the battlefield and involved in the great obstacles; being afraid of; thus surrendering before.....,

न तेषां जायते किंचिदशुभं रणसंकटे।
नापदं तस्य पश्यामि शोकदुःखभयं न हि।। 7।।

......(the nine Devis), he does not see inauspiciousness even in the crisis of war. I do not visualise any sort of misfortune, sorrow, danger/dread and suffering for him.

यैस्तु भक्त्या स्मृता नूनं तेषां वृद्धिः प्रजायते।
ये त्वां स्मरन्ति देवेशि रक्षसे तान्न संशयः।। 8।।

Those who remember always the presence of Devi with

devotion, they become prosperous. O Deveshi! Sovereign Supreme Mother! You always defend them undoubtedly.

प्रेतसंस्था तु चामुण्डा वाराही महिषासना।
ऐन्द्री गजसमारूढा वैष्णवी गरुडासना।। 9।।

Chamunda is seated on the preta-ghost, Varahi is seated on the buffalo. Aindri is seated on the elephant and Vaishnavi is on the Garuda.

माहेश्वरी वृषारूढा कौमारी शिखिवाहना।
लक्ष्मीः पद्मासना देवी पद्महस्ता हरिप्रिया।। 10।।

Maheshwari is seated on the bull, Kaumari on the peacock. Lakshmi on the lotus and holds a lotus in Her hand. Verily, She is the consort of Hari.

श्वेतरूपधरा देवी ईश्वरी वृषवाहना।
ब्राह्मी हंससमारूढा सर्वाभरणभूषिता।। 11।।

Ishwari, who is on the bull, has assumed white complexion. Brahmi's ride is on the swan, who is adorned with all the ornaments.

इत्येता मातरः सर्वाः सर्वयोगसमन्विताः।
नानाभरणशोभाढ्या नानारत्नोपशोभिताः।। 12।।

All these (nine) Mothers are the synthesis of Yogic Shakti. These are adorned with different ornaments and looking lustrous with multicoloured jewels.

दृश्यन्ते रथमारूढा देव्यः क्रोधसमाकुलाः।
शङ्खं चक्रं गदां शक्तिं हलं च मुसलायुधम्।। 13।।

Being on their rides, all these appear to be filled with great anger. Conch, discus, mace, Shakti, plough, pester are the missiles....,

खेटकं तोमरं चैव परशुं पाशमेव च।
कुन्तायुधं त्रिशूलं च शार्ङ्गमायुधमुत्तमम्।। 14।।

.....*khetaka* club, *tomara* lance, axe, noose, *kunta* spear, trident, horn are their arms and ammunition.

दैत्यानां देहनाशाय भक्तानामभयाय च।
धारयन्त्यायुधानीत्थं देवानां च हिताय वै।। 15।।

These are manifested to kill the *Daityas*-embodiments of ignorance and to grant protection to the devotees. They take up the arms for the welfare of the Devas.

नमस्तेऽस्तु महारौद्रे महाघोरपराक्रमे।
महाबले महोत्साहे महाभयविनाशिनि।। 16।।

Namaskar-prostration to *Maha Raudri*—the most Ferrocious mother! *Maha Ghora Parakrama*! Be my obeisance to *Mahabala* and *Mahotsa* and to *Maha-Bhaya-Vinashini*!

त्राहि मां देवि दुष्प्रेक्ष्ये शत्रूणां भयवर्धिनि।
प्राच्यां रक्षतु मामैन्द्री आग्नेय्यामग्निदेवता।। 17।।

Protect me O Devi! You create fear among the foes. It is too difficult to look at you. So, *Aindri* save me from the eastern direction, and *Agni Devata* from south east quater.

दक्षिणेऽवतु वाराही नैर्ऋत्यां खड्गधारिणी।
प्रतीच्यां वारुणी रक्षेद् वायव्यां मृगवाहिनी।। 18।।

Varahi may protect me from the southern direction. *Khadgadharini* protect me from the *Nairritya*-south west direction. Varuni from the west and *Mrigavahini* from the *Vayvi*/North-west direction.

उदीच्यां पातु कौमारी ऐशान्यां शूलधारिणी।
ऊर्ध्वं ब्रह्माणि मे रक्षेदधस्ताद् वैष्णवी तथा।। 19।।

Kaumari to protect me from the north, *Shuladharini* from the Ishan direction/north-east. Brahmani to protect me from the above and *Vaishnavi* from the below.

एवं दश दिशो रक्षेच्चामुण्डा शववाहना।
जया मे चाग्रतः पातु विजया पातु पृष्ठतः।। 20।।

So *Chamunda* to protect me from all the ten directions, who makes the ride on a corpse. *Jaya* to protect me in the front area, and *Vijaya* from the rear areas.

अजिता वामपार्श्वे तु दक्षिणे चापराजिता।
शिखामुद्योतिनी रक्षेदुमा मूर्ध्नि व्यवस्थिता।। 21।।

Ajita to protect from my left and *Aparajita* from the right. *Udyotini* to protect my tuft, *Uma* to protect my forehead.

मालाधरी ललाटे च भ्रुवौ रक्षेद् यशस्विनी।
त्रिनेत्रा च भ्रुवोर्मध्ये यमघण्टा च नासिके।। 22।।

Maladhari to protect my forehead, Yashasvini to protect both the eyebrows. *Trinetra* to protect the centre of the eyebrows and *Yamaghanta* to protect nostrils.

शङ्खिनी चक्षुषोर्मध्ये श्रोत्रयोर्द्वारवासिनी।
कपोलौ कालिका रक्षेत्कर्णमूले तु शांकरी।। 23।।

Shankhini to protect pituitary gland—the central part of my eyes and *Dvaravasini* to protect the base of my ears. Kalika *Devi* to protect my cheeks and *Shankari* to protect the base of my ears.

नासिकायां सुगन्धा च उत्तरोष्ठे च चर्चिका।
अधरे चामृतकला जिह्वायां च सरस्वती।। 24।।

Sughanda to protect my nose and the upper lip by *Charchika*; lower lip by *Amritakala* and my tongue to be protected by *Saraswati*.

दन्तान् रक्षतु कौमारी कण्ठदेशे तु चण्डिका।
घण्टिकां चित्रघण्टा च महामाया च तालुके।। 25।।

Kaumari may protect my teeth and the throat region by *Chandika*. *Chitraghanta* to protect my thyriod and palatal by *Mahamaya*.

कामाक्षी चिबुकं रक्षेद् वाचं मे सर्वमङ्गला।
ग्रीवायां भद्रकाली च पृष्ठवंशे धनुर्धरी।। 26।।

Kamakshi may protect my chin and *Sarvamangala* my speech. *Bhadrakali* to protect my neck and *Dhanurdhari* to protect my spine.

नीलग्रीवा बहिःकण्ठे नलिकां नलकूबरी।
स्कन्धयोः खड्गिनी रक्षेद् बाहू मे वज्रधारिणी।। 27।।

Nilagriva may protect my outer throat and the vocal chords by *Nalakuberi*. *Khadgini* may protect my both the shoulders and *Vajradharini* to protect my both the arms.

हस्तयोर्दण्डिनी रक्षेदम्बिका चाङ्गुलीषु च।
नखाञ्छूलेश्वरी रक्षेत्कुक्षौ रक्षेत्कुलेश्वरी।। 28।।

Dandini may protect my both the hands and *Ambika* to protect my fingers. *Shuleshvari* to protect my nails and *Kuleshvari* to protect my abdomen.

स्तनौ रक्षेन्महादेवी मनः शोकविनाशिनी।
हृदये ललिता देवी उदरे शूलधारिणी।। 29।।

Mahadevi may protect my both the nipples and *Shoka-Vinashani* to protect my mind. May *Lalita Devi* protect my heart region and *Shuladharini* to my gastro intestinal system!

नाभौ च कामिनी रक्षेद् गुह्यं गुह्येश्वरी तथा।
पूतना कामिका मेढ्रं गुदे महिषवाहिनी।। 30।।

May *Kamini* to protect my navel and *Guheshwari* to protect my anus. *Putana* and *Karnika* to my male organism and *Mahisha-Vahini* my rectum.

कट्यां भगवती रक्षेज्जानुनी विन्ध्यवासिनी।
जङ्घे महाबला रक्षेत्सर्वकामप्रदायिनी ।। 31।।

May *Bhagavati* protect my waist and *Vindyavasini* to protect my knees! *Mahabala* to protect my calf thighs, who is the fulfiller of the desires.

गुल्फयोर्नारसिंही च पादपृष्ठे तु तैजसी।
पादाङ्गुलीषु श्री रक्षेत्पादाधस्तलवासिनी।। 32।।

May *Narasimhi* protect my both the calf muscles/ankles and *Taijasi Devi* to protect my upper feet! *Shri* to protect fingers of the feet and *Talavasini* to protect the sole of my feet.

नखान् दंष्ट्रकराली च केशांश्चैवोर्ध्वकेशिनी।
रोमकूपेषु कौबेरी त्वचं वागीश्वरी तथा।। 33।।

Danashtrakarali to protect my nails and *Urdvakeshini* to my hair. May *Kauberi* protect my hair pores and *Vageshwari* may protect my skin!

रक्तमज्जावसामांसान्यस्थिमेदांसि पार्वती।
अन्त्राणि कालरात्रिश्च पित्तं च मुकुटेश्वरी।। 34।।

May *Parvati* protect my blood, fat, marrow, bones and ligaments! May *Kalaratri* protect my intestines and *Mukuteshwari* to protect my bile ducts!

पद्मावती पद्मकोशे कफे चूडामणिस्तथा।
ज्वालामुखी नक्षज्वालामभेद्या सर्वसंधिषु।। 35।।

May *Padmavati* protect the base of the spine and *Chudamani* to protect my phlegm! May *Jvalamukhi* to protect the redness of the nails and *Abheda* all the joints!

शुक्रं ब्रह्माणि मे रक्षेच्छयां छत्रेश्वरी तथा।
अहंकारं मनो बुद्धिं रक्षेन्मे धर्मधारिणी।। 36।।

May *Brahmani* protect my semen and *Chhatreshwari* to protect my shadow! May *Dharmadharini* to protect my ego, mind and intellect!

प्राणापानौ तथा व्यानमुदानं च समानकम्।
वज्रहस्ता च मे रक्षेत्प्राणं कल्याणशोभना।। 37।।

Vajrahasta may protect my breathing system-'*Prana-apana-*

Vyana-Udana and *Samana*'! *Kalyana-Shobhana* may protect my vital breath!

रसे रूपे च गन्धे च शब्दे स्पर्शे च योगिनी।
सत्त्वं रजस्तमश्चैव रक्षेन्नारायणी सदा।। 38।।

Yogini may protect my 'senses of taste, smell, touch, sound and perception, and *Narayani* may protect *Sattva-rajas-tamas.*

आयू रक्षतु वाराही धर्मं रक्षतु वैष्णवी।
यशः कीर्तिं च लक्ष्मीं च धनं विद्यां च चक्रिणी।। 39।।

Varahi may protect my longevity and *Vaishnavi* to protect my *Dharma*. *Lakshmi* to protect my fame, glory and assets, wealth/auspiciousness and *Chakrini* to protect *Vidya* aspect of knowledge.

गोत्रमिन्द्राणि मे रक्षेत्पशून्मे रक्ष चण्डिके।
पुत्रान् रक्षेन्महालक्ष्मीर्भार्यां रक्षतु भैरवी।। 40।।

Indrani may protect my *Gotra*-clan of Rishihood, *Chandi* to protect my cattle. *Mahalakshmi* may protect my progeny-sons and *Bhairavi* to protect my wife!

पन्थानं सुपथा रक्षेन्मार्गं क्षेमकरी तथा।
राजद्वारे महालक्ष्मीर्विजया सर्वतः स्थिता।। 41।।

My path may be protected by *Supantha* Devi and ways—roads by *Kshemakari*. My *Rajdvara*—officialdom or royel gates be protected by *Mahalakshmi* and *Vijaya* to protect me in all the situations.

रक्षाहीनं तु यत्स्थानं वर्जितं कवचेन तु।
तत्सर्वं रक्ष मे देवि जयन्ती पापनाशिनी।। 42।।

Whatsoever may be left over in this *Kavacham*, that may be protected by *Jayanti*—who removes all the sins.

पदमेकं न गच्छेत्तु यदीच्छेच्छुभमात्मनः।
कवचेनावृतो नित्यं यत्र यत्रैव गच्छति।। 43।।

If you want to have auspiciousness in your psycho-physical being, then put the apron of *Kavacham* and proceed ahead, wherever you want to go.

तत्र तत्रार्थलाभश्च विजयः सार्वकामिकः।
यं यं चिन्तयते कामं तं तं प्राप्नोति निश्चितम्।
परमैश्वर्यमतुलं प्राप्स्यते भूतले पुमान्।। 44।।

....There he attains prosperity, benefits, victory which gives him all-round prosperity. There and then, he attains all that what he longs for. He attains unparalalled sovereignity on this earth.

निर्भयो जायते मर्त्यः संग्रामेष्वपराजितः।
त्रैलोक्ये तु भवेत्पूज्यः कवचेनावृतः पुमान्।। 45।।

A man becomes fearless in the war-field and becomes victorious. He is adored in the *Triloki*—triple world, if he is enforced with the *Kavacham*.

इदं तु देव्याः कवचं देवानामपि दुर्लभम्।
यः पठेत्प्रयतो नित्यं त्रिसन्ध्यं श्रद्धयान्वितः।। 46।।

This Devi Kavacham is not easily accessible to the *Devas*, whosoever recites this *Kavacham* with determination during the *Tri-Sandhya*—three twilights...,

दैवी कला भवेत्तस्य त्रैलोक्येष्वपराजितः।
जीवेद् वर्षशतं साग्रमपमृत्युविवर्जितः।। 47।।

...he attains the identity with the *Devi Kala*—Devi's effulgence and becomes victorious in *Triloki*—the three worlds. He lives the full age of one hundred years and above and is not subjected to death because of the natural calamities.

नश्यन्ति व्याधयः सर्वे लूताविस्फोटकादयः।
स्थावरं जङ्गमं चैव कृत्रिमं चापि यद्विषम्।। 48।।

All his diseases like measles, leprosy, inflammatory problems are destroyed. The natural poison or otherwise got from inanimate and animate manifestations, all get subdued.

अभिचाराणि सर्वाणि मन्त्रयन्त्राणि भूतले।
भूचराः खेचराश्चैव जलजाश्चोपदेशिकाः।। 49।।

All the incantations through *Mantras* and *Yantras*, on this earth causing damage and destructions get neutralized. All the small *Devatas* having abode in water, space and earth get annihilated before a person, supported by this Kavacham.

सहजा कुलजा माला डाकिनी शाकिनी तथा।
अन्तरक्षिचरा घोरा डाकिन्यश्च महाबलाः।। 50।।

All the frightful-lamias (hell cats), *Dakinis* abiding in the sky, *Shakini* abiding in the greenery with ferrocious nature, *Sahaja*—born with birth, *Kulja*—born in clan, *Mala*—diseases in the throat and neck infirmities also are wiped off.

ग्रहभूतपिशाचाश्च यक्षगन्धर्वराक्षसाः।
ब्रह्मराक्षसवेतालाः कूष्माण्डा भैरवादयः।। 51।।

Influencing *Grahas*—star position, *Bhutas*—type of evil spirits, *Pishachas*—demon, *Yakshas*—the celestial treasury keepers, *Gandharvas*—celestial singers, *Rakshasas*—making movements during night, *Brahma Rakshasas*—cosmic forces of distiurbances, *Vetals*—goblins, *Kushmanda*—evil forces on the vegetations, *Bhairavas*—the forces of Shiva's armoury viz. (eight in number), etc.....

नश्यन्ति दर्शनात्तस्य कवचे हृदि संस्थिते।
मानोन्नतिर्भवेद् राज्ञस्तेजोवृद्धिकरं परम्।। 52।।

......all are destroyed at the sight of the person, who puts on this *Kavacham* in his heart. He attains fame, attains progress and recognition from the kings.

यशसा वर्धते सोऽपि कीर्तिमण्डितभूतले।
जपेत्सप्तशतीं चण्डीं कृत्वा तु कवचं पुरा।। 53।।

He gets all-round excellence, and his fame gets excelled on the earth Whosoever recites the *Sapta-Shati* after the investment of the *Kavacham*...,

यावद्भूमण्डलं धत्ते सशैलवनकाननम्।
तावत्तिष्ठति मेदिन्यां संततिः पुत्रपौत्रिकी।। 54।।

......he continues to maintain his geneology through sons, grandsons etc. till this earth exists with the jungles, mountains and forests.

देहान्ते परमं स्थानं यत्सुरैरपि दुर्लभम्।
प्राप्नोति पुरुषो नित्यं महामायाप्रसादतः।। 55।।

After leaving his mortal frame, he attains that state, which is very difficult to get by the Devas also. He is blessed with eternity through the grace of Mahamaya.

लभते परमं रूपं शिवेन सह मोदते।। ॐ।। 56।।

He attains the transcendental nature and becomes one with Shiva and gets blessed. Om.

इति देव्याः कवचं सम्पूर्णम्

Thus the Devi Kavacham is concluded.

अथार्गलास्तोत्रम्

ATHA ARGALA STOTRAM

(The Bolting)

ॐ अस्य श्रीअर्गलास्तोत्रमन्त्रस्य विष्णुर्ऋषिः, अनुष्टुप छन्दः, श्रीमहालक्ष्मीर्देवता, श्रीजगदम्बाप्रीतये सप्तशतीपाठाङ्गत्वेन जपे विनियोगः।।

Vishnu is the *Rishi*, *Anushtup* is *Chhanda*/metre, *Shri Mahalakshmi* is the *Devata* of this *Shri Argala-Stotra-Mantra.* For propitiation of *Shri Jagadamba*, the *Viniyoga*—accomplishment stands for the japam as the limb of *Sapta Shati patham*.

ॐ नमश्चण्डिकायै।।

Om Namaskar to Chandika

मार्कण्डेय उवाच

Markendeya said :

ॐ जयन्ती मङ्गला काली भद्रकाली कपालिनी।
दुर्गा क्षमा शिवा धात्री स्वाहा स्वधा नमोऽस्तु ते।। 1।।

OM Namaskar/prostrations to *Jayanti, Mangala, Kali, Bhadrakali, Kapalini, Durga, Kshama, Shiva, Dhatri, Svaha, Svadha.*

जय त्वं देवि चामुण्डे जय भूतार्तिहारिणि।
जयसर्वगते देवि कालरात्रि नमोऽस्तु ते।। 2।।

O Devi Chamunda! Be victorious! You are the remover of all

the afflictions—sufferings of all the living beings. Be victorious! O *Sarvagata*-omniscient one! O Devi! O *Kalaratri*! You are the very natrure of Jaya—victory. My Namaskar to you!

मधुकैटभविद्राविविधातृवरदे नमः।
रूपं देहि जयं देहि यशो देहि द्विषो जहि।। 3।।

You are the destroyer of *Madhu-Kaitabha*; the giver of boon to Brahma! My Namaskar to you. Be pleased and give me good physique, victory, fame and destroy my ill desires, and my enemies.

महिषासुरनिर्णाशि भक्तानां सुखदे नमः।
रूपं देहि जयं देहि यशो देहि द्विषो जहि।। 4।।

O the annihilator of *Mahishasura*! O the giver of boons to the devotees! My Namaskar to you. Be pleased and give me good physique, victory, fame and destroy my ill desires, and my enemies.

रक्तबीजवधे देवि चण्डमुण्डविनाशिनी।
रूपं देहि जयं देहि यशो देहि द्विषो जहि।। 5।।

O the slayer of *Raktabija*! The destroyer of *Chanda-Munda*! My Namaskar to you. Be pleased and give me good physique, victory, fame and destroy my ill desires, and my enemies.

शुम्भस्यैव निशुम्भस्य धूम्राक्षस्य च मर्दिनि।
रूपं देहि जयं देहि यशो देहि द्विषो जहि।। 6।।

O the extinguisher of *Shumbha-Nishumbha* and *Dhumraksha*! My Namaskar to you. Be pleased and give me good physique, victory, fame and destroy my ill desires, and my enemies.

वन्दिताङ्घ्रियुगे देवि सर्वसौभाग्यदायिनि।
रूपं देहि जयं देहि यशो देहि द्विषो जहि।। 7।।

Your feet are being adorned by all the Divine forces and you are the giver of all auspiciousness. Give me good physique, victory, fame and destroy my ill desises, and my enemies.

अचिन्त्यरूपचरिते सर्वशत्रुविनाशिनि।
रूपं देहि जयं देहि यशो देहि द्विषो जहि।। 8।।

You are the destroyer of all the foes and enemies and thus your *charitam*—description of your being is incomparable. Give me good physique, victory, fame and kill my enemies.

नतेभ्यः सर्वदा भक्त्या चण्डिके दुरितापहे।
रूपं देहि जयं देहि यशो देहि द्विषो जहि।। 9।।

O *Chandika*—the destroyer of all the sins! I always surrender at your feet. Please grant me good physique, victory, fame and destroy my ill desires and enemies.

स्तुवद्भ्यो भक्तिपूर्वं त्वां चण्डिके व्याधिनाशिनि।
रूपं देहि जयं देहि यशो देहि द्विषो जहि।। 10।।

O *Chandika*—the destroyer of all the ailments! Be pleased and give me good physique, victory, fame through my devotion to you and annihilate all my enemies.

चण्डिके सततं ये त्वामर्चयन्तीह भक्तितः।
रूपं देहि जयं देहि यशो देहि द्विषो जहि।। 11।।

O *Chandika*! Those who constantly approach you with *Stuti/ Archana*—recitation, to them you grant thriving physique, victory and fame. Also you destroy their enemies.

देहि सौभाग्यमारोग्यं देहि मे परमं सुखम्।
रूपं देहि जयं देहि यशो देहि द्विषो जहि।। 12।।

Grant me the excellent fortune, the highest prosperity and eternal peace. Grant me good physique, victory, fame and destroy my enemies.

विधेहि द्विषतां नाशं विधेहि बलमुच्चकैः।
रूपं देहि जयं देहि यशो देहि द्विषो जहि।। 13।।

Those who are envious of me, destroy them. Increase my strength and power. Give me health, fame, prosperity and destroy my enemies.

विधेहि देवि कल्याणं विधेहि परमां श्रियम्।
रूपं देहि जयं देहि यशो देहि द्विषो जहि।। 14।।

O Devi! Grant me welfare and give me Shri-excellent transcendence. Give me proper health, victory, excellence and destroy my enemies.

सुरासुरशिरोरत्ननिघृष्टचरणेऽम्बिके ।
रूपं देहि जयं देहि यशो देहि द्विषो जहि।। 15।।

O *Ambika*! Both the Suras—Divine forces and Asuras—anti-divine forces grind their crowns of jewels at your feet. Be pleased and grant me good physical being, victory, fame and destroy my enemies.

विद्यावन्तं यशस्वन्तं लक्ष्मीवन्तं जनं कुरु।
रूपं देहि जयं देहि यशो देहि द्विषो जहि।। 16।।

You make me well learned, flourishing with fame and make me wealthy and alike. Give us good physical health, victory, fame and destroy my enemies.

प्रचण्डदैत्यदर्पघ्ने चण्डिके प्रणताय मे।
रूपं देहि जयं देहि यशो देहि द्विषो जहि।। 17।।

O *Chandika*! You are the extinguisher of the false ego of forceful *Daityas*—anti divine beings. I have bowed before you at your feet, please grant me good and charmng physique, victory, fame and destroy my enemies.

चतुर्भुजे चतुर्वक्त्रसंस्तुते परमेश्वरि।
रूपं देहि जयं देहि यशो देहि द्विषो जहि।। 18।।

O *Chaturbhuja*! You do grace with your four arms to the four faced Brahma, who praises you. You are Parmesh-vari—Supreme Soverign Mother. Grant me good physique, victory, fame and destroy my enemies.

कृष्णेन संस्तुते देवि शश्वद्भक्त्या सदाम्बिके।
रूपं देहि जयं देहि यशो देहि द्विषो जहि।। 19।।

O *Ambika*! You are worshipped constantly by Shrikrishna (Vishnu), with supreme devotion. You grant me good physique, victory, fame and destroy my enemies.

हिमाचलसुतानाथसंस्तुते परमेश्वरि।
रूपं देहि जयं देहि यशो देहि द्विषो जहि।। 20।।

O *Parmeshvari*! You are being propitiated by (Lord Shiva)—the consort of *Himachala Suta—Parvati* the daughter of Himalaya mountaion. You grant me graceful form of physical being, victory, fame and destroy my enemies.

इन्द्राणीपतिसद्भावपूजिते परमेश्वरि।.
रूपं देहि जयं देहि यशो देहि द्विषो जहि।। 21।।

O *Parmeshvari*! You are being worshipped by Indrani Pati—the consort of *Indira* (Shachi) with greet reverance. Grant me good physique, victory, fame and destory my enemies.

देवि प्रचण्डदोर्दण्डदैत्यदर्पविनाशिनि।
रूपं देहि जयं देहि यशो देहि द्विषो जहि।। 22।।

You are the Devi, who has destroyed and crushed the ego of *Daityas*, possessed with powerful limbs. Please grant me charmng form, victory, fame and destory my enemies.

देवि भक्तजनोद्दामदत्तानन्दोदयेऽम्बिके।
रूपं देहि जयं देहि यशो देहि द्विषो जहि।। 23।।

O Devi Ambika! You are always gracing your devotees with eternal bliss. Give me good looking physique, victory, fame and annihilate my enemies.

पत्नीं मनोरमां देहि मनोवृत्तानुसारिणीम्।
तारिणीं दुर्गसंसारसागरस्य कुलोद्भवाम्।। 24।।

Bless me with charming and mentally evolved life partner following the pious norms of life and born of a noble family. She would help me to cross this oceanic world of birth and death.

इदं स्तोत्रं पठित्वा तु महास्तोत्रं पठेन्नरः।
स तु सप्तशतीसंख्यावरमाप्नोति सम्पदाम्।। ॐ ।।25।।

Whosoever recites the great *Patham* of Sapta Shati, after reciting this *Patham*, attains the great merits in number, of the Sapta Shati Patham and becomes the master of great fortune and wealth. Om.

इति देव्या अर्गलास्तोत्रं सम्पूर्णम्

Here the Argala Stotram is concluded.

अथ कीलकम्

ATHA KILKAM

(The Nailing)

ॐ अस्य श्रीकीलकमन्त्रस्य शिव ऋषिः, अनुष्टुप् छन्दः, श्रीमहासरस्वती देवता, श्रीजगदम्बाप्रीत्यर्थं सप्तशतीपाठाङ्गत्वेन जपे विनियोगः।

Shiva is the *Rishi*, *Anushtupa* is the metre, *Shri Mahasaraswati* is the Devata of this *Shri Kilaka Mantra*. The *Viniyoga*—accomplishment is for the Japam as being the limb of *Sapta Shati Patham*.

ॐ नमश्चण्डिकायै।।

OM Namaskar to Chandika

मार्कण्डेय उवाच

Markandeya Said :

ॐ विशुद्धज्ञानदेहाय त्रिवेदीदिव्यचक्षुषे।
श्रेयःप्राप्तिनिमित्ताय नमः सोमार्धधारिणे।। 1।।

He who holds the moon—crescent on his forehead, whose being is pure *Jnana*-complete knowledge; Veda Trayi—the three Vedas are his Divine eyes and who is the efficient cause of all bliss, to such Divinity (Shiva), I bow down.

सर्वमेतद्विजानीयान्मन्त्राणामभिकीलकम्।
सोऽपि क्षेममवाप्नोति सततं जाप्यतत्परः।। 2।।

What is 'Abhikilaka'—the obstacle remover of the curses in the forms of nailing in the Mantras, must be known strictly.

Thus he attains the highest merit, who knows the Sapta Shati *Patham* and its *Japam*.

सिद्ध्यन्त्युच्चाटनादीनि वस्तूनि सकलान्यपि।
एतेन स्तुवतां देवी स्तोत्रमात्रेण सिद्ध्यति।। 3।।

Inclination to attain liberation and perfection is possible through the adoration of Devi with this great stotarm/and is also attained through it. *Uchatan* everything undesirable and severe such desire is also attained.

न मन्त्रो नौषधं तत्र न किञ्चिदपि विद्यते।
विना जाप्येन सिद्ध्येत सर्वमुच्चाटनादिकम्।। 4।।

No other Mantra or any herb is needed as requirement in getting his actions/deeds accomplished. All his Uchattan actions are worked out without doing such Japam.

समग्राण्यपि सिद्ध्यन्ति लोकशङ्कामिमां हरः।
कृत्वा निमन्त्रयामास सर्वमेवमिदं शुभम्।। 5।।

All the wishes are achieved, with other incantations, such was the doubt with the devotees. *Hara*/Lord Shiva made it clear that the Sapta Shati alone exists everywhere and is all auspicious.

स्तोत्रं वै चण्डिकायास्तु तच्च गुप्तं चकार सः।
समाप्तिर्न च पुण्यस्य तां यथावन्नियन्त्रणाम्।। 6।।

Then Shiva concealed the Stotram of Shri Chandi. The merits are not destroyed in anyway to the person who performs the Patham of Sapta Shati, as it has been put to that effect with discipline.

सोऽपि क्षेममवाप्नोति सर्वमेवं न संशयः।
कृष्णायां वा चतुर्दश्यामष्टम्यां वा समाहितः।। 7।।

Who ever performs this worship, on the eighth or fourteenth lunar *tithi*/dates of dark fortnight, with single mindedness without any doubt...,

ददाति प्रतिगृह्णाति नान्यथैषा प्रसीदति।
इत्थंरूपेण कीलेन महादेवेन कीलितम्।। 8।।

.......and who surrenders everything before the Devi and later accepts it as Her *Prasadam* (blessings). With such a devotee, Devi is ever pleased otherwise not. Thus Mahadeva nailed this Stotram in that way.

यो निष्कीलां विधायैनां नित्यं जपति संस्फुटम्।
स सिद्धः स गणः सोऽपि गन्धर्वो जायते नरः।। 9।।

He who unnails it with strict discipline and recites properly the Stotram regularly, that devotee attains perfrection, becomes Her attendant and attains the position of Gandharva.

न चैवाप्यटतस्तस्य भयं क्वापीह जायते।
नापमृत्युवशं याति मृतो मोक्षमवाप्नुयात्।। 10।।

He does not get afraid of any thing, while he may be roaming anywhere. He does not die in short span of life and attains Moksha, after he casts off his mortal frame.

ज्ञात्वा प्रारभ्य कुर्वीत न कुर्वाणो विनश्यति।
ततो ज्ञात्वैव सम्पन्नमिदं प्रारभ्यते बुधैः।। 11।।

Start the *Patham* with the proper procedure. Otherwise, it would bring harm. Therefore, the learned one starts it after knowing its proper system/procedure.

सौभाग्यादि च यत्किञ्चिद् दृश्यते ललनाजने।
तत्सर्वं तत्प्रसादेन तेन जाप्यमिदं शुभम्।। 12।।

Whosoever you see in the womenfolk bestowed with grace, is but the grace of that Devi. Thus always perform the Japam of this great *Mantra*.

शनैस्तु जप्यमानेऽस्मिन् स्तोत्रे सम्पत्तिरुच्चकैः।
भवत्येव समग्रापि ततः प्रारभ्यमेव तत्।। 13।।

Those who recite it slowly also get prosperity, but to recite with coordination and concentration gives higher merits.

ऐश्वर्यं यत्प्रसादेन सौभाग्यारोग्यसम्पदः ।
शत्रुहानिः परो मोक्षः स्तूयते सा न किं जनै।। ॐ ।। 14 ।।

Its grace is to bestow sovereignity, well being, good health, fortune, destructoin of enemies and finally to grant Moksha. Therefore, why will not the human beings adore and propitiate the Devi? Om.

इति देव्याः कीलकस्तोत्रं सम्पूर्णम्

Here the Devi Kilkam is concluded.

अथ वेदोक्तं रात्रिसूक्तम्

VEDOKTAM RATRISUKTAM

(Vedic Ratri Suktam)

ॐ रात्रीत्याद्यष्टर्चस्य सूक्तस्य कुशिकः सौभरो रात्रिर्वा भारद्वाजो ऋषिः, रात्रिर्देवता, गायत्री छन्दः, देवीमाहात्म्यपाठे विनियोगः।

I resolve to recite the *Vedic Ratri Suktam* of eight *Suktas* in the Devi Mahatmya—*Patham. Kushika-Saubhara-Ratri-Bharadwaja* are the Rishis of the *Suktam. Ratri* is the *Devata* and *Gayatri* is the Metre and the application is for recitation of the Devi Mahatmyam

ॐ रात्री व्यख्यदायती पुरुत्रा देव्यक्षभिः। विश्वा अधि श्रियोऽधित ।। 1 ।।

OM! Ratri Devi is omniscient and She exists in all good or bad actions in this Universal manifestation. She grants the fruits of all the actions accordingly. She assumes Her entire effulgence.

ओर्वप्रा अमर्त्यानिवतो देव्युद्वतः। ज्योतिषा बाधते तमः ।। 2 ।।

The Ratri Devi is immortal, which fills the sky extensively. She is manifest below in the world and high above like bushes and trees. She dispells all ignorance of the embodied souls through Her Divine effulgence.

निरु स्वसारमस्कृतोषसं देव्यायती। अपेदु हासते तमः ।। 3 ।।

The Ratri Devi makes appear *Usha*—the dawn with which the darkness comes to an end, through its own innate nature.

सा नो अद्य यस्या वयं नि ते यामन्नविक्ष्महि। वृक्षे न वसतिं वयः ।। 4 ।।

May Ratri Devi be pleased with me! It is because of Her

influence, we go to sleep with ease, just as the birds go to sleep in their nests on the trees during night.

नि ग्रामासो अविक्षत नि पद्वन्तो नि पक्षिणः। नि श्येनासश्चिदर्थिनः ।। 5 ।।

She has enveloped all the human beings of this world and all the quadruped animals and birds, butterflies which fly with their wings in Her lap. Also the men moving around and birds like hawks take rest and sleep, alike.

यावया वृक्यं वृकं यवय स्तेनमूर्म्ये। अथ नः सुतरा भव।। 6 ।।

O Ratri Devi! Be pleased and make us free from the clutches of greed like that of she wolf and keep off ill impulses of wolf like a robber, hidden in us. Make our sleep comfortable!

उप मा पेपिशत्तमः कृष्णं व्यक्तमस्थित। उष ऋणेव यातय।। 7 ।।

O Usha—the presiding deity of the Night! The ignorance has enveloped us all around, which is dull and defused and that has approached me. Make me free from the debt in the hour of ignorance and clear it off like a debt!

उप ते गा इवाकरं वृणीष्व दुहितर्दिवः। रात्रि स्तोमं न जिग्युषे।। 8 ।।

O Ratri! You are the Milk giving cow. I pay my obeisance to you to make you considerate towards me. You are the daughter of the infinite sky. Be pleased and acept my Homa like eulogy of one eager to conquer!

अथ तन्त्रोक्तं रात्रिसूक्तम्

TANTROKTAM RATRISUKTAM

(Tantrik Ratri Suktam)

ॐ विश्वेश्वरीं जगद्धात्रीं स्थितिसंहारकारिणीम्।
निद्रां भगवतीं विष्णोरतुलां तेजसः प्रभुः।। 1।।

Om 'Jagatdhatri'—the supporter of the worlds, 'Sthiti'—Samharakarini'—the primal cause of sustenance and dissolution (of the universe) Nidra-Bhagavati—the Supreme deity of sleep and who is incomparable Shakti of Bhagvan Vishnu."

ब्रह्मोवाच

Brahma Said

त्वं स्वाहा त्वं स्वधा त्वं हि वषट्कारः स्वरात्मिका।
सुधा त्वमक्षरे नित्ये त्रिधा मात्रात्मिका स्थिता।। 2।।

"You are '*Svaha*'—the Vedic Mantra uttered when an 'Ahuti'—offerings is poured in the '*Agni*'—fire; you are '*Svadha*'—the Pauranik Mantra uttered when water oblations/offerings are made to *Pitris*—the departed souls. You are '*Vashatkara'*— a word of offering to the Devatas and you are the embodiment of '*Svara*' the immutable sound. You are '*Sudha*'—nectar. You are in the '*Nitya-akshara*'—eternal immutable word in the embodiment of 'Triple *Matra*'—Syllable and you are in the half *Matra*.

अर्धमात्रास्थिता नित्या यानुच्चार्या विशेषतः।
त्वमेव सन्ध्या सावित्री त्वं देवि जननी परा।। 3।।

You are, what cannot be uttered specifically. You are *Sandhya*—twilight. You are *Savitri*—the Pranava; *'Devi-Janani*—the Mother creatrix and *Para*—the transcendent one.

त्वयैतद्धार्यते विश्वं त्वयैतत्सृज्यते जगत् ।
त्वयैतत्पाल्यते देवि त्वमत्स्यन्ते च सर्वदा ।। 4 ।।

It is You, who hold this universe and create this world. By You this universe is protected.O Devi! You dissolve it at the end of *Kalpa.*

विसृष्टौ सृष्टिरूपा त्वं स्थितिरूपा च पालने।
तथा संहृतिरूपान्ते जागतोऽस्य जगन्मये ।। 5 ।।

You are *Srishtrirupa*—the very manifestation of existence, and you are *Sthiti rupa*—the existent and You sustain it. O *Jaganmayi Devi*—the Mother of universe. You are *Samhara rupa*—the consuming force at the time of dissolution of this world.

महाविद्या महामाया महामेधा महास्मृतिः।
महामोहा च भवती महादेवी महासुरी ।। 6 ।।

You are *'Mahavidya'*—the Great knowledge; *'Mahamaya'*—great illusion, *'Mahamedha'*—great intellect and *'Mahasmriti'*—great contemplation. You are *'Mahamoha'*—great delusion, *'Mahadevi'*—great divinity and *'Mahasuri'*—the great anti divinity.

प्रकृतिस्त्वं च सर्वस्य गुणत्रयविभाविनी।
कालरात्रिर्महारात्रिर्मोहरात्रिश्च दारुणा ।। 7 ।।

You are the Primal cause of everything, bringing into action all the three *Gunas*—qualities. You are *Kalaratri*—darknight, *Maharatri*—the great night, *Moharatri*—the night of delusion and *Daruna*—terrible night.

त्वं श्रीस्त्वमीश्वरी त्वं ह्रीस्त्वं बुद्धिर्बोधलक्षणा।
लज्जा पुष्टिस्तथा तुष्टिस्त्वं शान्तिः क्षान्तिरेव च ।। 8 ।।

You are *Shri*—the good fortune. You are *Ishvari*—Supreme Queen, you are *Hri*—modesty, *Buddhi*—intellect and *Bodhalakshana*—characterization of knowledge. You are *Lajja*—modesty, *Pushti*—nourishment and *Tushti* contentment. You are *Shanti*—tranquility and also *Kshanti* forbearance.

खड्गिनी शूलिनी घोरा गदिनी चक्रिणी तथा।
शङ्खिनी चापिनी बाणभुशुण्डीपरिघायुधा।। 9।।

You are *Khadgini*—the weilder of sword, *Shulini*—holder of spear and *Ghora*—club, *Chakrini*—holder of disc and You are *Shankhini*—the holder of a conch, *Chapini*—holder of bow and having the missiles of *Bana*—arrow, *Bhushundi*—slings and *Parigha*—iron mace.

सौम्या सौम्यतराशेषसौम्येभ्यस्त्वतिसुन्दरी।
परापराणां परमा त्वमेव परमेश्वरी।। 10।।

You are *Saumya*—pleasing, *Saumyatara*—more pleasing. You are verily, most pleasing than the pleasing things and You are *Sundari*—extremely beautiful. You are beyond the transcendent and immanent. Verily, You are the Supreme *Ishvari*—the Sovereign Queen.

यच्च किञ्चित् क्वचिद्वस्तु सदसद्वाखिलाात्मिके।
तस्य सर्वस्य या शक्तिः सा त्वं किं स्तूयसे तदा।। 11।।

Whatsoever is and wherever a thing exists, either real or unreal, is all that possessed by You in Yourself. You are *Akhilatmika* the universal self and You are the power behind all that. Who else is capable of extolling Your superiority?

यया त्वया जगत्स्रष्टा जगत्पात्यत्ति यो जगत्।
सोऽपि निद्रावशं नीतः कस्त्वां स्तोतुमिहेश्वरः।। 12।।

Myself as *Srashta* the creaetor and Vishnu, being the *Palaka*—the Sustainer also lies in great sleep. Who is capable of offering laudation to You?

विष्णुः शरीरग्रहणमहमीशान एव च।
कारितास्ते यतोऽतस्त्वां कः स्तोतुं शक्तिमान् भवेत्।। 13।।

Vishnu, myself as *Brahma, Ishana-Rudra* have been given embodied forms by You. Therefore, who is capable of offering the *Stuti*—laudation to You.

सा त्वमित्थं प्रभावैः स्वैरुदारैर्देवि संस्तुता।
मोहयैतौ दुराधर्षावसुरौ मधुकैटभौ।। 14।।

You are therefore, O Devi, being praised by Your own liberal influences. Be pleased and bewitch these two unassailable *Madhu* and *Kaitabha Asuras*—the demoniac forces.

प्रबोधं च जगत्स्वामी नीयतामच्युतो लघु।
बोधश्च क्रियतामस्य हन्तुमेतौ महासुरौ।। 15।।

May *Achutya*—the Lord of the universe be quickly awakened from sleep and be roused up in his action to slay these two great Asuras!

इति रात्रिसूक्तम्

The Ratri Suktam is concluded

After reciting Vedic and Ratri Suktam, the devotee must recite/perform Navarna Viniyoga, Nyasa, Dhyanam etc.

अथ नवार्णविधिः

The Procedure of Navarna

ॐ श्रीगणपतिर्जयति। 'ॐ अस्य श्रीनवार्णमन्त्रस्य ब्रह्मविष्णु-रुद्रा ऋषयः, गायत्र्युष्णिगनुष्टुभश्छन्दांसि, श्रीमहाकालीमहालक्ष्मी-महासरस्वत्यो देवताः, ऐं बीजम्, ह्रीं शक्तिः, क्लीं कीलकम्, श्रीमहाकालीमहालक्ष्मीमहासरस्वतीप्रीत्यर्थे जपे विनियोगः।'

Namaskar to *Shri Ganesha*, glory be to *Shri Ganesha*! *Brahma-Vishnu-Rudra* are the Rishis of *Shri Navarna Mantra*. The *Gayatri, Ushnik, Anushtup* are the metres. *Shri Mahakali, Mahalakshmi, Mahasarasvati* are the Devatas/deities. The Japam is dedicated to *Shri Mahakali- Mahalakshmi-Mahasarasvati*.

Pour the water while reciting this *Viniyoga*/ commitment/resolution mantra. The *Nyasas* are feeling the pulsation of the Divine Mother in one's own body while touching head, mouth, face, heart, anal place, feet and navel portion, with the fingers of right hand. It is mental appropriation of various parts of the body to tutelary deities.

The Nyasas are to be recited while touching the various limbs of the body with fingers and feeling the Divine effulgence within one's own psycho-physical being.

Rishi Nyasas is dedicated to the Rishis of the Durga-Sapta-Shati and the Rishis are Brahma, Vishnu and Rudra.

ऋष्यादिन्यासः

Rishi Nyasas

(Presence of Brahma, Vishnu and Rudra as Divinity in Rishi form)

ब्रह्मविष्णुरुद्रऋषिभ्यो नमः, शिरसि।

I bow to the presence of *Brahma, Vishnu* and *Rudra Rishi,* who are on my head.

गायत्र्युष्णिगनुष्टुप्छन्दोभ्यो नमः, मुखे।

I bow to the *Gayatri, Ushnik, Anushtup* metres who are in my mouth.

महाकालीमहालक्ष्मीमहासरस्वतीदेवताभ्यो नमः, हृदि।

I bow to *Mahakali, Mahalakshmi, Mahasarasvati* Devatas in my heart region.

ऐं बीजाय नमः, गुह्ये।

I bow to *Aim Beeja*/seed which is in the anal-portion.

ह्रीं शक्तये नमः, पादयोः।

I bow to *Hrim Shakti* which is in my feet.

क्लीं कीलकाय नमः, नाभौ।

I bow to *Klim-Kilaka*/nail which is in my navel portion. Recite the Mantra....

'ॐ ऐं ह्रीं क्लीं चामुण्डायै विच्चे'

(हस्तशुद्धिं कृत्वा करन्यासः)

Purify your hands with the *Navarna Mantra* and perform *Kara Nyasa.*

(Kara Nyasa is the feeling of Divinity through hands.)

करन्यासः

Kara Nyasa(Presence of Divinity in hand)

ॐ ऐं अङ्गुष्ठाभ्यां नमः

OM! Namaskar to *Aim,* which abides in the thumbs.

(Touch your both thumbs with the fore-fingers)

ॐ ह्रीं तर्जनीभ्यां नमः

OM! Namaskar to the *Hrim* which abides in fore-fingers.

(Touch your fore fingers with your thumbs).

ॐ क्लीं मध्यमाभ्यां नमः

OM! Namaskar to *Klim* , which abides in the mid-finger

(Touch your mid-fingers with thumbs)

ॐ चामुण्डायै अनामिकाभ्यां नमः

OM! Namaskar to *Chamunda*, which abides in the ring finger (Touch your ring-fingers with thumbs).

ॐ विच्चे कनिष्ठिकाभ्यां नमः

OM! Namaskar to *Vichche*, which abides in the small finger

(Touch your small fingers with your thumbs).

ॐ ऐं ह्रीं क्लीं चामुण्डायै विच्चे करतलकरपृष्ठाभ्यां नमः

OM! Namaskar to *Aim, Hrim, Klim, Chamundayai, Viche,* which abide in the palm and dorsal

(Touch your palms and in the reverse dorsal).

(After *Kara Nyasas,* perform *Hridya Nyasas* by touching the heart region with all the five fingers of right hand)

हृदयादिन्यासः

Hridya Adi-Nyasa

(Presence of Divine Mother in the heart region)

ॐ ऐं हृदयाय नमः

OM! Namaskar to *Aim*, which abides in the heart.

ॐ ह्रीं शिरसे स्वाहा

OM! Namaskar to *Hrim*, which abides in the head.

ॐ क्लीं शिखायै वषट्

OM! Namaskar to *Klim*, which abides in the tuft.

ॐ चामुण्डायै कवचाय हुम्

OM! Namaskar to *Chamunda* which abides in the armour on the *Hum* (Touch the left shoulder with your right fingers and right shoulder with your left fingers)

ॐ विच्चे नेत्रत्रयाय वौषट्

OM! Namaskar/*Voushat* – expression of exclamation to *Vichche*, which abide in the three eyes. (the third eye is the inner eye)

ॐ ऐं ह्रीं क्लीं चामुण्डायै विच्चे अस्त्राय फट्

OM! Namaskar/*Phat* to *Aim, Hrim, Klim, Chamundayai Vichche*, which abide in the *Astras*/missiles. (move your right hand around your head from left to right and clap your left hand palm with your mid finger and ring-finger)

(after the *Hridaya-adi Nyasa*, touch your tuft with all the five fingers of your right hand fingers and recite the *Akshara Nyasa*)

अक्षरन्यासः

(Presence of Divine Mother in the Akshara-Immutable Phoneme)

ॐ ऐं नमः, शिखायाम्।

OM! Namaskar to *Aim*, which is in the tuft.

ॐ ह्रीं नमः, दक्षिणनेत्रे।

OM! Namaskar to *Hrim*, which is in the right eye.

ॐ क्लीं नमः, वामनेत्रे।

OM! Namaskar to *Klim*, which is in the left eye.

ॐ चां नमः, दक्षिणकर्णे।

OM! Namaskar to *Cham*, which is in the right ear.

ॐ मुं नमः, वामकर्णे।

OM! Namaskar to *Mum*, which is in the left ear.

ॐ डां नमः, दक्षिणनासापुटे।

OM! Namaskar to *Dam*, which is in the right nostril.

ॐ यैं नमः, वामनासापुटे।

OM! Namaskar to *Yaim,* which is in the left nostril.

ॐ विं नमः, मुखे।

OM! Namaskar to *Vim,* which is in the mouth.

ॐ च्चें नमः, गुह्ये।

OM! Namaskar to *Chaim,* which is in the antral region.

(after doing the Nyasa, touch your body from head to feet with the Navarna Mantra and make snapping with the fingers for feeling the pulsation of Divinity. Then go in for Dik/Dinnyasa)

दिङ्न्यासः

(Presence of Divine Mother in all the directions)

ॐ ऐं प्राच्यै नमः।

OM! Namaskar to *Aim,* which is in the East.

ॐ ऐं आग्नेय्यै नमः।

OM! Namaskar to *Aim,* which is in the South East.

ॐ ह्रीं दक्षिणायै नमः।

OM! Namaskar to *Hrim,* which is in the South.

ॐ ह्रीं नैर्ऋत्यै नमः।

OM! Namaskar to *Hrim,* which is in the South West.

ॐ क्लीं प्रतीच्यै नमः।

OM! Namaskar to *Klim,* which is in the West.

ॐ क्लीं वायव्यै नमः।

OM! Namaskar to *Klim,* which is in the North West.

ॐ चामुण्डायै उदीच्यै नमः।

OM! Namaskar to *Chamunda,* which is in the North.

ॐ चामुण्डायै ऐशान्यै नमः।

OM! Namaskar to *Chamunda,* which is in the North West.

ॐ ऐं ह्रीं क्लीं चामुण्डायै विच्चे ऊर्ध्वायै नमः।

OM! Namaskar to *Aim Hrim Klim Chamundayai Vichche,* which is in the Ethereal direction.

ॐ ऐं ह्रीं क्लीं चामुण्डायै विच्चे भूम्यै नमः।

OM! Namaskar to *Aim Hrim Klim Chamundayai Vichche,* which is in the Down Earth direction.

(after completing the Nyasas, the devotee must meditate upon Shri Mahakali with the first *Dhyana Shloka,* Shri Mahalakshmi with the second *Dhyana Shloka* and Mahasaraswati with the third *Dhyana Shaloka* given at page 110).

ध्यानम्
Dhyanam

खड्गं चक्रगदेषु चापपरिघाञ्छूलं भुशुण्डीं शिरः
शङ्खं संदधतीं करैस्त्रिनयनां सर्वाङ्गभूषावृताम्।
नीलाश्मद्युतिमास्यपाददशकां सेवे महाकालिकां
यामस्तौत्स्वपिते हरौ कमलजो हन्तुं मधुं कैटभम्।। 1 ।।

I pay my adoration to *Mahakali*, who is with ten faces and ten feet. She holds sword, discus, mace, arrow, bow, club, spear, missile, skull and conch in Her hands. She is triple-eyed. Her limbs are all adorned with divine ornaments looking luminous like a blue jewel. She was worshipped with 'Stuti' by Brahma to kill *Madhu* and *Kaitabha*.

अक्षस्त्रक्परशुं गदेषुकुलिशं पद्मं धनुः कुण्डिकां
दण्डं शक्तिमसिं च चर्म जलजं घण्टां सुराभाजनम्।
शूलं पाशसुदर्शने च दधतीं हस्तैः प्रसन्नाननां
सेवे सैरिभमर्दिनीमिह महालक्ष्मीं सरोजस्थिताम्।। 2 ।।

I pay my obeisance to *Mahalakshmi*, who is seated on the *Saroja*-lotus, is of the complexion of coral and who holds *Akshamala*-rosary, axe, mace, arrow, thunderbolt, lotus, bow, pitcher, rod, *Shakti*, sword, shield, conch, bell, honey-cup, spear, noose and the *Sudarshana* discus, in Her hands. Her face is filled with smile and she is the destroyer of *Mahishasura*.

घण्टाशूलहलानि शङ्खमुसले चक्रं धनुः सायकं
हस्ताब्जैर्दधतीं घनान्तविलसच्छीतांशुतुल्यप्रभाम्।
गौरीदेहसमुद्भवां त्रिजगतामाधारभूतां महा-
पूर्वामत्र सरस्वतीमनुभजे शुम्भादिदैत्यार्दिनीम्।। 3 ।।

I do constantly meditate upon that *Mahasarasvati*, who holds *Ghanta*—bell, *Shula*—spike, *Hala*—plough, *Shankha*—Conch, *Musala*—pestle, *Chakra*—discus, *Dhanusha*—bow and *Bana*—arrow in her hands. She is effulgent like the moon of the harvest, at the fringe of a cloud. She, has issued forth from the being of *Gauri* and is the substrum of the three worlds. Verily, she is the destroyer of *Shumbha* and other *Asuras*.

After reciting the *Dhyana Mantras*, pay your obeisance to *Mala*/garland and recite :

ऐं ह्रीं अक्षमालिकायै नमः

OM! Namaskar to *Hrim*, which is in the Akshamala!

ॐ मां माले महामाये सर्वशक्तिस्वरूपिणि।
चतुर्वर्गस्त्वयि न्यस्तस्तस्मान्मे सिद्धिदा भव।।

OM! O Divine Mother! Mahamaya!You are the innate nature of absolute power. Be pleased and grant me perfection. All the *chaturvarga*—the four groups of phonemes are in your being.

ॐ अविघ्नं कुरु माले त्वं गृह्णामि दक्षिणे करे।
जपकाले च सिद्धयर्थं प्रसीद मम सिद्धये।।

OM! O Mala Ward off all the obstacles! Be pleased and grant me perfection during the *Japam, as* I hold you in my right hand.

ॐ अक्षमालाधिपतये सुसिद्धिं देहि देहि
सर्वमन्त्रार्थसाधिनि साधय साधय सर्वसिद्धिं
परिकल्पय परिकल्पय मे स्वाहा।

OM *Svaha* to the lord of *Aksha Mala* for grating me absolute perfection. You are the determining force of the meaning of all the *Mantras*.

(the devotee must perform-Japam of the Navarna Mantra 108 times with Akshamala :

ॐ ऐं ह्रीं क्लीं चामुण्डायै विच्चे

OM! *Aim Hrim Klim Chamundayai Vichche.*

After doing the Japam of 108 Mantra as above, recite the following Shloka :

गुह्यातिगुह्यगोप्त्री त्वं गृहाणास्मत्कृतं जपम्।
सिद्धिर्भवतु मे देवि त्वत्प्रसादान्महेश्वरि।।

O Devi! You are the protector of all mystic phenomenon. O Maheshvari! May I be blessed through your grace and attain perfection! You accept my Japam, as I make the supplication of the Japam, to please and propitiate You.

(after reciting the Shloka, surrender yourself at the feet of Devi and supplicate your Japam at the Devi's left hand)

सप्तशतीन्यासः

Presence of Divine Mother in the Sapta Shati text

प्रथममध्यमोत्तरचरित्राणां ब्रह्मविष्णुरुद्रा ऋषयः, श्रीमहाकालीमहालक्ष्मीमहासरस्वत्यो देवताः, गायत्र्युष्णिगनुष्टुभश्छन्दांसि, नन्दाशाकम्भरीभीमाः शक्तयः, रक्तदन्तिकादुर्गाभ्रामर्यो बीजानि, अग्निवायुसूर्यास्तत्त्वानि, ऋग्यजुःसामवेदा ध्यानानि, सकलकामनासिद्धये श्रीमहाकालीमहालक्ष्मीमहासरस्वतीदेवताप्रीत्यर्थे जपे विनियोगः।

The application of this *Nyasa* is for pleasing *Shri Mahakali, Mahalakshmi, Mahasarasvati* Devatas for attaining all the merits and perfection. *Brahma, Vishnu, Rudra* are the *Rishis* of the first, second and third episodes of the Sapta Shati. *Shri Mahakali, Mahalakshmi, Mahasarasvati* are the Devatas. *Gayatri-Ushnik-Anushtup* are the Metres, *Nanda-Shakambhari-Bhima* are the *Shaktis*/powers. *Agni-Vayu-Surya* are the cosmic principles. The *Rig-Yajur-Sama* Vedas are the *Dhyanas*/meditations, of this Sapta-Shati Nyasam.

ॐ खड्गिनी शूलिनी घोरा गदिनी चक्रिणी तथा।

शङ्खिनी चापिनी बाणभुशुण्डीपरिघायुधा।।

अङ्गुष्ठाभ्यां नमः

Om! You are *Khadgini*—the weilder of sword, *Shulini*—holder of spear and *Ghora*-holder of club, *Chakrini*—holder of discus. You are *Shankhini*—the holder of a conch, *Chapini*—holder of bow and having the missiles of *Bana*-arrow, *Bhushundi*—slings and *Parigha*—iron mace. The Devi with all the missiles abide in my thumb! (Recite this Mantra and touch your thumb with fore-finger.)

ॐ शूलेन पाहि नो देवि पाहि खड्गेन चाम्बिके।
घण्टास्वनेन नः पाहि चापज्यानिःस्वनेन च।।

तर्जनीभ्यां नमः

Om! Devi! Protect us with your *Shula*—spear. O Ambika! Protect us with your *Khadga*—sword. Protect us with the sound of your *Ghanta*—bell and by the twang of your *Chapajya* bow-string....., May the Devi with all the missiles abide in my fore finger! (Recite this Mantra and touch your fore finger with thumb.)

ॐ प्राच्यां रक्ष प्रतीच्यां च चण्डिके रक्ष दक्षिणे।
भ्रामणेनात्मशूलस्य उत्तरस्यां तथेश्वरि।।

मध्यमाभ्यां नमः

Om! Chandika! Guard us in the east, in the west, and O Ishvari! guard us in the north and the south by the movements of your *Shula*—spear. May the Devi with all the missiles abide in my mid-finger! (Recite this Mantra and touch your mid-finger with thumb.)

ॐ सौम्यानि यानि रूपाणि त्रैलोक्ये विचरन्ति ते।
यानि चात्यर्थघोराणि तै रक्षास्मांस्तथा भुवम्।।

अनामिकाभ्यां नमः

Om! Protect us and the earth with your lovely forms as well as of the terrible forms, which you manifest and which go on moving around the three worlds. The Devi with all the missiles abide in my ring-finger! (Recite this Mantra and touch your ring-finger with thumb!)

ॐ खड्गशूलगदादीनि यानि चास्त्राणि तेऽम्बिके।
करपल्लवसङ्गीनि तैरस्मान् रक्ष सर्वतः ।। कनिष्ठिकाभ्यां नमः

Om! Ambika! Protect us with your *Khadga*—sword; *Shula*—spear, *Gada*—club and whatever other missiles you have, which have been touched by your sprout-like hands. The Devi with all the missiles abide in my small finger. (Recite this Mantra and touch your small-finger with thumb.)

ॐ सर्वस्वरूपे सर्वेशे सर्वशक्तिसमन्विते।
भयेभ्यस्त्राहि नो देवि दुर्गे देवि नमोऽस्तु ते।।
करतलकरपृष्ठाभ्यां नमः

Om! O Durga Devi! I pay my obeisance to You, you are the innate nature of all forms. You are Supreme Sovereign Mother with all forces. May you protect us from all the obstacles and fears! You abide in my palm and dorsal and my Namaskar be to you by touching the palm and reversing on the dorsal. (Recite the below Mantra and touch your heart with your hands.)

ॐ खड्गिनी शूलिनी घोरा गदिनी चक्रिणी तथा।
शङ्खिनी चापिनी बाणभुशुण्डीपरिघायुधा।। हृदयाय नमः

Om! Recite the below Mantra and touch your head with your hands, and Namaskar be to it.

ॐ शूलेन पाहि नो देवि पाहि खड्गेन चाम्बिके।
घण्टास्वनेन नः पाहि चापज्यानिःस्वनेन च।। शिरसे स्वाहाः

Om! Recite the below Mantra and touch your tuft with your hands and Namaskar be to it.

ॐ प्राच्यां रक्ष प्रतीच्यां च चण्डिके रक्ष दक्षिणे।
भ्रामणेनात्मशूलस्य उत्तरस्यां तथेश्वरि।। शिखायै वषट्

Om Recite the below Mantra and touch your left shoulder with right hand and right shoulder with your left hand.

ॐ सौम्यानि यानि रूपाणि त्रैलोक्ये विचरन्ति ते।
यानि चात्यर्थघोराणि तै रक्षास्मांस्तथा भुवम्।।
कवचाय हुम्

Om! Recite the below Mantra and touch your eyes with your hands which is *Voushat*.

ॐ खड्गशूलगदादीनि यानि चास्त्राणि तेऽम्बिके।
करपल्लवसङ्गीनि तैरस्मान् रक्ष सर्वतः।।
नेत्रत्रयाय वौषट्

Om! Recite the below Mantra and touch your left hand with your right hand mid-finger and create the sound, which is 'phat'.

ॐ सर्वस्वरूपे सर्वेशे सर्वशक्तिसमन्विते।
भयेभ्यस्त्राहि नो देवि दुर्गे देवि नमोऽस्तु ते।।
अस्त्राय फट्

Om! After performing all the Nyasas, meditate upon Durga who is having three eyes and recite the following Dhyanam :

ध्यानम्
Contemplation

विद्युद्दामसमप्रभां मृगपतिस्कन्धस्थितां भीषणां
कन्याभिः करवालखेटविलसद्धस्ताभिरासेविताम्।
हस्तैश्चक्रगदासिखेटविशिखांश्चापं गुणं तर्जनीं
बिभ्राणामनलात्मिकां शशिधरां दुर्गां त्रिनेत्रां भजे।।

I meditate upon the *Trinetra Durga*—Divine Mother Durga having three eyes. Her being is illumined like the lightening. She is seated on the shoulders of lion and looks very terrific. Many divine girls with swords handling and shields in their hands are attending to Her. She holds *Chakra*—discus, sword, shield, arrow, bow and 'Tarjani mudra' in Her hands. Her *Svarupa*—innate form is of *Agni*—the fire element. She holds the lunar crown on Her forehead.

NOTE :

1. After going all the preliminaries of reciting the *Kavacha, Argala* and *Kilka* and the *Nyasa Mantras,* the devotee must recite or perform Homa under the instructions of a celebrated Guru, to start with the Shree Durga Sapta Shati's First Chapter to the Thirteenth Chapter.
2. Then the devotee must conclude with all the *Nyasas* as have been described in the beginning and recite *Rig Vedic Devi Shuktam* and *Tantrik Suktam, Pradhanik Rahasyam, Vaikritikam Rahasyam* and *Moorti Rahasyam.*
3. Then the devotee must recite *Kshama Prathna* appology for any mistake comitted knowingly/ unknowingly.
4. The Devotee must recite *Siddha-Kunjka-Stotram* as it conveys the secrets of the Sapta Shati Patham.

॥ श्रीदुर्गायै नमः ॥

अथ श्रीदुर्गासप्तशती

SHRI DURGA SAPTASHATI

प्रथमोऽध्यायः

FIRST CHAPTER

मेधा ऋषि का राजा सुरथ और समाधिको भगवती की महिमा बताते हुए मधु-कैटभ-वध का प्रसङ्ग सुनाना

(A narration of Medha Rishi about the glory of Divine Mother and Slaying of Madhu and Kaitabha to Raja Suratha and Samadhi Vaishya)

विनियोगः

ॐ प्रथमचरित्रस्य ब्रह्मा ऋषिः, महाकाली देवता, गायत्री छन्दः, नन्दा शक्तिः, रक्तदन्तिका बीजम्, अग्निस्तत्त्वम्, ऋग्वेदः स्वरूपम्, श्रीमहाकालीप्रीत्यर्थे प्रथमचरित्रजपे विनियोगः।

Om, Brahma is the *Rishi,* Mahakali is the *Devata,* Gayatri is the *Chhanda*—metre, Nanda is the *Shakti*—power, Raktadantika is the *Bijam*—seed, Agni is the *Tattvam*-cosmic principle, Rig Veda is the *Svarupam*—innate form of the first *Charitra*—episode. Thus the *Viniyoga*—deliberation is for obtaining Shri Mahakali's devotion in the *Japam* of the Pratham Charitram—first episode.

ध्यानम्

Meditation

खड्गं चक्रगदेषुचापपरिघाञ्छूलं भुशुण्डीं शिरः
शङ्खं संदधतीं करैस्त्रिनयनां सर्वाङ्गभूषावृताम्।
नीलाश्मद्युतिमास्यपाददशकां सेवे महाकालिकां
यामस्तौत्स्वपिते हरौ कमलजो हन्तुं मधुं कैटभम्।। 1।।

I submit to Mahakali, who is with ten faces and ten feet. She holds sword, discus, mace, arrow, bow, club, spear, missile, skull and conch in Her hands. She is triple-eyed. Her limbs are all adorned with divine ornaments looking luminous like a blue jewel. She was worshipped with *Stuti* /adoration by *Brahma* to kill *Madhu* and *Kaitabha*.

ॐ नमश्चण्डिकायै

Om Namaskar to Chandi

ॐ ऐं मार्कण्डेय उवाच।। 1।।

Om Aim Markandeya Uvacha (Said) :

सावर्णिः सूर्यतनयो यो मनुः कथ्यतेऽष्टमः।
निशामय तदुत्पत्तिं विस्तराद् गदतो मम।। 2।।

"Listen to the narrative, how 'Savarni' the 'Suryatanaya'—son of *Surya* is called as the eighth 'Manu'. I am explaining in detail how he took the birth.

महामायानुभावेन यथा मन्वन्तराधिपः।
स बभूव महाभागः सावर्णिस्तनयो रवेः।। 3।।

"How he the Ravi's son *Savarani / Suryatanaya*—became the Sovereign ruler of the *Manavantara*, with the grace of *Mahamaya*, I am describing you the episode in detail.

स्वारोचिषेऽन्तरे पूर्वं चैत्रवंशसमुद्भवः।
सुरथो नाम राजाभूत्समस्ते क्षितिमण्डले।। 4।।

In earlier times, there was a *Raja*—king by the name of *Suratha*, born of the *Chaitra-clan*. He was ruling the *Kshiti-maṇdala*—the whole world in the period of *Svarochisha Manvantara*.

तस्य पालयतः सम्यक् प्रजाः पुत्रानिवौरसान्।
बभूवुः शत्रवो भूपाः कोलाविध्वंसिनस्तदा।। 5।।

He would treat his subjects quite in accordance with the tenets of *Dharma*, like his own children. At that time, the *Kola Vidhvansinis*—the descendants of the Kola-Kshatreyas became enemies of the king.

तस्य तैरभवद् युद्धमतिप्रबलदण्डिनः।
न्यूनैरपि स तैर्युद्धे कोलाविध्वंसिभिर्जितः।। 6।।

Raja Suratha had a strong penal code of *Danda*—punishment. Inspite of having it, he was defeated in the battle, though the Kola Vidhavansinis were a small force.

ततः स्वपुरमायातो निजदेशाधिपोऽभवत्।
आक्रान्तः स महाभागस्तैस्तदा प्रबलारिभिः।। 7।।

He turned back to his capital, as his rule was then limited to his city alone. His great enemies, still mounted a war on that *Mahabhaga Raja*—the king of great accomplishment.

अमात्यैर्बलिभिर्दुष्टैर्दुर्बलस्य दुरात्मभिः।
कोशो बलं चापहृतं तत्रापि स्वपुरे ततः।। 8।।

His power of rule got diminished gradually. Thus, he was robbed off his treasury and forced to leave by his own powerful, vicious and ill-disposed ministers.

ततो मृगयाव्याजेन हृतस्वाम्यः स भूपतिः।
एकाकी हयमारुह्य जगाम गहनं वनम्।। 9।।

So the King lost his rule. Thus he alone rode on the horseback towards a dense forest. It was all under the pretension of making a hunt.

स तत्राश्रममद्राक्षीद् द्विजवर्यस्य मेधसः।
प्रशान्तश्वापदाकीर्णं मुनिशिष्योपशोभितम्।। 10।।

He saw there an *Ashram*—hermitage of the celebrated *Dvija Medha*—the distinguished among the Dvijas—twice born Medha Rishi; where the wild beasts were all peaceful as well. The place was graced by the disciples of the Muni.

तस्थौ कंचित्स कालं च मुनिना तेन सत्कृतः।
इतश्चेतश्च विचरंस्तस्मिन्मुनिवराश्रमे।। 11।।

On his reaching there, Muni greeted him. He then moved around here and there, as he stayed there for some time.

सोऽचिन्तयत्तदा तत्र ममत्वाकृष्टचेतनः।
मत्पूर्वैः पालितं पूर्वं मया हीनं पुरं हि तत्।। 12।।

There he was drawn towards attachment and felt into that deep thought : 'I donot know whether my city, which was properly cared for by my ancestors previously, and now deserted by me.....,

मद्भृत्यैस्तैरसद्वृत्तैर्धर्मतः पाल्यते न वा।
न जाने स प्रधानो मे शूरहस्ती सदामदः।। 13।।

is being properly looked after and guarded or ignored by my servants of evil nature. Knowing nothing about my chief elephant, who was heroic and always exhilirated.....,

मम वैरिवशं यातः कान् भोगानुपलप्स्यते।
ये ममानुगता नित्यं प्रसादधनभोजनैः।। 14।।

......and now fallen into the hands of my enemies. How is it being treated and given comforting enjoyment ? Those who were my constant followers and received favour, riches and food from me......,

अनुवृत्तिं ध्रुवं तेऽद्य कुर्वन्त्यन्यमहीभृताम्।
असम्यग्व्ययशीलैस्तैः कुर्वद्भिः सततं व्ययम्।। 15।।

.....they now certainly pay their respects to other kings. My riches would be spent lavishly by those spendthrifts.....,

संचितः सोऽतिदुःखेन क्षयं कोशो गमिष्यति।
एतच्चान्यच्च सततं चिन्तयामास पार्थिवः ।। 16 ।।

......and our own treasure, earned and attained with great efforts will get exhausted'. The king was continuously pondering over such and other problems.

तत्र विप्राश्रमाभ्याशे वैश्यमेकं ददर्श सः।
स पृष्टस्तेन कस्त्वं भो हेतुश्चागमनेऽत्र कः ।। 17 ।।

He saw a *Vaishya*—merchant near the hermitage of that Vipra—Brahmana, and asked him : "who are you ? What is the reason behind coming over here ?"

सशोक इव कस्मात्त्वं दुर्मना इव लक्ष्यसे।
इत्याकर्ण्य वचस्तस्य भूपतेः प्रणयोदितम् ।। 18 ।।

"Why you seem to be caught in the anxieties and why you look indifferent ?" Having heard the sympathetic words of the king.....,

प्रत्युवाच स तं वैश्यः प्रश्रयावनतो नृपम् ।। 19 ।।

.....the Vaishya bowed him respectfully and replied to the king with humble submission :

वैश्य उवाच ।। 20 ।।

Vaishya said

समाधिर्नाम वैश्योऽहमुत्पन्नो धनिनां कुले ।। 21 ।।

"I am a Vaishya, born in a wealthy *Kula*—clan and my name is *Samadhi*."

पुत्रदारैर्निरस्तश्च धनलोभादसाधुभिः।
विहीनश्च धनैर्दारैः पुत्रैरादाय मे धनम् ।। 22 ।।

I have been thrown out by my wicked wife and sons, because of their greed for my wealth. My wife and sons have misused my riches, and made me devoid of wealth.

वनमभ्यागतो दुःखी निरस्तश्चाप्तबन्धुभिः।
सोऽहं न वेद्मि पुत्राणां कुशलाकुशलात्मिकाम्।। 23।।

I have been cast out by my own kith and kin. I have come this forest, being grief-striken. I do not know anything about the conditions as being good or bad of my sons...,

प्रवृत्तिं स्वजनानां च दाराणां चात्र संस्थितः।
किं नु तेषां गृहे क्षेममक्षेमं किं नु साम्प्रतम्।। 24।।

.....of my own men and my wife, as I now dwell here. Nothing is known about their welfare regarding good or bad, to me.

कथं ते किं नु सद्वृत्ता दुर्वृत्ताः किं नु मे सुताः।। 25।।

How are my sons and how they live good or bad lives?"

राजोवाच।। 26।।

The king said :

यैर्निरस्तो भवाँल्लुब्धैः पुत्रदारादिभिर्धनैः।। 27।।

"Your covetous sons and wife who have deprived you of all the wealth and riches, then....,

तेषु किं भवतः स्नेहमनुबध्नाति मानसम्।। 28।।

....why it is so that your mind gets affectionately attached with and drawn towards them ?"

वैश्य उवाच।। 29।।

The Vaishya said :

एवमेतद्यथा प्राह भवानस्मद्गतं वचः।। 30।।

"what have been told by you, regarding myself is very true...,

किं करोमि न बध्नाति मम निष्ठुरतां मनः।
यैः संत्यज्य पितृस्नेहं धनलुब्धैर्निराकृतः।। 31।।

...but what can I do? My mind does not become hard; even the sons have not got any affection for a father, and those very persons have driven me out of wealth as they being very greedy....,

पतिस्वजनहार्दं च हार्दि तेष्वेव मे मनः।
किमेतन्नाभिजानामि जानन्नपि महामते।। 32।।

.....and the wife has lost all the love for me and kinsmen their attachment as well. O noble king! I do not comprehend, though I know it......,

यत्प्रेमप्रवणं चित्तं विगुणेष्वपि बन्धुषु।
तेषां कृते मे निःश्वासो दौर्मनस्यं च जायते।। 33।।

......how is it that the mind is still attached with love towards those worthless kiths and kins? I do have heavy sighs and feel dejected, because of their attitude.

करोमि किं यन्न मनस्तेष्वप्रीतिषु निष्ठुरम्।। 34।।

Still my mind does not become hard toward those unloving persons. What can I do now?"

मार्कण्डेय उवाय ।। 35।।

Markandeya said :

ततस्तौ सहितौ विप्र तं मुनिं समुपस्थितौ।। 36।।

"O Vipra! Then both of them approached the Muni with all reverence..,

समाधिर्नाम वैश्योऽसौ स च पार्थिवसत्तमः।
कृत्वा तु तौ यथान्यायं यथार्हं तेन संविदम्।। 37।।

.....and observing the proper etiquette, as per desired norms. 'Samadhi Vaishya' and 'Parthiva—'the king Suratha'....,

उपविष्टौ कथाः काश्चिच्चक्रतुर्वैश्यपार्थिवौ।। 38।।

.....sat down and conversed with the Muni on certain subjects".

राजोवाच।। 39।।

The king said :

भगवंस्त्वामहं प्रष्टुमिच्छाम्येकं वदस्व तत्।। 40।।

"I seek permission to ask you one thing. Be pleased to reply that question.

दुःखाय यन्मे मनसः स्वचित्तायत्ततां विना।
ममत्वं गतराज्यस्य राज्याङ्गेष्वखिलेष्वपि।। 41।।

I can not hold myself without asking you, as my mind is all full of sorrow. Though I have lost my kingdom and all other essentials...,

जानतोऽपि यथाज्ञस्य किमेतन्मुनिसत्तम।
अयं च निकृतः पुत्रैर्दारैर्भृत्यैस्तथोज्झितः।। 42।।

....I know it for certain that I have lost all that. O celebrated Muni! Still I have got attachment with it , as being like an ignorant man. This Vaishya has also been discarded by his children, wife and servants, hence.....,

स्वजनेन च संत्यक्तस्तेषु हार्दी तथाप्यति।
एवमेष तथाहं च द्वावप्यत्यन्तदुःखितौ।। 43।।

...disowned by his own people, but is still affectionate towards them without keeping any restraint. Thus both he and myself, are caught by miseries.

दृष्टदोषेऽपि विषये ममत्वाकृष्टमानसौ।
तत्किमेतन्महाभाग यन्मोहो ज्ञानिनोरपि।। 44।।

Thus we are drawn by attachments towards the objects, whose defect we know for certain. How this happens? O great sage Mahabhaga—revered one!

ममास्य च भवत्येषा विवेकान्धस्य मूढता।। 45।।

The delusion is very much apparent with both of us."

ऋषिरुवाच ।। 46 ।।

The Rishi said

ज्ञानमस्ति समस्तस्य जन्तोर्विषयगोचरे ।। 47 ।।

"Every being has the knowledge of objects, as perceived by the senses....,

विषयश्च महाभाग याति चैवं पृथक् पृथक् ।
दिवान्धाः प्राणिनः केचिद्रात्रावन्धास्तथापरे ।। 48 ।।

...O Mahabhaga/revered one! An object of sense reaches variously. Some beings are blind during day time and some others by the night.

केचिद्दिवा तथा रात्रौ प्राणिनस्तुल्यदृष्टयः ।
ज्ञानिनो मनुजाः सत्यं किं तु ते न हि केवलम् ।। 49 ।।

There are also other beings, who have equal sight by both day and night. Human beings are certainly endowed with Jnanam/congnition, but they are not the only beings......,

यतो हि ज्ञानिनः सर्वे पशुपक्षिमृगादयः ।
ज्ञानं च तन्मनुष्याणां यत्तेषां मृगपक्षिणाम् ।। 50 ।।

.....for cattle, birds, animals and other beings, also have the power of cognition. The knowledge that men possesses, is possessed by animals and birds as well.

मनुष्याणां च यत्तेषां तुल्यमन्यत्तथोभयोः ।
ज्ञानेऽपि सति पश्यैतान् पतङ्गाञ्छावचञ्चुषु ।। 51 ।।

Birds and beasts also have the cognizance as that human beings have. Look at these birds, they have knowledge, they do put the particles of grain in the beaks of their young ones....,

कणमोक्षादृतान्मोहात्पीड्यमानानपि क्षुधा ।
मानुषा मनुजव्याघ्र साभिलाषाः सुतान् प्रति ।। 52 ।।

...although they remain themselves hungry. O tiger among men, human beings are attached to their children for...,

लोभात्प्रत्युपकाराय नन्वेतान् किं न पश्यसि।
तथापि ममतावर्त्ते मोहगर्ते निपातिता:।। 53।।

...receiving the return help from them. Do not you see it? Even the men are caught in the net of Moha/delusion.

महामायाप्रभावेण संसारस्थितिकारिणा।
तन्नात्र विस्मय: कार्यो योगनिद्रा जगत्पते:।। 54।।

The existence of *Samsara*—world is caused through the power of *Mahamaya*. She is verily, the *Yoganidra*—the mystic sleep of *Jagatpati*,who is *Vishnu*—the sustainer of the universe. Therefore, you should not be astonished.

महामाया हरेश्चैषा तया सम्मोह्यते जगत्।
ज्ञानिनामपि चेतांसि देवी भगवती हि सा।। 55।।

It is by the power of *Mahamaya*, that the world is deluded. Verily, She, the *Bhagavati Mahamaya* draws even the consciousness power of...,

बलादाकृष्य मोहाय महामाया प्रयच्छति।
तया विसृज्यते विश्वं जगदेतच्चराचरम्।। 56।।

....the men of *Jnanam*—the knowledgeable persons, forcibly and throws them into delusion. She alone creates this universe which is both static and dynamic.

सैषा प्रसन्ना वरदा नृणां भवति मुक्तये।
सा विद्या परमा मुक्तेर्हेतुभूता सनातनी।। 57।।

When she gets appeased, becomes the *Varda*—boon-giver for Mukti—the final release. She is *Vidya*—the great spiritual knowledge and *Sanatani*—the Eternal one and the casue of final liberation...,

संसारबन्धहेतुश्च सैव सर्वेश्वरेश्वरी।। 58।।

......and the primal cause of the bondage of the world. She is 'Sarveshvareshvari'—the Sovereign Supreme Lady.

राजोवाच ।। 59 ।।

The king said :

भगवन् का हि सा देवी महामायेति यां भवान् ।। 60 ।।

"O Bhagvan—the Venerable one! Who is that lady to whom you call Mahamaya?

ब्रवीति कथमुत्पन्ना सा कर्मास्याश्च किं द्विज ।
यत्प्रभावा च सा देवी यत्स्वरूपा यदुद्भवा ।। 61 ।।

O Dvija ! How did She came into being? What are her actions? What constitutes her nature? Where from did she originate? What is her force?....,

तत्सर्वं श्रोतुमिच्छामि त्वत्तो ब्रह्मविदां वर ।। 62 ।।

....I would like to hear from you all that. O you are Proficient among the knowers of 'Brahma Vidya'—the Absolute knowledge."

ऋषिरुवाच ।। 63 ।।

The Rishi Said :

नित्यैव सा जगन्मूर्तिस्तया सर्वमिदं ततम् ।। 64 ।।

"She is eternal, She is embodiment of *Jagat*—the universe. Although this universe is pervaded by Her alone....,

तथापि तत्समुत्पत्तिर्बहुधा श्रूयतां मम ।
देवानां कार्यसिद्ध्यर्थमाविर्भवति सा यदा ।। 65 ।।

.....yet I have heard of Her incarnations variously. Whenever, She manifests Herself in order to fulfill the purposes of the *Devas*—brilliant ones...,

उत्पन्नेति तदा लोके सा नित्याप्यभिधीयते ।
योगनिद्रां यदा विष्णुर्जगत्येकार्णवीकृते ।। 66 ।।

...then She is said to be born in the world, though She is eternal. Vishnu—the Lord of the Universe took to the mystic slumber, while making the universe one with ocean...,

आस्तीर्य शेषमभजत्कल्पान्ते भगवान् प्रभुः।
तदा द्वावसुरौ घोरौ विख्यातौ मधुकैटभौ।। 67।।

..then at the end of *Kalpa, Bhagavan Prabhu*—the adorable Lord was stretched out on Shesha—the Lord of serpents, who supports the earth planet. Two terrible asuras—the well known *Madhu* and *Kaitabha*.....,

विष्णुकर्णमलोद्भूतौ हन्तुं ब्रह्माणमुद्यतौ।
स नाभिकमले विष्णोः स्थितो ब्रह्मा प्रजापतिः।।68।।

...sprung into being out of the wax of Vishnu's ears. Brahma—the creator of beings was at that time sitting on the navel lotus of Vishnu, when those two asuras were ready to kill him.

दृष्ट्वा तावसुरौ चोग्रौ प्रसुप्तं च जनार्दनम्।
तुष्टाव योगनिद्रां तामेकाग्रहृदयस्थितः।। 69।।

Seeing those two fierce asuras and *Janardhana Lord Vishnu* in his sleep, *Brahma* with single minded concentration praised 'Yoganidra' for.....

विबोधनार्थाय हरेर्हरिनेत्रकृतालयाम्।
विश्वेश्वरीं जगद्धात्रीं स्थितिसंहारकारिणीम्।। 70।।

...awakening Hari, who was dwelling in the eyes of Hari. Brahma extolled *Vishveshvari*—the Supreme Sovereign Queen, *Jagatdhatri*—the supporter of the worlds, *Sthiti—Samharakarini*—the primal cause of sustenance and dissolution (of the universe)....

निद्रां भगवतीं विष्णोतरतुलां तेजसः प्रभुः।। 71।।

...*Nidra-Bhagavati*—the Supreme deity of sleep and who is incomparable Shakti of Bhagvan Vishnu."

ब्रह्मोवाच।। 72।।

Brahma Said :

त्वं स्वाहा त्वं स्वधा त्वं हि वषट्कारःस्वरात्मिका।। 73।।

"You are *Svaha*—the Vedic Mantra uttered when an *Ahuti*—offerings is poured in the *Agni*—fire; you are *Svadha*—the Pauranik Mantra uttered when water oblations / offerings are made to *Pitris*—the departed souls. You are *Vashatkara*— a word of offering to the Devatas and you are the embodiment of *Svara* the immutable sound...,

सुधा त्वमक्षरे नित्ये त्रिधा मात्रात्मिका स्थिता।
अर्धमात्रास्थिता नित्या यानुच्चार्या विशेषतः।। 74।।

...You are *Sudha*—nectar. You are in the 'Nitya-akshara'—eternal immutable word in the embodiment of *Triple Matra*—Syllable and you are in the half Matra. You are, what cannot be uttered specifically.

त्वमेव संध्या सावित्री त्वं देवि जननी परा।
त्वयैतद्धार्यते विश्वं त्वयैतत्सृज्यते जगत्।। 75।।

You are *Sandhya*—twilight. You are *Savitri*—the Pranava; *Devi, Janani*—the Divine Mother creatrix and *Para*—the transcendent one. It is You, who hold this universe and create this world.

त्वयैतत्पाल्यते देवि त्वमत्स्यन्ते च सर्वदा।
विसृष्टौ सृष्टिरूपा त्वं स्थितिरूपा च पालने।। 76।।

By You, this universe is protected O Devi! You dissolve it at the end of Kalpa. You are *Srishtrirupa*—the very manifestation of existence, and you are *Sthiti rupa*—the existent and You sustain it.

तथा संहृतिरूपान्ते जगतोऽस्य जगन्मये।
महाविद्या महामाया महामेधा महास्मृतिः।। 77।।

O *Jaganmayi Devi*—the Mother of universe. You are *Samhara rupa*—the consuming force at the time of dissolution of this world. You are *Mahavidya*—the Great eternal knowledge; *Mahamaya*—great illusion, *Mahamedha*—great intellect and *Mahasmriti*—great contemplation.

महामोहा च भवती महादेवी महासुरी।
प्रकृतिस्त्वं च सर्वस्य गुणत्रयविभाविनी।। 78।।

You are *Mahamoha*—great delusion, *Mahadevi*—great divinity and *Mahasuri*—the great anti divinity. You are the Primal cause of everything, bringing into action all the three *Gunas*—qualities.

कालरात्रिर्महारात्रिर्मोहरात्रिश्च दारुणा।
त्वं श्रीस्त्वमीश्वरी त्वं ह्रीस्त्वं बुद्धिर्बोधलक्षणा।। 79।।

You are *Kalaratri*—darknight, *Maharatri*—the great night, *Moharatri*—the light of delusion and *Daruna*—terrible night. You are *Shri*—the good fortune. You are *Ishvari*—Supreme Queen, you are *Hri*—modesty, *Buddhi*—intellect and *Bodhalakshana*—characterization of knowledge.

लज्जा पुष्टिस्तथा तुष्टिस्त्वं शान्तिः क्षान्तिरेव च।
खड्गिनी शूलिनी घोरा गदिनी चक्रिणी तथा।। 80।।

You are *Lajja*—modesty, *Pushti*—nourishment and *Tushti* contentment. You are *Shanti*—tranquility and also *Kshanti* forbearance. You are *Khadgini*—the weilder of sword, *Shulini*—holder of spear and of *Ghora*—club, *Chakrini*—holder of disc and....

शङ्खिनी चापिनी बाणभुशुण्डीपरिघायुधा।
सौम्या सौम्यतराशेषसौम्येभ्यस्त्वतिसुन्दरी।। 81।।

....You are *Shankhini*—the holder of a conch, *Chapini*—holder of bow and having the missiles of *Bana*—arrow, *Bhushundi*—slings and *Parigha*—iron mace. You are *Saumya*—pleasing, *Saumyatara*—more pleasing. You are verily, most pleasing than the pleasing things and You are *Sundari*—extremely beautiful.

परापराणां परमा त्वमेव परमेश्वरी।
यच्च किंचित्क्वचिद्वस्तु सदसद्वाखिलात्मके।। 82।।

You are beyond the transcendent and immanent. Verily, You are the Supreme *Ishvari*—the Sovereign Queen. Whatsoever is and wherever a thing exists, either real or unreal, is all that possessed by You in Yourself. You are *Akhilatmika* the universal self...,

तस्य सर्वस्य या शक्तिः सा त्वं किं स्तूयसे तदा।
यया त्वया जगत्स्त्रष्टा जगत्पात्यत्ति यो जगत्।। 83।।

...and You are the power behind all that. Who else is capable of extolling Your superiority? Myself as *Srashta* the creaetor and Vishnu, being the *Palaka*—the Sustainer......

सोऽपि निद्रावशं नीतः कस्त्वां स्तोतुमिहेश्वरः।
विष्णुः शरीरग्रहणमहमीशान एव च।। 84।।

......also lies in great sleep. Who is capable of offering laudation to You? Vishnu, myself as Brahma, Ishana-Rudra....,

कारितास्ते यतोऽतस्त्वां कः स्तोतुं शक्तिमान् भवेत्।
सा त्वमित्थं प्रभावैः स्वैरुदारैर्देवि संस्तुता।। 85।।

....have been given embodied forms by You. Therefore, who is capable of offering the *Stuti*—laudatoin to You. You are therefore, O Devi, being praised by Your own liberal influences.

मोहयैतौ दुराधर्षावसुरौ मधुकैटभौ।
प्रबोधं च जगत्स्वामी नीयतामच्युतो लघु।। 86।।

Be pleased and bewitch these two unassailable Madhu and Kaitabha *Asuras*—the demoniac forces. May Achutya—the Lord of the universe be quickly awakened from sleep...

बोधश्च क्रियतामस्य हन्तुमेतौ महासुरौ।। 87।।

..and be roused up in his action to slay these two great Asuras!"

ऋषिरुवाच।। 88 ।।

The Rishi Said :

एवं स्तुता तदा देवी तामसी तत्र वेधसा।। 89 ।।

"Thus the Devi *Tamasi* was extolled by Brahma the creator...,

विष्णोः प्रबोधनार्थाय निहन्तुं मधुकैटभौ।
नेत्रास्यनासिकाबाहुहृदयेभ्यस्तथोरसः।। 90 ।।

...in order to awaken Vishnu for slaying Madhu and Kaitabha. From eyes, mouth, nostrils, arms, heart and breast...,

निर्गम्य दर्शने तस्थौ ब्रह्मणोऽव्यक्तजन्मनः।
उत्तस्थौ च जगन्नाथस्तया मुक्तो जनार्दनः।। 91 ।।

...She Herself came out of Vishnu's being and appeared before Brahma of the inscrutable mysterious birth. *Janardana* being the lord of the Universe, quitted by Her, rose up....,

एकार्णवेऽहिशयनात्ततः स ददृशे च तौ।
मधुकैटभौ दुरात्मानावतिवीर्यपराक्रमौ।। 92 ।।

......from His couch of *Sheshanaga* in the waters of *Ekarnava*—Universal ocean. Madhu-Kaitabha of exceeding heroism and power......,

क्रोधरक्तेक्षणावत्तुं ब्रह्माणं जनितोद्यमौ।
समुत्थाय ततस्ताभ्यां युयुधे भगवान् हरिः।। 93 ।।

..having their eyes red with anger, were extremely ready to devour Brahma. Thereupon the Lord of the Universe—Bhagvana Hari got up, and fought with them....

पञ्चवर्षसहस्राणि बाहुप्रहरणो विभुः।
तावप्यतिबलोन्मत्तौ महामायाविमोहितौ।। 94 ।।

.....for five thousand years, using His arms as weapons. They got violently excited with their exceeding power thus being deluded by Mahamaya....,

उक्तवन्तो वरोऽस्मत्तो व्रियतामिति केशवम्॥95॥

...so they exclaimed to Keshava : 'Ask for a boon from us'?

श्रीभगवानुवाच॥96॥

Shri Bhagavana Said :

भवेतामद्य मे तुष्टौ मम वध्यावुभावपि॥ 97॥

"If you are satisfied with me, then both of you must be slain by Me.

किमन्येन वरेणात्र एतावद्धि वृतं मम॥ 98॥

There is no need of asking any other boon here. My choice is only this indeed."

ऋषिरुवाच॥99॥

The Rishi Said :

वञ्चिताभ्यामिति तदा सर्वमापोमयं जगत्॥100॥

Being thus bewitched (by the words), they found the whole world full of water.

विलोक्य ताभ्यां गदितो भगवान् कमलेक्षणः।
आवां जहि न यत्रोर्वी सलिलेन परिप्लुता॥ 101॥

They asked Bhagvana *Kamalekshana*—the lotus eyed Lord: 'Slay us there, where the earth be without water'.

ऋषिरुवाच॥102॥

The Rishi Said :

तथेत्युक्त्वा भगवता शङ्खचक्रगदाभृता।
कृत्वा चक्रेण वै च्छिन्ने जघने शिरसी तयोः॥103॥

"Bhagavana Vishnu, the weilder of conch, discus and mace took them on His loins, thereafter saying 'be it so'. And then severed their heads with His discus.

एवमेषा समुत्पन्ना ब्रह्मणा संस्तुता स्वयम्।
प्रभावमस्या देव्यास्तु भूयः शृणु वदामि ते ।। ऐं ॐ।। 104।।

Mahamaya—the Great Power got incarnated Herself, when praised by Brahma. Now you listen to the further glory of this Devi. I tell you'. Aim Aum.

इति श्रीमार्कण्डेयपुराणे सावर्णिके मन्वन्तरे देवीमाहात्म्ये
मधुकैटभवधो नाम प्रथमोऽध्यायः।। 1।।

The first Chapter entitled *Slaying of Madhu-Kaitabha* of the Devi Mahatmya, during the time span of *Savarni*—the Manu occuring in the *Markandeya Purana* is concluded.

उवाच 14, अर्धश्लोकाः 24, श्लोकाः 66, एवमादितः।। 104।।

Narrated mantras : 14, half Shlokas : 24,
full Shlokas : 66, in all 104 Shlokas, concluded

द्वितीयोऽध्यायः

SECOND CHAPTER

देवताओं के तेज से देवी का प्रादुर्भाव और महिषासुर की सेना का वध

Dawn of Devi's Being, through the effulgence of the Devatas and destruction of the Mahishasura's force

विनियोगः

Application

ॐ मध्यमचरित्रस्य विष्णुर्ऋषिः, महालक्ष्मीर्देवता, उष्णिक् छन्दः शाकम्भरी शक्तिः, दुर्गा बीजम्, वायुस्तत्त्वम्, यजुर्वेदः स्वरूपम्, श्रीमहालक्ष्मीप्रीत्यर्थं मध्यमचरित्रजपे विनियोगः।

Om, Vishnu is the *Rishi*, Mahalakshmi is the *Devata*, Ushnika is the *Chhanda*—metre, Shakambari is the *Shakti*—power, Durga is the *Bijam*—seed, Vayu is the *Tattva*, Yajurveda is the *Svarupam*—innate/self formation of the Second Charitra. Thus the *Viniyoga*—application is for pleasing Shri Mahalakshmi with the Japam of the Madhyam Charitra.

ध्यानम्

Meditation

ॐ अक्षस्रक्परशुं गदेषुकुलिशं पद्मं धनुष्कुण्डिकां
दण्डं शक्तिमसिं च चर्म जलजं घण्टां सुराभाजनम्।
शूलं पाशसुदर्शने च दधतीं हस्तैः प्रसन्नाननां
सेवे सैरिभमर्दिनीमिह महालक्ष्मीं सरोजस्थिताम्।।

Om. I pay my obeisance to Mahalakshmi, who is seated on

the '*Saroja*'—lotus. She is of the complexion of coral. She holds in Her hands, '*Akshamala*—rosary, axe, mace, arrow, thunderbolt, lotus, bow, pitcher, rod, 'Shakti', sword, shield, conch, bell, honey cup, spear, noose and the *Sudarshana* discus. Her face is ever smiling and She is the destroyer of Mahishasura.

ॐ ह्रीं ऋषिरुवाच।। 1।।

Om Hrim Rishi Said :

देवासुरमभूद्युद्धं पूर्णमब्दशतं पुरा।
महिषेऽसुराणामधिपे देवानां च पुरन्दरे।। 2।।

"Of long past, there was a war between *Devas* and *Asuras* for a full one hundred (celestial) years. *Mahishasura* was the lord of '*Asuras*'/anti-divinity and *Purandara* (Indra) was the lord of 'Devas'—divinity.

तत्रासुरैर्महावीर्यैर्देवसैन्यं पराजितम्।
जित्वा च सकलान् देवानिन्द्रोऽभून्महिषासुरः।। 3।।

In that war, forces of the Devas were vanquished by the valarous '*Asuras*'. After conquering all the 'Devas', *Mahishasura* become the '*Indra*' of (*Svarga*—heaven).

ततः पराजिता देवाः पद्मयोनिं प्रजापतिम्।
पुरस्कृत्य गतास्तत्र यत्रेशगरुडध्वजौ।। 4।।

Then the defeated Devas headed by 'Padamayoni-Prajapati' (Brahma) went to that place, where 'Isha/Shiva' and 'Garudadhvaja—Vishnu' had their abode.

यथावृत्तं तयोस्तद्वन्महिषासुरचेष्टितम्।
त्रिदशाः कथयामासुर्देवाभिभवविस्तरम्।। 5।।

The Devas narrated to them, the detail of their woe, as it happened to them, at their defeat, by the hands of Mahishasura.

सूर्येन्द्राग्न्यनिलेन्दूनां यमस्य वरुणस्य च।
अन्येषां चाधिकारान् स स्वयमेवाधितिष्ठति।। 6।।

They said : He (Mahishasura) has taken over himself the

power and jurisdiction of *Surya, Indra, Agni, Anila Indu, Yama* and *Varuna* along with the host of other Devas.

स्वर्गान्निराकृताः सर्वे तेन देवगणा भुवि।
विचरन्ति यथा मर्त्या महिषेण दुरात्मना।। 7।।

On being thrown out from '*Svarga*'—heaven by the wicked and ill natured Mahishasura, the Devas have been then wandering like mortals on the earth.

एतद्वः कथितं सर्वममरारिविचेष्टितम्।
शरणं वः प्रपन्नाः स्मो वधस्तस्य विचिन्त्यताम्।। 8।।

We have narrated to you, all that what has been done by the enemy of the Devas, so we have sought shelter under both of you. May You both be pleased and think of the strategy for his killing!

इत्थं निशम्य देवानां वचांसि मधुसूदनः।
चकार कोपं शम्भुश्च भ्रुकुटीकुटिलाननौ।। 9।।

Madhusudana got angry, after hearing the words of the Devas, so got *Shiva* also angry and their face became twisted with their eyebrows frowned.

ततोऽतिकोपपूर्णस्य चक्रिणो वदनात्ततः।
निश्चक्राम महत्तेजो ब्रह्मणः शंकरस्य च।। 10।।

A great 'Tejas'—light emitted from the face of *Chakrin*—Vishnu, who was full of intense anger. From the bodies of Brahma and Shankara too an intense 'Tejas'—light sprung forth.

अन्येषां चैव देवानां शक्रादीनां शरीरतः।
निर्गतं सुमहत्तेजस्तच्चैक्यं समगच्छत।। 11।।

Likewise, the great *Tejas* issued forth from the bodies of Indra and other 'Devas'. All the *Tejas* got accumulated together.

अतीव तेजसः कूटं ज्वलन्तमिव पर्वतम्।
ददृशुस्ते सुरास्तत्र ज्वालाव्याप्तदिगन्तरम्।। 12।।

The Devas witnessed a huge mass of 'Tejas' like an excessively blazing mountain, pervading in all the quarters, with its flames.

अतुलं तत्र तत्तेजः सर्वदेवशरीरजम्।
एकस्थं तदभून्नारी व्याप्तलोकत्रयं त्विषा।। 13।।

A *Nari*—manifestatin in the woman form, evolved with the lustre of that incomparable unified Tejas, produced from the bodies/forms of all the Devas, pervading in the triple world.

यदभूच्छाम्भवं तेजस्तेनाजायत तन्मुखम्।
याम्येन चाभवन् केशा बाहवो विष्णुतेजसा।। 14।।

Her face came into being by the 'Tejas' of Shambu; by Yama's, Her hair sprung, by Vishnu's Tejas, the arms.

सौम्येन स्तनयोर्युग्मं मध्यं चैन्द्रेण चाभवत्।
वारुणेन च जङ्घोरू नितबस्तेजसा भुवः।। 15।।

....by Somas Tejas the two breasts. By Indra's Tejas Her waist, by Varuna's Tejas Her shank and thigh. By 'Bhuva's Her hips...,

ब्रह्मणस्तेजसा पादौ तदङ्गुल्योऽर्कतेजसा।
वसूनां च कराङ्गुल्यः कौबेरेण च नासिका।। 16।।

by Brahma's 'Tejas' Her feet, by Arka's-'Tejas' Her toes, by Vasu's 'Tejas' Her fingers and by Kubera's 'Tejas' Her nose....,

तस्यास्तु दन्ताः सम्भूताः प्राजापत्येन तेजसा।
नयनत्रितयं जज्ञे तथा पावकतेजसा।। 17।।

....by the 'Teja's of Prajapati Her teeth come into being and likewise by the 'Tejas' of 'Pavaka', Her three eyes were formed.....,

भ्रुवौ च संध्ययोस्तेजः श्रवणावनिलस्य च।
अन्येषां चैव देवानां सम्भवस्तेजसां शिवा।। 18।।

...eyebrows came into formation by the 'Tejas' of two 'Sandhyas' the ears became with the 'Tejas' of 'Anila'. The manifestations of other Devas also became cause of the being of Shiva—the auspicious Devi.

ततः समस्तदेवानां तेजोराशिसमुद्भवाम्।
तां विलोक्य मुदं प्रापुरमरा महिषार्दिताः।। 19।।

All the Devas oppressed by Mahishasura became joyful, when they looked at Her, Who had come into being from the unified 'Tejas' of all the Devas.

शूलं शूलाद्विनिष्कृष्य ददौ तस्यै पिनाकधृक्।
चक्रं च दत्तवान् कृष्णः समुत्पाद्य स्वचक्रतः।।20।।

A 'Shula'—trident was presented to Her, bringing forth from his own trident by the *Pinakadharin—Shiva;* and *Krishna-Vishnu* offered Her one *Chakra,* created by his own *Chakra.....,*

शङ्खं च वरुणः शक्तिं ददौ तस्यै हुताशनः।
मारुतो दत्तवांश्चापं बाणपूर्णे तथेषुधी।। 21।।

...*Varuna* gave Her conch and *Hutashana* offered Shakti; *Maruta* presented Her a bow and two quivers full of arrows....,

वज्रमिन्द्रः समुत्पाद्य कुलिशादमराधिपः।
ददौ तस्यै सहस्राक्षो घण्टामैरावताद् गजात्।।22।।

...*Sahsraksha* the Indra with hundred eyes brought forth thunderbolt from his own *Vajra*—thunderbold and one *Ghanta*—bell taken from his elephant Airavata..,

कालदण्डाद्यमो दण्डं पाशं चाम्बुपतिर्ददौ।
प्रजापतिश्चाक्षमालां ददौ ब्रह्मा कमण्डलुम्।।23।।

...*Yama* offered one staff to Her from *Kaladanda* and *Ambupati/ Varuna*—the lord of all oceans presented a noose; and *Prajapati*—Brahma gave an *Akshamala*—string of Aksha and one Kamandalu...,

समस्तरोमकूपेषु निजरश्मीन् दिवाकरः।
कालश्च दत्तवान् खड्गं तस्याश्चर्म च निर्मलम्।।24।।

...Divakara Surya—the Sun put his own rays on all Her pores and 'Kala'/Yama gave Her a spotless sword and shield.

क्षीरोदश्चामलं हारमजरे च तथाम्बरे।
चूडामणिं तथा दिव्यं कुण्डले कटकानि च॥ 25॥

Kshirasagara—the Ocean of Milk offered a crystal necklace and a pair of undecaying garments, a divine crest of *Chudamani*—jewel—two ear-rings, and bracelets..,

अर्धचन्द्रं तथा शुभ्रं केयूरान् सर्वबाहुषु।
नूपुरौ विमलौ तद्वद् ग्रैवेयकमनुत्तमम्॥ 26॥

..a brilliant *Ardhachandra*—crescent ornament, armlet on all arms, a pair of radiant anklets, a best one necklace...,

अङ्गुलीयकरत्नानि समस्तास्वङ्गुलीषु च।
विश्वकर्मा ददौ तस्यै परशुं चातिनिर्मलम्॥ 27॥

and excellent diamond rings on all the fingers. *Vishvakarma* gave Her the brilliant axe..,

अस्त्राण्यनेकरूपाणि तथाभेद्यं च दंशनम्।
अम्लानपङ्कजां मालां शिरस्युरसि चापराम्॥ 28॥

...also weapon of various forms and an impenetrable armour. The unfading garland of lotuses for Her head and another for Her breast...,

अददज्जलधिस्तस्यै पङ्कजं चातिशोभनम्।
हिमवान् वाहनं सिंहं रत्नानि विविधानि च॥ 29॥

...were given by *Jaladhi*—the ocean, besides a lovely lotus in Her palm. Himavan presented a lion for Her vehicle to ride and varieties of jewels.

ददावशून्यं सुरया पानपात्रं धनाधिपः।
शेषश्च सर्वनागेशो महामणिविभूषितम्॥ 30॥

Dhanadhipa—Kuvera offered a drinking cup, fully filled with wine. Properly ornamented with *Mahamani*, the best of jewels, the Lord of all serpent race Shesha....,

नागहारं ददौ तस्यै धत्ते यः पृथिवीमिमाम्।
अन्यैरपि सुरैर्देवी भूषणैरायुधैस्तथा।। 31।।

......made a gift of *Nagahara* —a serpent necklace properly bedecked. It is he, who holds this earth. The Devi was also offered with ornaments, weapons by other Devas....,

सम्मानिता ननादोच्चैः साट्टहासं मुहुर्मुहुः।
तस्या नादेन घोरेण कृत्स्नमापूरितं नभः।। 32।।

......who honoured Her. She gave out a loud roar with *Attahas*—defying laugh frequently again and again. By Her extremely great roaring, the whole space was filled with a loud roar....,

अमायतातिमहता प्रतिशब्दो महानभूत्।
चुक्षुभुः सकला लोकाः समुद्राश्च चकम्पिरे।। 33।।

....causing great reverberation in the sky. It shook all the worlds and trembling occured in the oceans.

चचाल वसुधा चेलुः सकलाश्च महीधराः।
जयेति देवाश्च मुदा तामूचुः सिंहवाहिनीम्।। 34।।

The earth quaked and all the moutains got rocked. The Devas exclaimed *Jaya*—victory to *Simhavahini*—the rider on the lion.

तुष्टुवुर्मुनयश्चैनां भक्तिनम्रात्ममूर्तयः।
दृष्ट्वा समस्तं संक्षुब्धं त्रैलोक्यममरारयः।। 35।।

The Munis, bowed their physical beings before Her, with gerat devotion. The enemies of *Amara's*—immortals who are the Devatas, witnessed *Triloki*—the three worlds in agitation....,

सन्नद्धाखिलसैन्यास्ते समुत्तस्थुरुदायुधाः।
आः किमेतदिति क्रोधादाभाष्य महिषासुरः।। 36।।

...those Asuras mobilised all the armies and rose up together with their arms lifted up, 'What is happening, all this?', Said Mahishasura in great anger.

अभ्यधावत तं शब्दमशेषैरसुरैर्वृतः।
स ददर्श ततो देवीं व्याप्तलोकत्रयां त्विषा।। 37।।

He rushed towards the roaring spot, surrounded by multitude of Asuras. He observed Devi pervading the 'Triloki'—the three worlds with full lustre.

पादाक्रान्त्या नतभुवं किरीटोल्लिखिताम्बराम्।
क्षोभिताशेषपातालां धनुर्ज्यानिःस्वनेन ताम्।। 38।।

The earth got bent with Her footstep, and the space/sky got scrapped with Devi's diadem, shaking the *Patala* nether most world with the twang of Her bowstring...,

दिशो भुजसहस्रेण समन्ताद् व्याप्य संस्थिताम्।
ततः प्रववृते युद्धं तया देव्या सुरद्विषाम्।। 39।।

...She kept standing and pervading all the sectors around with Her thousand arms. Then the great battle began between that Devi and the enemies of the Devas.

शस्त्रास्त्रैर्बहुधा मुक्तैरादीपितदिग्न्तरम्।
महिषासुरसेनानीश्चिक्षुराख्यो महासुरः।। 40।।

All the quarters of the sky got illumined by the arms and missiles hurdled in the diverse directions. *Chikshura*—the general of *Mahishasura* was a great Asura....,

युयुधे चामरश्चान्यैश्चतुरङ्गबलान्वितः।
रथानामयुतैः षड्भिरुदग्राख्यो महासुरः।। 41।।

....and *Charmara* also alongwith (Chikshura) began to fight with their *Chaturanga bala*— a four fold force. A great Asura named *Udagara* fought alongwith sixty thousand chariots...,

अयुध्यतायुतानां च सहस्रेण महाहनुः।
पञ्चाशद्भिश्च नियुतैरसिलोमा महासुरः।। 42।।

....and *Mahahanu* (Asura) with ten million (of chariots) gave a battle to Devi. *Asiloma* the great Asura fought alongwith five million Asuras....,

अयुतानां शतैः षड्भिर्बाष्कलो युयुधे रणे।
गजवाजिसहस्रौघैरनेकैः परिवारितः ।। 43 ।।

.....and *Bashkala* along with six million Asuras fought in that battle. *Parivarita* along with thousands of elephants and horses......,

वृतो रथानां कोट्या च युद्धे तस्मिन्नयुध्यत।
बिडालाख्योऽयुतानां च पञ्चाशद्भिरथायुतैः ।। 44 ।।

...and surrounded by ten million chariots, fought the fierceful battle. A great *Asura Bidala* fought the battle surrounded with five hundred million charioteers..,

युयुधे संयुगे तत्र रथानां परिवारितः।
अन्ये च तत्रायुतशो रथनागहयैर्वृताः ।। 45 ।।

....and also fought thousands of great 'Asura', alongwith chariots, elephants and horses, who gathered there....,

युयुधुः संयुगे देव्या सह तत्र महासुराः।
कोटिकोटिसहस्त्रैस्तु रथानां दन्तिनां तथा ।। 46 ।।

.......to fight with the Devi. They came there in tens of millions of the army of chariots and.....,

हयानां च वृतो युद्धे तत्राभून्महिषासुरः।
तोमरैर्भिन्दिपालैश्च शक्तिभिर्मुसलैस्तथा ।। 47 ।।

..... horses with the great Asura Mahishasura himself to fight the great war. All others armed with *Tomar*—lance *Bhindipalas*—Javelin Shakti'—missile, *Musala*—pestle..,

युयुधुः संयुगे देव्या खड्गैः परशुपट्टिशैः।
केचिच्च चिक्षिपुः शक्तीः केचित्पाशांस्तथापरे ।। 48 ।।

...*Khadga*—sword, *Parshu*—axe, '*Pattisha*'—three pointed weapon etc. and some threw '*Shakti*' and some '*Pasha*'—noose over the Devi in that fierceful war.

देवीं खड्गप्रहारैस्तु ते तां हन्तुं प्रचक्रमुः।
सापि देवी ततस्तानि शस्त्राण्यस्त्राणि चण्डिका ।। 49 ।।

Some other Asuras tried to strike the Devi with swords, in order to kill Her. Devi Chandika also cut their arms and weapons....,

लीलयैव प्रचिच्छेद निजशस्त्रास्त्रवर्षिणी।
अनायास्तानना देवी स्तूयमाना सुरर्षिभिः ।। 50 ।।

...with Her mere '*Lila*'—play, which were thrown upon Her. Devi also without any trace of strain on Her face, was extolled by the 'Devas' and 'Rishis'.

मुमोचासुरदेहेषु शस्त्राण्यस्त्राणि चेश्वरी।
सोऽपि क्रुद्धो धुतसटो देव्या वाहनकेसरी।। 51 ।।

Ishvari also threw arms and missiles at the bodies of '*Asuras*'. Lion—the vehicle of Devi got enraged and shaking its mane...,

चचारासुरसैन्येषु वनेष्विव हुताशनः।
निःश्वासान् मुमुचे यांश्च युध्यमाना रणेऽम्बिका।। 52 ।।

... while roaming among the multitude of the Asuras like a huge burning fire in the jungle. While fighting the Asuras in the battle-field, She heaved many heavy sighs. Breathed by Ambika, the sighs...,

त एवं सद्यः सम्भूता गणाः शतसहस्त्रशः।
युयुधुस्ते परशुभिर्भिन्दिपालासिपट्टिशैः।। 53 ।।

...became simultaneously Her '*Ganas*' fighting by hundreds of thousands in number. They fought with 'Parshu'—axes, 'Bhindipalas', 'Asi'—swords; 'Pattishas'—missiles.

नाशयन्तोऽसुरगणान् देवीशक्त्युपबृंहिताः।
अवादयन्त पटहान् गणाः शङ्खांस्तथापरे।। 54 ।।

Those '*Ganas*' beat drums, some blew conchs, thus killing the Asuric forces, with the spread of the Shakti of the Devi.....,

मृदङ्गांश्च तथैवान्ये तस्मिन् युद्धमहोत्सवे।
ततो देवी त्रिशूलेन गदया शक्तिवृष्टिभिः।। 55 ।।

....and other played on *Mridanga*, in that great martial festival. After it, the Devi showered '*Trishula*'—trident, 'Gada'—club and 'Shakti'—missile....,

खड्गादिभिश्च शतशो निजघान महासुरान्।
पातयामास चैवान्यान् घण्टास्वनविमोहितान्।। 56।।

.... also, She killed hundreds of '*Mahasuras*'—the great Asuras with swords and the like, threw others down, who became unconscious with the noise of the '*Ghanta*'—bell.

असुरान् भुवि पाशेन बद्ध्वा चान्यानकर्षयत्।
केचिद् द्विधा कृतास्तीक्ष्णैः खड्गपातैस्तथापरे।। 57।।

Asuras were bound by '*Pasha*'—noose and She dragged them to the ground. Some were split into two by the sharp slashes of Her sword.

विपोथिता निपातेन गदया भुवि शेरते।
वेमुश्च केचिद्रुधिरं मुसलेन भृशं हताः।। 58।।

Others got smashed with the blows of Her mace, and laid down on the ground. Some vomitted blood, when they were severely harmed by Her club.

किचिन्निपतिता भूमौ भिन्ना शूलेन वक्षसि।
निरन्तराः शरौघेण कृताः केचिद्रणाजिरे।। 59।।

Some fell down dead, just after being pierced by Her trident in their breasts. In that great war-field, most of the *Asuras* gave up their lives after being pierced by the arrows constantly.

श्येनानुकारिणः प्राणान् मुमुचुस्त्रिदशार्दनाः।
केषांचिद् बाहवश्छिन्नाश्छिन्नग्रीवास्तथापरे।। 60।।

Many of the enemies of Devas lost their lives, who were like hawks falling on their prey. Some had their arms cut off, some got their necks broken.....,

शिरांसि पेतुरन्येषामन्ये मध्ये विदारिताः।
विच्छिन्नजङ्घास्त्वपरे पेतुरुर्व्यां महासुराः।। 61।।

...To some, their heads were rolled down. Some others were torn into pieces in the middle of trunk. Some great Asuras fell on the ground with their legs cut off.

एकबाह्वक्षिचरणाः केचिद्देव्या द्विधा कृताः।
छिन्नेऽपि चान्ये शिरसि पतिताः पुनरुत्थिताः।।62।।

Some rendered one armed, one eyed and one legged and pierced them in two parts by the Devi Herself. While others, though rendered headless, fell and rose again.

कबन्धा ययुधुर्देव्या गृहीतपरमायुधाः।
ननृतुश्चापरे तत्र युद्धे तूर्यलयाश्रिताः।। 63।।

'Kabandhas'—headless trunks fought with the Devi, taking in their hands the best of weapons. Some of these headless trunks danced there in that battle to the rhythem corresponding to the musical instruments.

कबन्धाश्छिन्नशिरसः खड्गशक्त्यृष्टिपाणयः।
तिष्ठ तिष्ठेति भाषन्तो देवीमन्ये महासुराः।। 64।।

Many Kabandhas with their severed heads taking swords, spears and lances still in their hands, were running and other great Asuras roaring : 'Stop! Stop O Devi!'

पातितै रथनागाश्वैरसुरैश्च वसुन्धरा।
अगम्या साभवत्तत्र यत्राभूत्स महारणः।। 65।।

That part of the earth became unapproachable, where the battle was fought, with the felling of Asuras, their chariots, elephants and horses.

शोणितौघा महानद्यः सद्यस्तत्र प्रसुस्त्रुवुः।
मध्ये चासुरसैन्यस्य वारणासुरवाजिनाम्।। 66।।

Amidst that *Asura*-army, profuse blood of the Asuras, elephants and horses flowed instantaneously like large rivers.

क्षणेन तन्महासैन्यमसुराणां तथाम्बिका।
निन्ये क्षयं यथा वह्निस्तृणदारुमहाचयम्।। 67।।

Devi Ambika destroyed that huge army of Asuras in single 'Kshana' which is the twinkle of an eye, as fire consumes a huge heap of straw and wood.

स च सिंहो महानादमुत्सृजन्धुतकेसरः।
शरीरेभ्योऽमरारीणामसूनिव विचिन्वति।। 68।।

Her vehicle lion thundering loudly with roars and shaking his mane, jumped around in the battle-field, appearing for the search out the *pranas*—the vital breaths from the bodies of the enemies of 'Amaras'—the Devas.

देव्या गणैश्च तैस्तत्र कृतं युद्धं महासुरैः।
यथैषां तुतुषुर्देवाः पुष्पवृष्टिमुचो दिवि।। ॐ।। 69।।

In that war-field, the *Ganas* of Devi fought with Asuras with full valour, thus the 'Devas' showered flowers from the sky and praised them (the ganas).

इति श्रीमार्कण्डेयपुराणे सावर्णिके मन्वन्तरे देवीमाहात्म्ये
महिषासुरसैन्यवधो नाम द्वितीयोऽध्यायः।। 2।।

The Second Chapter entitled '*Slaying of Mahishasura*' of the *Devi Mahatmya,* during the time-span of Savarni—the Manu, occuring in the *Markandeya Purana* is concluded.

उवाच1, श्लोकाः 68, एवम् 69, एवमादितः 173।।

Narrated Shlokas 1, Shlokas 68, total in this chapter 69, total in all 173.

तृतीयोऽध्यायः

THIRD CHAPTER

सेनापतियों सहित महिषासुर का वध

The Slaying of Mahishasura alongwith his Commanders

ध्यानम्

Dhyanam/Meditation

ॐ उद्यद्भानुसहस्त्रकान्तिमरुणक्षौमां शिरोमालिकां
रक्तालिप्तपयोधरां जपवटीं विद्यामभीतिं वरम्
हस्ताब्जैर्दधतीं त्रिनेत्रविलसद्वक्त्रारविन्दश्रियं
देवीं बद्धहिमांशुरत्नमुकुटां वन्देऽरविन्दस्थिताम्।।

Om, I pay my obeisence with devotion to Devi, whose radiance of the limbs is that of thousands of the rising suns. She is garmented with the silken red robes. Her neck is decorated with the '*Mundamala*'—garland of skulls. Both of the breasts are annointed with the '*Rakta-chandana*'/red sandal paste. She holds in Her lotus like hands, '*Japamala*' '*Vidya*', '*Abhaya*' and '*Vara*' mudras. She is triple eyed. Her face gives bloomy brilliance like a lotus. A jewel alongwith the moon in crowned on Her forehead. I bow to that Devi, who is seated on the '*Arvinda*/lotus.

ॐ ऋषिरुवाच।। 1।।

Om The Rishi Said :

निहन्यामानं तत्सैन्यमवलोक्य महासुरः।
सेनानीश्चिक्षुरः कोपाद्ययौ योद्धुमथाम्बिकाम्।। 2।।

"Army chief—the Great Asura Chikshura got too enraged,

when he saw his army being slain at the hands of the Devi, he advanced in anger to fight with Ambika.

स देवीं शरवर्षेण ववर्ष समरेऽसुरः।
यथा मेरुगिरेः शृङ्गं तोयवर्षेण तोयदः।। 3।।

That Asura rained the showers of arrows on the Devi in that battle, as if clouds showered rain on the peaks of *Mount Meru.*

तस्यच्छित्त्वा ततो देवी लीलयैव शरोत्करान्।
जघान तुरगान् बाणैर्यन्तारं चैव वाजिनाम्।। 4।।

Then the Devi, playfully cut asunder his numberless arrows, killed his horses and his horsemen with Her arrows.

चिच्छेद च धनुः सद्यो ध्वजं चातिसमुच्छ्रितम्।
विव्याध चैव गात्रेषु छिन्नधन्वानमाशुगैः।। 5।।

She cut his bow and the lofty banner forthwith, and pierced the limbs of his body, after his bow was cut and pierced.

सच्छिन्नधन्वा विरथो हताश्वो हतसारथिः।
अभ्यधावत तां देवीं खड्गचर्मधरोऽसुरः।। 6।।

Then that Asura armed with a sword and shield rushed at the Devi, after his bow was broken, his horses got killed, his charioteer killed and chariot smashed.

सिंहमाहत्य खड्गेन तीक्ष्णधारेण मूर्धनि।
आजघान भुजे सव्ये देवीमप्यतिवेगवान्।। 7।।

He—the Asura swiftly injured the lion on the head with his sharp edged sword and struck the Devi on Her left arm.

तस्याः खड्गो भुजं प्राप्य पफाल नृपनन्दन।
ततो जग्राह शूलं स कोपादरुणलोचनः।। 8।।

O Nripa Nandan—the best among kings! His sword broke into pieces, as and when it touched Her arm. Thereupon his eyes turned red with anger, took his Shula—spike (spear) in his hand...,

चिक्षेप च ततस्तत्तु भद्रकाल्यां महासुरः।

जाज्वल्यमानं तेजोभी रविबिम्बमिवाम्बरात्।। 9 ।।

...... and the great '*Asura*', threw the spike on *Bhadrakali*. Blazing with reflected light, it was like the hurling of the sun from the skies.

दृष्ट्वा तदापतच्छूलं देवी शूलममुञ्चत।
तच्छूलं शतधा तेन नीतं स च महासुरः।। 10 ।।

On seeing the spike coming towards Herself, the Devi hurled Her spike pierced it into hundred directions, alongwith the great 'Asura' Chikshura.

हते तस्मिन्महावीर्ये महिषस्य चमूपतौ।
आजगाम गजारूढश्चामरस्त्रिदशार्दनः।। 11 ।।

Chamara, the great terror to the Devas mounted on the horse and advanced, after seeing the Mahishasura's valient chief of army slain.....

सोऽपि शक्तिं मुमोचाथ देव्यास्तामम्बिका द्रुतम्।
हुंकाराभिहतां भूमौ पातयामास निष्प्रभाम्।। 12 ।।

...he also hurled '*Shakti*'—missile at the Devi. Ambika quickly assailed it with a '*Humkara*'—the divine roar, and made it lustreless and it fell to the ground.

भग्नां शक्तिं निपतितां दृष्ट्वा क्रोधसमन्वितः।
चिक्षेप चामरः शूलं बाणैस्तदपि साच्छिनत्।। 13 ।।

On seeing the '*Shakti*'—missile broken and fallen, *Chamara* got highly enraged and threw a *Shula*—the spike. Devi cut it into pieces with Her arrows.

ततः सिंहः समुत्पत्य गजकुम्भान्तरे स्थितः।
बाहुयुद्धेन युयुधे तेनोच्चैस्त्रिदशारिणा।। 14 ।।

The lion then leapt up and sat at the centre of the elephant's forehead, and got engaged in hand to hand fight with the enemy of the foes.

युद्धयमानौ ततस्तौ तु तस्मान्नागान्महीं गतौ।
युयुधातेऽतिसंरब्धौ प्रहारैरतिदारुणैः।। 15।।

Both of them came down, while fighting from the back of the elephant and fought vehemently, striking the most terrible blows at each other.

ततो वेगात् खमुत्पत्य निपत्य च मृगारिणा।
करप्रहारेण शिरश्चामरस्य पृथक्कृतम्।। 16।।

The lion, then sprung up quickly towards the sky and while descending, severed Chamara's head with a blow of its paws.

उदग्रश्च रणे देव्या शिलावृक्षादिभिर्हतः।
दन्तमुष्टितलैश्चैव करालश्च निपातितः।। 17।।

Udagara Asura was also killed in the battle by the Devi with stones, trees and the like. *Karala Asura* also was struck down to death by Her teeth, fists and slaps.

देवी क्रुद्धा गदापातैश्चूर्णयामास चोद्धतम्।
वाष्कलं भिन्दिपालेन बाणैस्ताम्रं तथान्धकम्।। 18।।

The Devi got enraged and grounded *Uddhata Asura* with the blows of Her club and killed '*Vashkala Asura*' with '*Bhindipala*' missile—the dart and destroyed '*Tamara*' and '*Andhaka*' with arrows.

उग्रास्यमुग्रवीर्यं च तथैव च महाहनुम्।
त्रिनेत्रा च त्रिशूलेन जघान परमेश्वरी।। 19।।

'*Trinetra Parmeshvari*'—the 'three eyed Supreme Devi' killed '*Ugarasya*', '*Ugravirya*' and '*Mahahanu*' with Her '*Trishula*'—trident.

बिडालस्यासिना कायात्पातयामास वै शिरः।
दुर्धरं दुर्मुखं चोभौ शरैर्निन्ये यमक्षयम्।। 20।।

Bidal's head was severed from his body, with the Devi's sword and dent. Both '*Durdhara*' and '*Durmukha*' were sent to the Yama's abode with Her arrows.

एवं संक्षीयमाणे तु स्वसैन्ये महिषासुरः।
माहिषेण स्वरूपेण त्रासयामास तान् गणान्।। 21।।

Then Mahishasura transformed himself into a *Mahisha*—buffalo, after seeing his army being thus destroyed. He then began to terrify the '*Ganas*'—troops of the Devi.

कांश्चित्तुण्डप्रहारेण खुरक्षेपैस्तथापरान्।
लाङ्गूलताडितांश्चान्याञ्छृङ्गाभ्यां च विदारितान्।। 22।।

To some, he struck them down with the blow of his 'Tunda'—snout, to some, he stamped with his hooves, some by the lashes of his tail and others by the force of his horns....,

वेगेन कांश्चिदपरान्नादेन भ्रमणेन च।
निःश्वासपवनेनान्यान् पातयामास भूतले।। 23।।

...to some, he struck them down on the earth, by his forceful speed, to some he shattered with his roar and the others by the blast of his exhaling breath.

निपात्य प्रमथानीकमभ्यधावत सोऽसुरः।
सिंहं हन्तुं महादेव्याः कोपं चक्रे ततोऽम्बिका।। 24।।

That Asura rushed to slay the lion of the Mahadevi after having destroyed the force of the army. Thus Ambika got enraged.

सोऽपि कोपान्महावीर्यः खुरक्षुण्णमहीतलः।
शृङ्गाभ्यां पर्वतानुच्चांश्चिक्षेप च ननाद च।। 25।।

The great in valour, Mahishasura uprooted the earth with his hooves in rage. He tossed up the high mountain with his horns and roared a violent outcry.

वेगभ्रमणविक्षुण्णा मही तस्य व्यशीर्यत।
लाङ्गूलेनाहतश्चाब्धिः प्लावयामास सर्वतः।। 26।।

The earth got disturbed and disintegrated, by the force of his roaring. The sea then overflowed the earth everywhere, when he lashed it by his tail.

धुतशृङ्गविभिन्नाश्च खण्डं खण्डं ययुर्घनाः।
श्वासानिलास्ताः शतशो निपेतुर्नभसोऽचलाः।। 27।।

The clouds got fragmented into pieces on being pierced by his swaying horns, and the mountains fell down from the sky, when he heaved high breaths.

इति क्रोधसमाध्मातमापतन्तं महासुरम्।
दृष्ट्वा सा चण्डिका कोपं तद्वधाय तदाकरोत्।। 28।।

The great Asura got swollen with rage and made instant advances towards the Devi. She—the Chandika exhibited Her wrath, merely to crush him to death.

सा क्षिप्त्वा तस्य वै पाशं तं बबन्ध महासुरम्।
तत्याज माहिषं रूपं सोऽपि बद्धो महामृधे।। 29।।

She cast Her noose over him and bound the great Asura. Then he quitted his buffalo form, when got rounded in that great war.

ततः सिंहोऽभवत्सद्यो यावत्तस्याम्बिका शिरः।
छिनत्ति तावत्पुरुषः खड्गपाणिरदृश्यत।। 30।।

He then appeared in the form of a lion suddenly. When Ambika severed off the head, he instantaneously took the appearance of a man with a sword in hand.

तत एवाशु पुरुषं देवी चिच्छेद सायकैः।
तं खड्गचर्मणा सार्धं ततः सोऽभून्महागजः।। 31।।

The Devi immediately with Her arrow chopped the man off his sword and shield as well. Then he took the form of a big elephant.

करेण च महासिंहं तं चकर्ष जगर्ज च।
कर्षतस्तु करं देवी खड्गेन निरकृन्तत।। 32।।

The elephant made a great roaring trumpet and tugged at Her great lion. The Devi then cut his trunk off with her sword.

ततो महासुरो भूयो माहिषं वपुरास्थितः।
तथैव क्षोभयामास त्रैलोक्यं सचराचरम्।। 33।।

He, the great Asura then assumed his buffalo shape and put all the three worlds of animate and inanimate beings to trouble.

ततः क्रुद्धा जगन्माता चण्डिका पानमुत्तमम्।
पपौ पुनः पुनश्चैव जहासारुणलोचना।। 34।।

'Jaganmata'—the Mother creatrix Chandika got enraged. She had a divine drink repeatedly and laughed. Her eyes became red.

ननर्द चासुरः सोऽपि बलवीर्यमदोद्धतः।
विषाणाभ्यां च चिक्षेप चण्डिकां प्रति भूधरान्।। 35।।

Asura became all the more intoxicated with his power and valour. He roared and began to throw the mountains from his horns on the Chandika.

सा च तान् प्रहितांस्तेन चूर्णयन्ती शरोत्करैः।
उवाच तं मदोद्धूतमुखरागाकुलाक्षरम्।। 36।।

She smashed off all the hurled mountains, reducing them to dust and said to him. While speaking, the colour of Her face turned red with the intoxication of the '*Madhu*'—the divine elixir.

देव्युवाच।। 37।।

The Devi Said :

गर्ज गर्ज क्षणं मूढ मधु यावत्पिबाम्यहम्।
मया त्वयि हतेऽत्रैव गर्जिष्यन्त्याशु देवताः।। 38।।

"Roar and roar for a moment O fool, till I take the *Madhu*—the divine elixir. You will be put to end by me now and the Devas will soon roar in this place."

ऋषिरुवाच।। 39।।

The Rishi Said :

एवमुक्त्वा समुत्पत्य साऽऽरूढा तं महासुरम्।
पादेनाक्रम्य कण्ठे च शूलेनैनमताडयत्।। 40।।

Having thus said so, She jumped on that great Asura and landed on him. She then crumbled him on the neck with Her foot and struck him with the Shula—missile.

ततः सोऽपि पदाऽऽक्रान्तस्तया निजमुखात्ततः।
अर्धनिष्क्रान्त एवासीद् देव्या वीर्येण संवृतः।।41।।

Mahishasura was even caught up under Her foot. He got issued forth in half, from his own mouth, but was fully overcome by the valour of the Devi.

अर्धनिष्क्रान्त एवासौ युध्यमानो महासुरः।
तया महासिना देव्याशिरश्छित्त्वा निपातितः।।42।।

The great Asura was laid out by the Devi, Who chopped off his head with Her great sword, in the condition of fighting with his half-revealed form.

ततो हाहाकृतं सर्वं दैत्यसैन्यं ननाश तत्।
प्रहर्षं च परं जग्मुः सकला देवतागणाः।। 43।।

The whole army of the Asuras got perished, while they were crying in confusion and desperation. The whole multitude of Devas exclaimed with exciting joy.

तुष्टुवुस्तां सुरा देवीं सह दिव्यैर्महर्षिभिः।
जगुर्गन्धर्वपतयो ननृतुश्चाप्सरोगणाः।। ॐ ।। 44।।

Devas alongwith the Divine Mahrishis praised the Great Devi. The Gandharva chiefs sang and the 'Apsaras' made the celestial dance. Om.

इति श्रीमार्कण्डेय पुराणे सावर्णिके मन्वन्तरे देवीमाहात्म्ये
महिषासुरवधो नाम तृतीयोऽध्यायः।। 3।।

The third chapter entitled '*Slaying of Mahishasura*' of the Devi-Mahatmya, during the time span of *Savarni*—the Manu occuring in the Markendeya Purana is concluded.

उवाच, 3, श्लोका: 41, एवम् 44, एवमादित: 217 ।।

Narrated Mantras 3, Shlokas 41, in this Chapter 44, total Shlokas : 217.

चतुर्थोऽध्यायः

FOURTH CHAPTER

इन्द्रादि देवताओं द्वारा देवी की स्तुति

Devi's Stuti—laudation by Indra and other Devas

ध्यानम्

Dhyanam/Meditation

ॐ कालाभ्राभां कटाक्षैररिकुलभयदां मौलिबद्धेन्दुरेखां
शङ्खं चक्रं कृपाणं त्रिशिखमपि करैरुद्वहन्तीं त्रिनेत्राम्।
सिंहस्कन्धाधिरूढां त्रिभुवनमखिलं तेजसा पूरयन्तीं
ध्यायेद् दुर्गां जयाख्यां त्रिदशपरिवृतां सेवितां सिद्धिकामैः ।।

'*Jaya*', who is adored by the men seeking after *Siddhi*—perfection, is surrounded by the '*Devas*'. The appearance of Her limbs resembles like that of the black clouds. She, with Her glance is a symbol of terror to the foes. The crescent shines on Her forehead. She holds conch, discus, sword, trident in Her hands. She is triple eyed and emits Her lustre upon the three worlds. She rides on the shoulders of a lion. Durga with such name of the Jaya be meditated upon!

ॐ ऋषिरुवाच ।। 1 ।।

Om, The Rishi Said :

शक्रादयः सुरगणा निहतेऽतिवीर्ये
तस्मिन्दुरात्मनि सुरारिबले च देव्या।
तां तुष्टुवुः प्रणतिनम्रशिरोधरांसा
वाग्भिः प्रहर्षपुलकोद्गमचारुदेहाः ।। 2 ।।

Shakra—Indra and other Devas bowed with reverence their necks and shoulders before the Devi. They lauded Her with the best words of praises, after being the bold, valourous duratman—evil natured Mahishasura and his army killed by the Devi. The Devas were feeling highly exalted in their beings, on this triumph.

देव्या यया ततमिदं जगदात्मशक्त्या
निश्शेषदेवगणशक्तिसमूहमूर्त्या।
तामम्बिकामखिलदेवमहर्षिपूज्यां
भक्त्या नताः स्म विदधातु शुभानि सा नः।।3।।

All the accumulated power of the Devas is verily, the embodiment of the Devi. She has enveloped the whole universe with Her own power. We do bow to that Ambika, with devotion, Who alone is worthy of worship by the Devas and Mahrishis. May she grant us auspicious things!

यस्याः प्रभावमतुलं भगवाननन्तो
ब्रह्मा हरश्च न हि वक्तुमलं बलं च।
सा चण्डिकाखिलजगत्परिपालनाय
नाशाय चाशुभभयस्य मतिं करोतु।।4।।

Bhagavan Ananta, Brahma and *Hara* are unable to describe Her incomparable greatness. May Chandika be thoughtful on protecting the whole world and be gracious for destroying the fear of inauspiciousness!

या श्रीः स्वयं सुकृतिनां भवनेष्वलक्ष्मीः
पापात्मनां कृतधियां हृदयेषु बुद्धिः।
श्रद्धा सतां कुलजनप्रभवस्य लज्जा
तां त्वां नताः स्म परिपालय देवि विश्वम्।।5।।

It is 'She' Who dwells as 'Shri'—auspiciousness in the dwellings of the virtuous and as '*Alakshmi*'—inauspiciousness in those of the vicious and ill natured. She dwells in the forms of '*Buddhi*'—the intellect in the hearts of the learned, and '*Shraddha*'—veneration in the hearts of the true beings and '*Lajja*'—modesty in the hearts of the noble beings. We do bow to You and be pleased to protect the universe!

किं वर्णयाम तव रूपमचिन्त्यमेतत्।
किं चातिवीर्यमसुरक्षयकारि भूरि।
किं चाहवेषु चरितानि तवाद्भुतानि
सर्वेषु देव्यसुरदेवगणादिकेषु।। 6।।

O Devi, how are we competent to describe Your inconceivable form and Your surpassing valour that destroys the 'Asuras'? Also how are we able to narrate Your wonderful '*Charita*'—feats and actions displayed in the battles between the host of Devas and Asuras?

हेतुः समस्तजगतां त्रिगुणापि दोषै-
र्न ज्ञायसे हरिहरादिभिरप्यपारा।
सर्वाश्रयाखिलमिदं जगदंशभूत-
मव्याकृता हि परमा प्रकृतिस्त्वमाद्या।। 7।।

O Devi! You are the primal cause of the origin of all the worlds. Though You are possessed of the *Triguna's Sattva*, rajas and tamas qualities yet You are devoid of the 'Doshas'—the defects. Devas like Hari and Hara cannot have any of Your comprehension. You are the resort of all and one. This entire world is only an '*amsha*'—portion of Your being, because You are the *Parama-Prakriti* the—Primordial nature, beyond any mutation modification.

यस्याः समस्तसुरता समुदीरणेन
तृप्तिं प्रयाति सकलेषु मखेषु देवि।
स्वाहासि वै पितृगणस्य च तृप्तिहेतु-
रुच्चार्यसे त्वमत एव जनैः स्वधा च।। 8।।

O Devi! You are verily, '*Svaha*'—the utterance of which gives satisfaction to the 'Devas' in all the sacrifices. You are also '*Svadha*', which grants satisfaction to the manes. Thus the people chant your name as 'Svaha-Svadha'.

या मुक्तिहेतुरविचिन्त्यमहाव्रता त्व-
मभ्यस्यसे सुनियतेन्द्रियतत्त्वसारैः।
मोक्षार्थिभिर्मुनिभिरस्तसमस्तदोषै-
र्विद्यासि सा भगवती परमा हि देवि।।9।।

O Devi ! You are that Bhagavati, which is the cause of '*Mukti*'—final liberation. You are inconceivable '*Mahavrata*'—great penances. You are devoid of all the 'Doshas'/defects. You are meditated upon by the '*Munis*' with their senses well controlled, for attaining 'Moksha'—final libration. You are really 'Para Vidya'—transcendental knowledge.

शब्दात्मिका सुविमलर्ग्यजुषां निधान-
मुद्गीथरम्यपदपाठवतां च साम्नाम्।
देवी त्रयी भगवती भवभावनाय
वार्ता च सर्वजगतां परमार्तिहन्त्री।। 10।।

You are verily, the embodiment of '*Shabda*'—the Eternal Word. You are very sacred *Rik* and *Yajur* hymns and You are '*Saman*' with the Udagitha having the beautiful recitation of words. You are '*Trayi*'—embodying the three Vedas. You are *Bhagavati*, whereby life is sustained. You are the Supreme destroyer of the pain (suffering) of this whole world.

मेधासि देवि विदिताखिलशास्त्रसारा
दुर्गासि दुर्गभवसागरनौरसङ्गा।
श्रीः कैटभारिहृदयैककृताधिवासा
गौरी त्वमेव शशिमौलिकृतप्रतिष्ठा।। 11।।

O Devi! You are 'Medha'—intellect by which the essence of all the 'Shastras'—scriptues is well grasped. You are 'Durga' as being the ship that takes human beings across the difficult ocean of worldly existence. You are devoid of attachment. You are '*Shri*'—who has taken Her placement in the heart of 'Hari'. You are verily, '*Gauri*'—of the fair complexion, who has identified Herself with '*Shashimauli Shiva*'—who holds the moon crescent for the crown.

ईषत्सहासममलं परिपूर्णचन्द्र-
बिम्बानुकारि कनकोत्तमकान्तिकान्तम्।
अत्यद्भुतं प्रहृतमात्तरुषा तथापि
वक्त्रं विलोक्य सहसा महिषासुरेण।। 12।।

You have a gentle smile on Your face, resembling the 'Puranachandra' full moon's orb. It is like the magnificience of the pure gold on your face. Still it is very strange that Mahishasura got enraged and he suddenly struck Your face, is really very strange.

दृष्ट्वा तु देवि कुपितं भ्रुकुटीकराल-
मुद्यच्छशाङ्कसदृशच्छवि यन्न सद्यः।
प्राणान्मुमोच महिषस्तदतीव चित्रं
कैर्जीव्यते हि कुपितान्तकदर्शनेन।। 13।।

O Devi! When the same face turned terrible with its frowns, red like the rising moon and horrible with the lightening of the eyebrows, then it is far strange that after witnessing your such face Mahishasura did not forthwith give up his vital-breath. For who can live after viewing the wrathful Antaka's Darshana—the very sight of Death?

देवि प्रसीद परमा भवती भवाय
सद्यो विनाशयसि कोपवती कुलानि।
विज्ञातमेतदधुनैव यदस्तमेत-
न्नीतं बलं सुविपुलं महिषासुरस्य।। 14।।

O Devi, be pleased! You are 'Parma'—highly Supreme and being pleased, You extend welfare to the world. When you get enraged, You forthwith detroy the 'Kulas'—families of 'Asuras'. This we have learnt by viewing how the extensive force of Mahishasura was put to an end.

ते सम्मता जनपदेषु धनानि तेषां
तेषां यशांसि न च सीदति धर्मवर्गः।
धन्यास्त एवं निभृतात्मजभृत्यदारा
येषां सदाभ्युदयदा भवती प्रसन्ना।। 15।।

They alone are indeed worthy to live in a habitat, with whom You are well pleased. Riches and glories are their fortunes. Their acts of righteousness never cease. They are indeed, blessed of their servants, sons and wives. You are always generous in bestowing gifts and grace to them.

धर्म्याणि देवि सकलानि सदैव कर्मा-
ण्यत्यादृतः प्रतिदिनं सुकृती करोति।
स्वर्गं प्रयाति च ततो भवतीप्रसादा-
ल्लोकत्रयेऽपि फलदा ननु देवि तेन।। 16।।

O Devi, by Your grace alone the individuals perform the rightful actions with great care, and thereby attain the *Svarga*—heaven. You are verily, O Devi, the bestower of great merits in 'Lokatraya'—the three worlds.

दुर्गे स्मृता हरसि भीतिमशेषजन्तोः
स्वस्थैः स्मृता मतिमतीव शुभां ददासि।
दारिद्र्यदुःखभयहारिणि का त्वदन्या
सर्वोपकारकरणाय सदाऽऽर्द्रचित्ता।। 17।।

O Durga! You remove fear from every person, when they remember You at the times of crisis. You grant the highest wisdom, when You are remembered with the right and pious conduct. O Devi! You are the dispeller of poverty, pain and fear. You are having a sympathetic heart for helping every person.

एभिर्हतैर्जगदुपैति सुखं तथैते
कुर्वन्तु नाम नरकाय चिराय पापम्।
संग्राममृत्युमधिगम्य दिवं प्रयान्तु
मत्वेति नूनमहितान् विनिहंसि देवि।। 18।।

O Devi! You destroy the enemies with the intention that the world may attain happiness by the slaying of these 'Asuras'. These '*Asuras*' have committed heneious sins, and stay for long in '*Naraka*'—hell. Let these (Asuras) also attain heaven by meeting death at Your hands in the battle and that is Your strategy.

दृष्ट्वैव किं न भवती प्रकरोति भस्म
सर्वासुरानरिषु यत्प्रहिणोषि शस्त्रम्।
लोकान् प्रयान्तु रिपवोऽपि हि शस्त्रपूता
इत्थं मतिर्भवति तेष्वपि तेऽतिसाध्वी।। 19।।

Why do you direct Your weapons against the '*Asuras*'—foes? Why do not you reduce to ashes all the 'Asuras' by your mere sight? You do so, purely with the intention that these 'Asuras' may be purified and attain higher places by the mere touch of your sacred weapons. Such is your most kind intention towards them.

खड्गप्रभानिकरविस्फुरणैस्तथोग्रैः
शूलाग्रकान्तिनिवहेन दृशोऽसुराणाम्।
यन्नागता विलयमंशुमदिन्दुखण्ड-
योग्याननं तव विलोकयतां तदेतत्।। 20।।

Eyes of the Asuras could not be out by the terrible flashes emitted from Your sword or by the radiance of Your spear—point lustre. It s only because that they would be getting cool rays while seeing Your face, which resembles the moon.

दुर्वृत्तवृत्तशमनं तव देवि शीलं
रूपं तथैतदविचिन्त्यमतुल्यमन्यैः।
वीर्यं च हन्तृ हृतदेवपराक्रमाणां
वैरिष्वपि प्रकटितैव दया त्वयेत्थम्।। 21।।

O Devi! Your nature is to overcome and defect the conduct of the wicked. Yours is the inconceivable matchless form. Your power is to detroy those, who have deprived the Devas of their glory and prowess. You have also bestowed your compassion even towards the enemies.

केनोपमा भवतु तेऽस्य पराक्रमस्य
रूपं च शत्रुभयकार्यतिहारि कुत्र।
चित्ते कृपा समरनिष्ठुरता च दृष्टा
त्वय्येव देवि वरदे भुवनत्रयेऽपि।। 22।।

O Devi Varda—the bestower of boons! How can Your power be compared to? Is there this beauty of Your most charming self possible anywhere, which is striking fear among the foes? You have compassion in Your consciousness, but mercilesseness in the battlefield. You alone have such qualities in the three worlds.

त्रैलोक्यमेतखिलं रिपुनाशनेन
त्रातं त्वया समरमूर्धनि तेऽपि हत्वा।
नीता दिवं रिपुगणा भयमप्यपास्त-
मस्माकमुन्मदसुरारिभवं नमस्ते।। 23।।

O Devi Namaskar be to you! 'We bow you! You have saved the three worlds by destroying the enemies of these worlds. Having killed them in the battle field, You have despatched those hosts of enemies to heaven. You have removed our fear from the violent excitement of the enemies of the Devas.'

शूलेन पाहि नो देवि पाहि खड्गेन चाम्बिके।
घण्टास्वनेन नः पाहि चापज्यानिःस्वनेन च।। 24।।

'O Devi! Protect us with your *'Shula'*—spear. O Ambika! Protect us with your 'Khadga'—sword. Protect us with the sound of Your 'Ghanta'—bell and by the twang of Your 'Chapjya'—the bow string.....,

प्राच्यां रक्ष प्रतीच्यां च चण्डिके रक्ष दक्षिणे।
भ्रामणेनात्मशूलस्य उत्तरस्यां तथेश्वरि।। 25।।

.....O Chandika! Guard us in the east, in the west, and O Ishvari, guard us in the north and the south by the movement of Your 'shula'—the spear.

सौम्यानि यानि रूपाणि त्रैलोक्ये विचरन्ति ते।
यानि चात्यर्थघोराणि तै रक्षास्मांस्तथा भुवम्।। 26।।

Protect us and the earth with Your lovely forms, as well the terrible forms, which You do have and which go on moving around the three worlds.

खड्गशूलगदादीनि यानि चास्त्राणि तेऽम्बिके।
करपल्लवसङ्गीनि तैरस्मान् रक्ष सर्वतः।। 27।।

O Ambika! Protect us with your '*Khadga*'—the sword; 'Shula'—the spear, 'Gada'—the club and whatever other missiles, which have been touched by your sprout like hands.

ऋषिरुवाच।। 28।।

The Rishi Said :

एवं स्तुता सुरैर्दिव्यैः कुसुमैर्नन्दनोद्भवैः।
अर्चिता जगतां धात्री तथा गन्धानुलेपनैः।। 29।।

"Having thus praised 'Jagaddhatri'—the Mother creatrix by the 'Suras'—brilliant ones with celestial flowers that blossomed in the '*Nandana*'—the celestial garden and made 'Archana'/laudation with '*Ghanda*'—'*Anulepana*'—annointed with perfumes.

भक्त्या समस्तैस्त्रिदशैर्दिव्यैर्धूपैस्तु धूपिता।
प्राह प्रसादसुमुखी समस्तान् प्रणतान् सुरान्।। 30।।

With devotion, all of them offered divine 'Dhupa'—incense to the Devi. She spoke to the Devas with the expression of Her serene face, who were assembled there with submission and prayer.

देव्युवाच।। 31।।

The Devi Said :

व्रियतां त्रिदशाः सर्वे यदस्मत्तोऽभिवाञ्छितम्।। 32।।

"O all of you Devas! Choose whatever you desire of me."

देवा ऊचुः।। 33।।

The Devas Said :

भगवत्या कृतं सर्वं न किंचिदवशिष्यते।। 34।।

Bhagvati has accomplished all the works, and nothing remains to be done.

यदयं निहतः शत्रुरस्माकं महिषासुरः।
यदि चापि वरो देयस्त्वयास्माकं महेश्वरि।। 35।।

O Maheshvari! Since our enemy Mahishasura has been slain by You. Even then You intend to grace us with your boon.....,

संस्मृता संस्मृता त्वं नो हिंसेथाः परमापदः।
यश्च मर्त्यः स्तवैरेभिस्त्वां स्तोष्यत्यमलानने।। 36।।

...then, whenever we think of You again, You be pleased to destroy our direct afflictions and misfortunes. O '*Amalanana*'— the Mother of spotless beauty! Whosoever mortal shall praise you with these hymns....,

तस्य वित्तर्द्धिविभवैर्धनदारादिसम्पदाम्।
वृद्धयेऽस्मत्प्रसन्ना त्वं भवेथाः सर्वदाम्बिके।। 37।।

....O Ambika! May you make an increase in his wealth and other fortunes, alongwith riches, prosperity, glory and life companion. Be always pleased with us!

ऋषिरुवाच।। 38।।

The Rishi Said

इति प्रसादिता देवैर्जगतोऽर्थे तथाऽऽत्मनः।
तथेत्युक्त्वा भद्रकाली बभूवान्तर्हिता नृप।। 39।।

O king! Thus being appeased by the Devas, for their own sake and for the sake of the world, the *Bhadrakali* said : 'Be it so, and became 'Antarhita'—invisible out of their sight.

इत्येतत्कथितं भूप सम्भूता सा यथा पुरा।
देवी देवशरीरेभ्यो जगत्त्रयहितैषिणी।। 40।।

O king! I have narrated you how the Devi made Her appearance, out of the bodies of the Devas for the welfare of the three worlds in the times of ancient past as being 'Hitaishini'—the well wisher of all.

पुनश्च गौरीदेहात्सा समुद्भूता यथाभवत्।
वधाय दुष्टदैत्यानां तथा शुम्भनिशुम्भयोः।। 41।।

And again, as happened, how She appeared in the form of Gauri for slaying of Shumbha-Nishumbha along with other wicked 'Daityas'/anti divine forces....

रक्षणाय च लोकानां देवानामुपकारिणी।
तच्छृणुष्व मयाऽऽख्यातं यथावत्कथयामि ते।। ह्रीं ॐ।। 42।।

.....for the protection of the worlds and for the 'Upakara'—benefication of the Devas. I shall tell you as it took place, listen to me as I relate it to you. Hrim Om.

इति श्रीमार्कण्डेयपुराणे सावर्णिके मन्वन्तरे देवीमाहात्म्ये
शक्रादिस्तुतिर्नाम चतुर्थोऽध्यायः।। 4।।

The fourth Chapter entitled '*Praises* by *Shakra* and others', of the Devimahatmya in the Markendeya Purana, occuring during the period of Savarni—the Manu is thus concluded.

उवाच 5, अर्धश्लोकौ 2, श्लोकाः 35, एवम् 42, एवमादितः 259।।

Narrated Mantras 5, half Shlokes 2, Shloka 35, (total 42 shloka) in all 259 Shlokas, concluded.

पंचमोऽध्यायः

FIFTH CHAPTER

देवताओं द्वारा देवी की स्तुति, चण्ड-मुण्ड के मुख से अम्बिका के रूप की प्रशंसा सुनकर शुम्भ का उनके पास दूत भेजना और दूत का निराश लौटना

Stuti/Laudation of the Devatas to Devi. Chanda and Munda giving the description of the beauty of Ambika. Shumbha's sending of Duta before Ambika with the marriage proposal and his return with unresolved proposal.

विनियोगः

Ritualistic Regulation/Application

ॐ अस्य श्रीउत्तरचरित्रस्य रुद्र ऋषिः, महासरस्वती देवता, अनुष्टुप् छन्दः, भीमा शक्तिः, भ्रामरी बीजम्, सूर्यस्तत्त्वम्, सामवेदः स्वरूपम्, महासरस्वतीप्रीत्यर्थे उत्तरचरित्रपाठे विनियोगः।

Om! Rudra is the *Rishi*, Mahasarasvati is Devata, Anushtup is *Chhanda*—the metre, *Bhima* is *Shakti*—the power, *Bhramari* is the Bijam, Surya is *Tattvam* of the cosmic Principle. *Samveda* is *Svarupam*—the innate form of Uttaracharita. Thus the *Viniyoga*—application is for Mahasarasvati, in the Japam/ Patham of the Uttarcharitra.

ध्यानम्

Meditation

ॐ घण्टाशूलहलानि शङ्खमुसले चक्रं धनुः सायकं
हस्ताब्जैर्दधतीं घनान्तविलसच्छीतांशुतुल्यप्रभाम्।

गौरीदेहसमुद्भवां त्रिजगतामाधारभूतां महा-
पूर्वामत्र सरस्वतीमनुभजे शुम्भादिदैत्यार्दिनीम्।।

I do constantly meditate upon the Mahasarasvati Devi, who holds 'Ganta'—the bell, 'Shula'—the spike, 'Hala'—the plough, 'Shankha'—the Conch; 'Musala'—the pestle, 'Chakra'—the discus, 'Dhanusha'—the bow and 'Bana—the arrow. She, who is effulgent like the harvest, at the fringe of a cloud. She, who has issued forth from the being of Gauri and is the substrum of the three worlds. Verily, She is the destroyer of *Shumbha* and other Asuras.

ॐ क्लीं ऋषिरुवाच।। 1।।

Om Klim Rishi Said :

पुरा शुम्भनिशुम्भाभ्यामसुराभ्यां शचीपतेः।
त्रैलोक्यं यज्ञभागाश्च हृता मदबलाश्रयात्।। 2।।

In the ancient past, Shumbha and Nishumbha took away the sovereignty of three worlds from Shachipati—Indra, under the force of the intoxicated pride and strength. Also they took away the portion of Yajna—sacrifices.

तावेव सूर्यतां तद्वदधिकारं तथैन्दवम्।
कौबेरमथ याम्यं च चक्राते वरुणस्य च।। 3।।

These two Asuras themselves took over the authority of the Sun, of the Moon, of *Kubera*, of *Yama* and of *Varuna* alike.

तावेव पवनर्द्धिं च चक्रतुर्वह्निकर्म च।
ततो देवा विनिर्धूता भ्रष्टराज्याः पराजिताः।। 4।।

They also exercised the powers of *Vayu* and *Agni*. The Devas were defeated and deprived of their sovereignity and authority.

हृताधिकारास्त्रिदशास्ताभ्यां सर्वे निराकृताः।
महासुराभ्यां ता देवीं संस्मरन्त्यपराजिताम्।। 5।।

When they were deprived of their powers and functions, also when they were expelled by these two *Mahasuras*, all the Devas thought of *Aparajita*—the unconquerable Mother.....,

तयास्माकं वरो दत्तो यथाऽऽपत्सु स्मृताखिलाः।
भवतां नाशयिष्यामि तत्क्षणात्परमापदः।। 6।।

.....that She had granted a *Vara*—boon to them : "As and when the calamities will befall, think of me, I will put an end instantaneously from the wrost misfortunes".

इति कृत्वा मतिं देवा हिमवन्तं नगेश्वरम्।
जग्मुस्तत्र ततो देवीं विष्णुमायां प्रतुष्टुवुः।। 7।।

Having made such a resolve, the Devas went to *Himavant*—the Lord of mountains and made obeisance to the *Devi Vishnumaya*—the illusive power of Vishnu.

देवा ऊचुः।। 8।।

The Devas Said :

नमो देव्यै महादेव्यै शिवायै सततं नमः।
नमः प्रकृत्यै भद्रायै नियताः प्रणताः स्म ताम्।। 9।।

Namaskar to the Devi, namaskar to '*Mahadevi*', who is 'Shiva'—ever auspicious. Namaskar to Her, who is 'Prakrti'—the primordial nature and 'Bhadra'—sustainer. With full attention, we pay obeisance to Her.

रौद्रायै नमो नित्यायै गौर्यै धात्र्यै नमो नमः।
ज्योत्स्नायै चेन्दुरूपिण्यै सुखायै सततं नमः।। 10।।

Namaskar to '*Radura*'—the terrible and ferrocious, to '*Nitya*'—the eternal, '*Gauri*'—of the fair complexion, *Dhatri*—the supporter. Namaskar to Jyotsna—the moon, Indurupa—the moonlight and Sukha—the happiness itself.

कल्याण्यै प्रणतां वृद्ध्यै सिद्ध्यै कुर्मो नमो नमः।
नैर्ऋत्यै भूभृतां लक्ष्म्यै शर्वाण्यै ते नमो नमः।। 11।।

Namaskar to *Kalyani*—the welfare, '*Vraddha*'—the prosperity, *Siddha*—the perfection. Namaskar to '*Nairrtya*'—the wealth of Rakshasas, the 'Lakshmi' of the king's prosperity and 'Sharvani'—the consort of Shiva.

दुर्गायै दुर्गपारायै सारायै सर्वकारिण्यै।
ख्यात्यै तथैव कृष्णायै धूम्रायै सततं नमः ।। 12 ।।

Repeated Namaskars to the 'Durga', Who is not easily accessible, the 'Durgapara' Devi, who takes across the difficult world, '*Sara*— the Supreme essence, *Sarvakarini*— the creator of everything, *Khyati*—the fame, 'Krishna'—the Shakti of Vishnu (of the black hue), and also the '*Dhumra*'— of smoke like complexion.

अतिसौम्यातिरौद्रायै नतास्तस्यै नमो नमः।
नमो जगत्प्रतिष्ठायै देव्यै कृत्ये नमो नमः ।। 13 ।।

Namaskar again and again to '*Atisomya-Radura*'—most gentle and most terrible. Namaskar to the Devi, who is '*Jagatpratistha*'—the support of the world. Namaskar to '*Krti*'—the creativity.

या देवी सर्वभूतेषु विष्णुमायेति शब्दिता।
नमस्तस्यै ।। 14 ।। नमस्तस्यै ।। 15 ।। नमस्तस्यै नमो नमः ।। 16 ।।

Namaskar to the Devi, who is being called as '*Vishnumaya*'— the illusive power of Vishnu in all being. Namaskar to that Devi. Again and again Namaskar be to Her.

या देवी सर्वभूतेषु चेतनेत्यभिधीयते।
नमस्तस्यै ।। 17 ।। नमस्तस्यै ।। 18 ।। नमस्तस्यै नमो नमः ।। 19 ।।

Namaskar to the Devi, who abides in all the beings in the form of '*Chetna*'—the consciousness. Namaskar to that Devi. Again and again Namaskar be to Her.

या देवी सर्वभूतेषु बुद्धिरूपेण संस्थिता।
नमस्तस्यै ।। 20 ।। नमस्तस्यै ।। 21 ।। नमस्तस्यै नमो नमः ।। 22 ।।

Namaskar to that Devi, who abides in all beings in the form of '*Buddhi*'—the intelligence. Namaskar to that Devi. Again and again Namaskar be to Her.

या देवी सर्वभूतेषु निद्रारूपेण संस्थिता।

नमस्तस्यै ।। 23 ।। नमस्तस्यै ।। 24 ।। नमस्तस्यै नमो नमः ।। 25 ।।

Namaskar to that Devi, who abides in all beings in the form of '*Nidra*'/sleep. Namaskar to that Devi. Again and again Namaskar be to Her.

या देवी सर्वभूतेषु क्षुधारूपेणा संस्थिता।

नमस्तस्यै ।। 26 ।। नमस्तस्यै ।। 27 ।। नमस्तस्यै नमो नमः ।। 28 ।।

Namaskar to that Devi, who abides in all beings in the form of '*Kshudha*'—hunger. Namaskar to that Devi. Again and again Namaskar be to Her.

या देवी सर्वभूतेषुच्छायारूपेण संस्थिता।

नमस्तस्यै ।। 29 ।। नमस्तस्यै ।। 30 ।। नमस्तस्यै नमो नमः ।। 31 ।।

Namaskar to that Devi, who abides in all beings in the form of '*Chhaya*' the reflection. Namaskar to that Devi. Again and again Namaskar be to Her.

या देवी सर्वभूतेषु शक्तिरूपेण संस्थिता।

नमस्तस्यै ।। 32 ।। नमस्तस्यै ।। 33 ।। नमस्तस्यै नमो नमः ।। 34 ।।

Namaskar to that Devi, who abides in all beings in the form of '*Shakti*'—the power; Namaskar to that Devi. Again and again, Namaskar be to Her.

या देवी सर्वभूतेषु तृष्णारूपेण संस्थिता।

नमस्तस्यै ।। 35 ।। नमस्तस्यै ।। 36 ।। नमस्तस्यै नमो नमः ।। 37 ।।

Namaskar to that Devi, who abides in all beings in the form of '*Trishna*'—the thirst; Namaskar to that Devi. Again and again, Namaskar be to Her.

या देवी सर्वभूतेषु क्षान्तिरूपेण संस्थिता।

नमस्तस्यै ।। 38 ।। नमस्तस्यै ।। 39 ।। नमस्तस्यै नमो नमः ।। 40 ।।

Namaskar to that Devi, who abides in all beings in the form of '*Kshanti*'—the forgiveness; Namaskar to that Devi. Again and again, Namaskar be to Her.

या देवी सर्वभूतेषु जातिरूपेण संस्थिता।
नमस्तस्यै ।। 41 ।। नमस्तस्यै ।। 42 ।। नमस्तस्यै नमो नमः ।। 43 ।।

Namaskar to that Devi, who abides in all beings in the form of '*Jati*'—the genus; Namaskar to that Devi. Again and again, Namaskar be to Her.

या देवी सर्वभूतेषु लज्जारूपेण संस्थिता।
नमस्तस्यै ।। 44 ।। नमस्तस्यै ।। 45 ।। नमस्तस्यै नमो नमः ।। 46 ।।

Namaskar to that Devi, who abides in all beings in the form of '*Lajja*'—modesty. Namaskar to that Devi. Again and again, Namaskar be to Her.

या देवी सर्वभूतेषु शान्तिरूपेण संस्थिता।
नमस्तस्यै ।। 47 ।। नमस्तस्यै ।। 48 ।। नमस्तस्यै नमो नमः ।। 49 ।।

Namaskar to that Devi, who abides in all beings in the form of '*Shanti*'—the peace; Namaskar to that Devi. Again and again, Namaskar be to Her.

या देवी सर्वभूतेषु श्रद्धारूपेण संस्थिता।
नमस्तस्यै ।। 50 ।। नमस्तस्यै ।। 51 ।। नमस्तस्यै नमो नमः ।। 52 ।।

Namaskar to that Devi, who abides in all beings in the form of '*Shraddha*'—the faith. Namaskar to that Devi. Again and again, Namaskar be to Her.

या देवी सर्वभूतेषु कान्तिरूपेण संस्थिता।
नमस्तस्यै ।। 53 ।। नमस्तस्यै ।। 54 ।। नमस्तस्यै नमो नमः ।। 55 ।।

Namaskar to that Devi, who abides in all beings in the form of '*Kanti*'—the luminosity. Namaskar to that Devi. Again and again, Namaskar be to Her.

या देवी सर्वभूतेषु लक्ष्मीरूपेण संस्थिता।
नमस्तस्यै ।। 56 ।। नमस्तस्यै ।। 57 ।। नमस्तस्यै। नमो नमः । 58 ।।

Namaskar to that Devi, who abides in all beings in the form

of *'Lakshmi'*—the good fortunes. Namaskar to that Devi. Again and again, Namaskar be to Her.

या देवी सर्वभूतेषु वृत्तिरूपेण संस्थिता।
नमस्तस्यै ।। 59 ।। नमस्तस्यै ।। 60 ।। नमस्तस्यै नमो नमः ।। 61 ।।

Namaskar to that Devi, who abides in all beings in the form of *'Vrtti'*—the activity/mode of life. Namaskar to that Devi. Again and again, Namaskar be to Her.

या देवी सर्वभूतेषु स्मृतिरूपेण संस्थिता।
नमस्तस्यै ।। 62 ।। नमस्तस्यै ।। 63 ।। नमस्तस्यै नमो नमः ।। 64 ।।

Namaskar to that Devi, who abides in all beings in the form of *'Smrti'*—the memory. Namaskar to that Devi. Again and again, Namaskar be to Her.

या देवी सर्वभूतेषु दयारूपेण संस्थिता।
नमस्तस्यै ।। 65 ।। नमस्तस्यै ।। 66 ।। नमस्तस्यै नमो नमः ।। 67 ।।

Namaskar to that Devi, who abides in all beings in the form of *'Daya'*—the compassion. Namaskar to that Devi. Again and again, Namaskar be to Her.

या देवी सर्वभूतेषु तुष्टिरूपेण संस्थिता।
नमस्तस्यै ।। 68 ।। नमस्तस्यै ।। 69 ।। नमस्तस्यै नमो नमः ।। 70 ।।

Namaskar to that Devi, who abides in all beings in the form of *'Tushti'*— contentment. Namaskar to that Devi. Again and again, Namaskar be to Her.

या देवी सर्वभूतेषु मातृरूपेण संस्थिता।
नमस्तस्यै ।। 71 ।। नमस्तस्यै ।। 72 ।। नमस्तस्यै नमो नमः ।। 73 ।।

Namaskar to that Devi, who abides in all beings in the form of *'Matrirupa'*—the mother. Namaskar to that Devi. Again and again, Namaskar be to Her.

या देवी सर्वभूतेषु भ्रान्तिरूपेण संस्थिता।
नमस्तस्यै ।। 74 ।। नमस्तस्यै ।। 75 ।। नमस्तस्यै नमो नमः ।। 76 ।।

Namaskar to that Devi, who abides in all beings in the form of *'Bhranti'*—the illusion; Namaskar to that Devi. Again and again, Namaskar be to Her.

इन्द्रियाणामधिष्ठात्री भूतानां चाखिलेषु या।
भूतेषु सततं तस्यै व्याप्तिदेव्यै नमो नमः ।। 77 ।।

Again and again, Namaskar be to that *'Adhisthatri Devi'*—the Supreme Controller, who constantly presides over the senses and is all pervading and controls all the elements.

चितिरूपेण या कृत्स्नमेतद् व्याप्य स्थिता जगत्।
नमस्तस्यै ।। 78 ।। नमस्तस्यै ।। 79 ।। नमस्तस्यै नमो नमः ।। 80 ।।

Namaskar to that Devi, who abides in all beings in the form of *'Chiti'*—the consciousness and who pervades the entire world. Namaskar to that Devi. Again and again, Namaskar be to Her.

स्तुता सुरैः पूर्वभभीष्टसंश्रया-
त्तथा सुरेन्द्रेण दिनेषु सेविता।
करोतु सा नः शुभहेतुरीश्वरी
शुभानि भद्राण्यभिहन्तु चापदः ।। 81 ।।

The Devas have invoked You in the ancient past, for the sake of their desired object and You have been adored regularly by *'Surendra'*—the Lord of Devas. May that 'Ishvari', the source of all auspiciousness grant all the best to us and make an end to our calamities.

या साम्प्रतं चोद्धतदैत्यतापितै-
रस्माभिरीशा च सुरैर्नमस्यते।
या च स्मृता तत्क्षणमेव हन्ति नः
सर्वापदो भक्तिविनम्रमूर्तिभिः ।। 82 ।।

Being tormented by the arrogant 'Daityas', the Devatas invoked Her and prostrated before Her. May She destroy all of our calamities, as She does to those, who remember Her with devotion and humility!

ऋषिरुवाच।। 83।।

The Rishi Said :

एवं स्तवादियुक्तानां देवानां तत्र पार्वती।
स्नातुमभ्याययौ तोये जाह्नव्या नृपनन्दन।। 84।।

Nripanandana! Prince! having thus praised by the Devas, the Parvati Devi came there to have a dip in the waters of *Jahanvi*/ the Ganga."

साब्रवीत्तान् सुरान् सुभ्रूर्भवद्भिः स्तूयतेऽत्र का।
शरीरकोशतश्चास्याः समुद्भूताब्रवीच्छिवा।। 85।।

She the lovely eyebrowed Devi said to those Suras : "To whom do you praise here?" Śhiva thus sprang forth from Her physical sheath, and She spoke :

स्तोत्रं ममैतत् क्रियते शुम्भदैत्यनिराकृतैः।
देवैः समेतैः समरे निशुम्भेन पराजितैः।। 86।।

"You the Devas are all assembled here, as being humiliated by Shumbha and routed in battle by Nishumbha, are praying to me."

शरीरकोशाद्यत्तस्याः पार्वत्या निःसृताम्बिका।
कौशिकीति समस्तेषु ततो लोकेषु गीयते।। 87।।

Then Ambika came out from the physical sheath of Parvati, so She is glorified in all the worlds as '*Kaushiki*'—having Her origin in *Parvati's Kosha*—sheath.

तस्यां विनिर्गतायां तु कृष्णाभूत्सापि पार्वती।
कालिकेति समाख्याता हिमाचलकृताश्रया।। 88।।

After She had issued forth, then Parvati turned dark and was renowned as '*Kalika*' to have Her abode in the Himalaya mountains.

ततोऽम्बिकां परं रूपं बिभ्राणां सुमनोहरम्।
ददर्श चण्डो मुण्डश्च भृत्यौ शुम्भनिशुम्भयोः।। 89।।

Then the two servants '*Chanda* and *Munda*' of '*Shumbha*' and '*Nishumbha* saw that excellent, beautiful and charming form of that Ambika.

ताभ्यां शुम्भाय चाख्याता अतीव सुमनोहरा।
काप्यास्ते स्त्री महाराज भासयन्ती हिमाचलम्।। 90।।

Then they (Chanda and Munda) went before *Shumbha* and said : "O king ! A most beautiful woman dwells there and shedding lusture on the Himalaya mountain.

नैव तादृक् क्वचिद्रूपं दृष्टं केनचिदुत्तमम्।
ज्ञायतां काप्यसौ देवी गृह्यतां चासुरेश्वर।। 91।।

Such surpassingly beauty must not have ever been seen by any one so far anywhere. 'O Chief of the Asuras, ascertain who that Devi is and take hold of Her.'

स्त्रीरत्नमतिचार्वङ्गी द्योतयन्ती दिशस्त्विषा।
सा तु तिष्ठति दैत्येन्द्र तां भवान् द्रष्टुमर्हति।। 92।।

She is a jem among women having exquisitely beautiful limbs. She illuminates all the directions with Her lustre. O *Daityendra*—Chief of the Daityas! "She is still there (on Himalayas); you should see Her".

यानि रत्नानि मणयो गजाश्वादीनि वै प्रभो।
त्रैलोक्ये तु समस्तानि साम्प्रतं भान्ति ते गृहे।। 93।।

O *Prabhu*—Lord! Whatever the jems, elephants, horses and other precious jewels are in three worlds, they are now placed in your house.

ऐरावतः समानीतो गजरत्नं पुरन्दरात्।
पारिजाततरुश्चायं तथैवोच्चैःश्रवा हयः।। 94।।

'*Airavata*' is the gem among elephants, which has been taken away by you from '*Purandara*'—Indra and so also is this *Parijata* tree and the '*Uccaishrava*' horse.

विमानं हंससंयुक्तमेतत्तिष्ठति तेऽङ्गणे।
रत्नभूतमिहानीतं यदासीद्वेधसोऽद्भुतम्।। 95।।

Here stands the wonderful aeroplane yoked with *Hamsa*—Swan, in your courtyard. This aeroplane with wonderful gems, which originally belonged to Brahma, has been brought here.

निधिरेष महापद्मः समानीतो धनेश्वरात्।
किञ्जल्किनीं ददौ चाब्धिर्मालामम्लानपङ्कजाम्।। 96 ।।

You have brought the treasure named '*Mahapadma*' from the '*Dhaneshwara*'—Kubera. The '*Kinjalkini*' garland made of unfading lotus flowers has been given to you by the ocean.

छत्रं ते वारुणं गेहे काञ्चनस्रावि तिष्ठति।
तथायं स्यन्दनवरो यः पुराऽऽसीत्प्रजापतेः।। 97 ।।

Your house/dwelling place looks exceedingly beautiful with the gold-showering umbrella of *Varuna*. Here is the best chariot, that previously belonged to Prajapati.

मृत्योरुत्क्रान्तिदा नाम शक्तिरीश त्वया हृता।
पाशः सलिलराजस्य भ्रातुस्तव परिग्रहे।। 98 ।।

You have snatched the *Mrityu's*—death's '*Utkrantida Shakti*', which is encroaching power. The '*Pasha*'—noose of '*Salilraja*'—the Ocean king is in the possession of your brother (Nishumbha).

निशुम्भस्याब्धिजाताश्च समस्ता रत्नजातयः।
वह्निरपि ददौ तुभ्यमग्निशौचे च वाससी।। 99 ।।

All kinds of jems produced in the ocean are in the custody of Nishumbha. '*Vahni*'—Fire has also given you the two garments which are purified by fire.

एवं दैत्येन्द्र रत्नानि समस्तान्याहृतानि ते।
स्त्रीरत्नमेषा कल्याणी त्वया कस्मान्न गृह्यते।। 100 ।।

O *Daityendra*/Chief among Daityas! You have thus accumulated all the jems, and why not this beautiful '*Striratna*'—the 'Lady-jewel' is being siezed by you?"

ऋषिरुवाच ।। 101 ।।

The Rishi Said :

निशम्येति वचः शुम्भः स तदा चण्डमुण्डयोः ।
प्रेषयामास सुग्रीवं दूतं देव्या महासुरम् ।। 102 ।।

Having heard those words of *Chanda* and *Munda, Shumbha* commissioned *Sugriva* the great Asura, as messenger to the Devi...,

इति चेति च वक्तव्या सा गत्वा वचनान्मम ।
यथा चाभ्येति सम्प्रीत्या तथा कार्यं त्वया लघु ।। 103 ।।

....and said : 'Go and tell her these words on my behalf, in such a manner, so that She may be pleased to come close to me in love with affection'.

स तत्र गत्वा यत्रास्ते शैलोद्देशेऽतिशोभने ।
सा देवी तां ततः प्राह श्लक्ष्णं मधुरया गिरा ।। 104 ।।

He went there, where the Devi was staying at a very lovely spot on the mountain. He spoke to the Devi in refined and sweet language.

दूत उवाच ।। 105 ।।

The Messenger said :

देवि दैत्येश्वरः शुम्भस्त्रैलोक्ये परमेश्वरः ।
दूतोऽहं प्रेषितस्तेन त्वत्सकाशमिहागतः ।। 106 ।।

'O Devi, Daityashvara *Shumbha* is the Lord of Daityas and is the *Parmeshvara*—Supreme Sovereign of *Triloki*—the three worlds. I am his *Duta*—messenger, sent by him to your presence.

अव्याहताज्ञः सर्वासु यः सदा देवयोनिषु ।
निर्जिताखिलदैत्यारिः स यदाह शृणुष्व तत् ।। 107 ।।

Hear what I say, for him : "All the Devas obey to him with

one voice. His orders are never resisted by the Devas. It is he, who has defeated all the foes of the Daityas.

मम त्रैलोक्यमखिलं मम देवा वशानुगाः।
यज्ञभागानहं सर्वानुपाश्नामि पृथक् पृथक्।। 108।।

All the three worlds belong to me and the Devas are under my influence and obedience. I enjoy all the shares of Yajna—sacrifices separately.

त्रैलोक्ये वररत्नानि मम वश्यान्यशेषतः।
तथैव गजरत्नं च हृत्वा देवेन्द्रवाहनम्।। 109।।

All the best gems of the three worlds are in my possession and command. The vehicle of *Devendra*, lord of the Devas, is like the gem of elephants, which has been taken away by me.

क्षीरोदमथनोद्भूतमश्वरत्नं ममामरैः।
उच्चैःश्रवससंज्ञं तत्प्रणिपत्य समर्पितम्।। 110।।

'*Amaras*'/Devas themselves offered me with submissions at my feet that gem-horse named *Ucchaishravas*, which sprang forth at the churning time of "*Kshirasagara*'the 'milk-ocean.'

यानि चान्यानि देवेषु गन्धर्वेषूरगेषु च।
रत्नभूतानि भूतानि तानि मय्येव शोभने।। 111।।

O Shobana—the beautiful lady! All the rare objects of '*Ratnas*'/jewels which existed with the *Devas, Gandharvas*—celestial musicians and *Urgas*—the cobras are now with me.

स्त्रीरत्नभूतां त्वां देवि लोके मन्यामहे वयम्।
सा त्वमस्मानुपागच्छ यतो रत्नभुजो वयम्।। 112।।

We do look upon you, O Devi, as the jewel of women-folk in the world! You are verily, as such. We only are to enjoy the rare objects. so You come to us.

मां वा ममानुजं वापि निशुम्भमुरुविक्रमम्।
भज त्वं चञ्चलापाङ्गि रत्नभूतासि वै यतः।। 113।।

O Devi! We acknowledge You in the very existence of a jewel. You come to me or my younger brother Nishumbha, who is of great prowess. You are verily, an unsteady eyed.

परमैश्वर्यमतुलं प्राप्स्यसे मत्परिग्रहात्।
एतद् बुद्ध्या समालोच्य मत्परिग्रहतां व्रज॥ 114॥

You will be the owner of great and incomparable, opulence/wealth, which you will get by marrying me. Think with Your determining intellect and be my wife".

ऋषिरुवाच॥ 115॥

The Rishi Said :

इत्युक्ता सा तदा देवी गम्भीरान्तःस्मिता जगौ।
दुर्गा भगवती भद्रा ययेदं धार्यते जगत्॥ 116॥

On hearing the words of the *Duta*—messenger, the Devi Durga who is adorable and auspicious, and by whom this universe is supported, became serene in Her mind and said :

देव्युवाच॥ 117॥

The Devi Said :

सत्यमुक्तं त्वया नात्र मिथ्या किंचित्त्वयोदितम्।
त्रैलोक्याधिपतिः शुम्भो निशुम्भश्चापि तादृशः॥ 118॥

"What you spoke is true, nothing false has been told by you in this regard. Shumbha is indeed the sovereign of the triple world and likewise is Nishumbha too.

किं त्वत्र यत्प्रतिज्ञातं मिथ्या तत्क्रियते कथम्।
श्रूयतामल्पबुद्धित्वात्प्रतिज्ञा या कृता पुरा॥ 119॥

But in this regard, how can my promise as made by Me be false? You please listen to My promise, as made by Me earlier, because of My lesser intellect.

यो मां जयति संग्रामे यो मे दर्पं व्यपोहति।
यो मे प्रतिबलो लोके स मे भर्ता भविष्यति॥ 120॥

He alone can be My husband, who will conquer Me in the battle-field, who would let My pride down and would be equal in My prowess in the world.

तदागच्छतु शुम्भोऽत्र निशुम्भो वा महासुरः।
मां जित्वा किं चिरेणात्र पाणिं गृह्णातु मे लघु।। 121।।

Shumbha or Nishumbha, the great Asuras, may come here. They may win Me over here and let him soon take My hand in marriage. What need of delay?"

दूत उवाच।। 122।।

Duta—the messenger said :

अवलिप्तासि मैवं त्वं देवि ब्रूहि ममाग्रतः।
त्रैलोक्ये कः पुमांस्तिष्ठेदग्रे शुम्भनिशुम्भयोः।। 123।।

"O Devi! You are haughty and full of pride. Talk not so tall before me. Who can equal and stand before *Shumbha* and *Nishumbha* in the three worlds.

अन्येषामपि दैत्यानां सर्वे देवा न वै युधि।
तिष्ठन्ति सम्मुखे देवि किं पुनः स्त्री त्वमेकिका।। 124।।

O Devi! All the Devas verily, can never stand face to face with other Daityas in the battle-field. How can you stand all alone there?

इन्द्राद्याः सकला देवास्तस्थुर्येषां न संयुगे।
शुम्भादीनां कथं तेषां स्त्री प्रयास्यसि सम्मुखम्।। 125।।

Indra and all other Devas could not resist before Shumbha and other Asuras in the battle-field. How can you stand before them?

सा त्वं गच्छ मयैवोक्ता पार्श्वं शुम्भनिशुम्भयोः।
केशाकर्षणनिर्धूतगौरवा मा गमिष्यसि।। 126।।

Thus so you go to Shumbha and Nishumbha, as per my word

itself. Let it not be that you go to them with your hair being dragged and your dignity lost".

देव्युवाच ।। 127 ।।

The Devi Said :

एवमेतद् बली शुम्भो निशुम्भश्चातिवीर्यवान्।
किं करोमि प्रतिज्ञा मे यदनालोचिता पुरा ।। 128 ।।

Yes it is true, what you say. Shumbha and Nishumbha is of course, exceedingly valourous and strong. What can I do, as I have made a vow, an ill considered one, taken much earlier.

स त्वं गच्छ मयोक्तं ते यदेतत्सर्वमादृतः ।
तदाचक्ष्वासुरेन्द्राय स च युक्तं करोतु तत् ।। ॐ ।। 129 ।।

So you go back and tell the Daitya Chief with great care all that what has been said by me to you. Let him do, whatsoever he considers proper.

इति श्रीमार्कण्डेयपुराणे सावर्णिके मन्वन्तरे देवीमाहात्म्ये देव्या
दूतसंवादो नाम पञ्चमोऽध्यायः ।। 5 ।।

The fifth Chapter entitled "*Dialogue between Duta and the Devi*" of the Devi Mahatmya, during the time-span of Savarni—the Manu, occuring in the Markandeya Purana is concluded.

उवाच 9, त्रिपान्मन्त्राः 66, श्लोकाः 54, एवम् 129,
एवमादिताः 388 ।।

Narrated Mantra 9, Tripanmantra 66, Shloka 54, Total in this chapter 129, Total in all 388.

षष्ठोऽध्याय:

SIXTH CHAPTER

धूम्रलोचन-वध

Slaying of Dhumralochana

ध्यानम्

Meditation

ॐ नागाधीश्वरविष्टरां फणिफणोत्तंसोरुरत्नावली-
भास्वद्देहलतां दिवाकरनिभां नेत्रत्रयोद्भासिताम्।
मालाकुम्भकपालनीरजकरां चन्द्रार्धचूडां परां
सर्वज्ञेश्वरभैरवाङ्कनिलयां पद्मावतीं चिन्तये।।

I meditate upon the most excellent *Padmavati Devi,* whose abode is in the lap of 'Sarvajneshvara-Bhairva'—the Omniscient Bhairva. She is seated on the *Nagaraja*—lord of serpants. Her being shines with Her lustre, and by the magnificient garland of the cobra gems. Her radiance is that of the Sun. Her looks are supremely superb with Her three eyes. She holds '*Mala*'—garland; '*Kumbha*'—pot, '*Kapala*'—skull and '*Kamal*'—lotus in Her hands and the crown of half-moon gives a vibrant look.

ॐ ऋषिरुवाच।। 1।।

Om Rishi Said :

इत्याकर्ण्य वचो देव्याः स दूतोऽमर्षपूरितः।
समाचष्ट समागम्य दैत्यराजाय विस्तरात्।। 2।।

On hearing the words of the Devi, the Duta felt slighted with indignation, returned to the king of 'Daityas' and related all in detail.

तस्य दूतस्य तद्वाक्यमाकर्ण्यासुरराट् ततः।
सक्रोधः प्राह दैत्यानामधिपं धूम्रलोचनम्।। 3।।

On hearing the words of the Devi from his Duta, the king of Asuras got enraged and told *Dhumralochana*—the Chieftain of the Daityas :

हे धूम्रलोचनाशु त्वं स्वसैन्यपरिवारितः।
तामानय बलाद् दुष्टां केशाकर्षणविह्वलाम्।। 4।।

"O! Dhumralochana! Make haste together with your army and bring that '*Dushta*'—ill-natured shrewed lady by force, to be distressed when dragged by her hair.

तत्परित्राणदः कश्चिद्यदि वोत्तिष्ठतेऽपरः।
स हन्तव्योऽमरो वापि यक्षो गन्धर्व एव वा।। 5।।

Or if any one comes to Her rescue as Her saviour; let he be slain, may be he an '*Amara*', '*Yaksha*' or *Gandharva*".

ऋषिरुवाच।। 6।।

The Rishi Said :

तेनाज्ञप्तस्ततः शीघ्रं स दैत्यो धूम्रलोचनः।
वृतः षष्ट्या सहस्त्राणामसुराणां द्रुतं ययौ।। 7।।

On receiving such a command from (Shumbha), *Dhumralochana* went forth quickly, accompanied by sixty thousand Asuras.

स दृष्ट्वा तां ततो देवीं तुहिनाचलसंस्थिताम्।
जगादोच्चैः प्रयाहीति मूलं शुम्भनिशुम्भयोः।। 8।।

He asked the Devi loudly, to come before the presence of Shumbha and Nishumbha, Who was stationed on the snowy mountain.

न चेत्प्रीत्याद्य भवती मद्भर्तारमुपैष्यति।
ततो बलान्नयाम्येष केषाकर्षणविह्वलाम्।। 9।।

"If yo donot submit before my lord with pleasure and love,

I will take you by force then, distressed you will be, when dragged by hair."

देव्युवाच ।। 10 ।।

The Devi Said :

दैत्येश्वरेण प्रहितो बलवान् बलसंवृतः।
बलान्नयसि मामेवं ततः किं ते करोम्यहम्।। 11 ।।

"You have been sent here by the lord of Daityas, accompanied by the army and mighty you are as well. If you take Me by force, then what can I do to you?"

ऋषिरुवाच ।। 12 ।।

The Rishi Said :

इत्युक्तः सोऽभ्यधावत्तामसुरो धूम्रलोचनः।
हुंकारेणैव तं भस्म सा चकाराम्बिका ततः ।। 13 ।।

"Having said so by the Devi, the Asura Dhumralochana rushed towards Her and thereupon Ambika reduced him to ashes with the heave of the sound 'Hum'."

अथ क्रुद्धं महासैन्यमसुराणां तथाम्बिका।
ववर्ष सायकैस्तीक्ष्णैस्तथा शक्तिपरश्वधैः ।। 14 ।

Then the great army of Asuras became enraged and showered sharp '*Sayakas*'—arrows, '*Shakti*'—missiles and '*Parshu*'—axes.

ततो धुतसटः कोपात्कृत्वा नादं सुभैरवम्।
पपातासुरसेनायां सिंहो देव्याः स्ववाहनः ।। 15 ।।

Lion—the vehicle of the Devi got enraged and shaking its mane in anger, made the most terrific roar. It fell amidst the army of the '*Asuras*'.

कांश्चित् करप्रहारेण दैत्यानास्येन चापरान्।
आक्रम्य चाधरेणान्यान् स जघान महासुरान्।। 16 ।।

To some of the Asuras, it killed with a blow of its fore paws, to others with its jaws and the rest of the Asuras by the hind legs....,

केषांचित्पाटयामास नखैः कोष्ठानि केसरी।
तथा तलप्रहारेण शिरांसि कृतवान् पृथक्।। 17।।

...*Kesari*—the lion tore the hearts of some Asuras and cut off heads, from their body, and others with its mouth, with the blow of its paws, and...

विच्छिन्नबाहुशिरसः कृतास्तेन तथापरे।
पपौ च रुधिरं कोष्ठादन्येषां धुतकेसरः।। 18।।

...it cut off arms and heads from others; while shaking its mane. It drank the blood from the hearts of others.

क्षणेन तद्बलं सर्वं क्षयं नीतं महात्मना।
तेन केसरिणा देव्या वाहनेनातिकोपिना।। 19।।

Being highly enraged and highly spirited that lion who bore the Devi, in a moment annihilated that army of Asuras.

श्रुत्वा तमसुरं देव्या निहतं धूम्रलोचनम्।
बलं च क्षयितं कृत्स्नं देवीकेसरिणा ततः।। 20।।

Having heard that 'Asura' Dhumralochana was killed by the Devi and all his army has been reduced to naught by the lion of the Devi...,

चुकोप दैत्याधिपतिः शुम्भः प्रस्फुरिताधरः।
आज्ञापयामास च तौ चण्डमुण्डौ महासुरौ।। 21।।

...Shumbha the lord of Daityas got infuriated. His lips quivered and then he commanded to *Chanda* and *Munda* the two great Asuras :

हे चण्ड हे मुण्ड बलैर्बहुभिः परिवारितौ।
तत्र गच्छत गत्वा च सा समानीयतां लघु।। 22।।

"O Chanda! O Munda! Go along with the large force and bring Her immediately here...

केशेष्वाकृष्य बद्ध्वा वा यदि वः संशयो युधि।
तदाशेषायुधैः सर्वैरसुरैर्विनिहन्यताम्।। 23।।

.....either by binding or by dragging Her by hair. But if you presume and doubt about that, then all the Asuras need to engage Her in fight and kill with mighty weapons...,

तस्यां हतायां दुष्टायां सिंहे च विनिपातिते।
शीघ्रमागम्यतां बद्ध्वा गृहीत्वा तामथाम्बिकाम्।। ॐ ।। 24।।

....and sieze that Ambika quickly, on being Her wounded and killed alongwith her lion, then bring Her bound.

इति श्रीमार्कण्डेयपुराणे सावर्णिके मन्वन्तरे देवीमाहात्म्ये
शुम्भनिशुम्भसेनानीधूम्रलोचनवधो नाम षष्ठोऽध्यायः।। 6।।

The Sixth chapter entitled 'Slaying of Dhumralochana, the Army Chief of Shumbha-Nishumbha of the '*Devi Mahatmaya*', during the time span of *Savarni*—the Manu, occuring in the Shri Markandeya Purana is concluded.

उवाच 4, श्लोकाः 20, एवम् 24, एवामादितः 412।।

Narrations 4, Shlokas 20, total in the chapter 24, total in all 412 shlokas.

सप्तमोऽध्यायः
SEVENTH CHAPTER

चण्ड और मुण्ड का वध
Slaying of Chanda and Munda

ध्यानम्
Meditation

ॐ ध्यायेयं रत्नपीठे शुककलपठितं शृण्वतीं श्यामलाङ्गीं
न्यस्तैकाङ्घ्रिं सरोजे शशिशकलधरां वल्लकीं वादयन्तीम्।
कह्लाराबद्धमालां नियमितविलसच्चोलिकां रक्तवस्त्रां
मातङ्गीं शङ्खपात्रां मधुरमधुमदां चित्रकोद्भासिभालाम्।।

I meditate upon *Matangi Devi*, who is listening to the sweet words (tune) of the speaking parrot, on the couch decorated with gems. Her complexion is '*Shyama*'—'blue-black'. She has kept one of Her feet on the lotus and holds the half-moon on Her forehead. She plays on '*Vina*', and has worn the garland of '*Kahlar*' flowers and has kept Her limbs properly tight with '*Cholika*' garment. Her apron is red and is holding a Conch like pot in Her hand. A slight effect of elixir is felt on Her face and the *Chitraka* '*Bindi*'—small mark of Vermilion is giving a grand look on Her forehead.

ॐ ऋषिरुवाच।। 1।।

Om the Rishi Said :

आज्ञप्तास्ते ततो दैत्याश्चण्डमुण्डपुरोगमाः।
चतुरङ्गबलोपेता ययुरभ्युद्यतायुधाः।। 2।।

"Under the instructions of (Shumbha), Chanda and Munda

Daityas, alongwith *Chaturanga*—the four fold division of army, marched ahead, being fully armed.

ददृशुस्ते ततो देवीमीषद्धासां व्यवस्थिताम्।
सिंहस्योपरि शैलेन्द्रशृङ्गे महति काञ्चने।।3।।

They saw the Devi, who was smiling gently and was seated upon the lion at *Shailendra Shringa*—the peak of the Himalaya mountain, which was of huge gold.

ते दृष्ट्वा तां समादातुमुद्यमं चक्रुरुद्यताः।
आकृष्टचापासिधरास्तथान्ये तत्समीपगाः।। 4।।

On seeing Her, some of the Daityas got excited themselves and made a bid to capture Her. Some came before Her with bows bent and sword drawn.

ततः कोपं चकारोच्चैरम्बिका तानरीन् प्रति।
कोपेन चास्या वदनं मषीवर्णमभूत्तदा।। 5।।

Thereupon, Ambika got terribly enraged with those foes, and with Her '*Kopa*'—anger, her complexion became dark as '*Mashi*'—black ink itself is.

भ्रुकुटिकुटिलात्तस्या ललाटफलकाद्दुतम्।
काली करालवदना विनिष्क्रान्तासिपाशिनी।।6।।

From Her forehead, fierce with frown, sprung forth '*Kali*' with '*Karalvadana*—the terrific expression of face, armed with '*Asi*'—the sword and '*Pasha*', the noose...,

विचित्रखट्वाङ्गधरा नरमालाविभूषणा।
द्वीपिचर्मपरीधाना शुष्कमांसातिभैरवा।। 7।।

...She held the strange '*Khatvanga*'—a staff/stick decorated with a garland of skulls, and wrapped with a tiger's skin. She was only skeleton, with all the flesh on the body dried off, and looked very fearful....,

अतिविस्तारवदना जिह्वाललनभीषणा।
निमग्नारक्तनयना नादापूरितदिङ्मुखा।। 8।।

...with highly extended mouth, fearful with Her sprawling

tongue out, deep-sunk reddish eyes and filled all the directions of the sky with Her terrible roars...,

सा वेगेनाभिपतिता घातयन्ती महासुरान्।
सैन्ये तत्र सुरारीणामभक्षयत तद्बलम्।। 9।।

.....She was falling upon with great force upon the *Asuras* and slaughtering their great army. She ate up the foes/ enemies of the 'Suras'—Devas.

पार्ष्णिग्राहाङ्कुशग्राहियोधघण्टासमन्वितान्।
समादायैकहस्तेन मुखे चिक्षेप वारणान्।। 10।।

She was snatching the elephants with one hand and putting them in the mouth alongwith their bells; together with their rearing guards, who were *Ankusha-grahi*/elephant driver *Mahawats* with goads..

तथैव योधं तुरगै रथं सारथिना सह।
निक्षिप्य वक्त्रे दशनैश्चर्वयन्त्यतिभैरवम्।। 11।।

Taking the cavalry with the horses, chariot and the charioteer, in the similar process, She chewed them in the most frightful manner with Her teeth.

एकं जग्राह केशेषु ग्रीवायामथ चापरम्।
पादेनाक्रम्य चैवान्यमुरसान्यमपोथयत्।। 12।।

She would catch one hold of the hair, and another by the neck. To one, She would crush by the weight of Her foot and another with the push of Her breast.

तैर्मुक्तानि च शस्त्राणि महास्त्राणि तथासुरैः।
मुखेन जग्राह रुषा दशनैर्मथितान्यपि।। 13।।

She would catch the arm and the missiles of the Asuras with Her mouth, shot by them and would ground them with Her teeth in fury.

बलिनां तद् बलं सर्वमसुराणां दुरात्मनाम्।
ममर्दाभक्षयच्चान्यानन्यांश्चाताडयत्तथा।। 14।।

She killed all the multitude of mighty and evil-designed

Asuras. To some, She devoured and to others, She beat them with blows.

असिना निहताः केचित्केचित्खट्वाङ्गताडिताः।
जग्मुर्विनाशमसुरा दन्ताग्राभिहतास्तथा।। 15।।

Some were killed with the swords, some were beaten with "*Khatvanga*—a club sharped foot of a cot with the garland of skulls and others met their end with the grinding off their beings by the edge of Her teeth.

क्षणेन तद् बलं सर्वमसुराणां निपातितम्।
दृष्ट्वा चण्डोऽभिदुद्राव तां कालीमतिभीषणाम्।। 16।।

Thus the Devi destroyed all the mighty force of the Asuras in a moment. On seeing all this, *Chanda* rushed towards that *Kali*, who was all the more terrible in appearance.

शरवर्षैर्महाभीमैर्भीमाक्षीं तां महासुरः।
छादयामास चक्रैश्च मुण्डः क्षिप्तैः सहस्रशः।। 17।।

The '*Mahasura*'—great Rakshasa hurled showers of dreadful arrows and '*Munda*' hurled discus in thousands, on the terrible-eyed Devi, thus covering Her with *Chakras*.

तानि चक्राण्यनेकानि विशमानानि तन्मुखम्।
बभुर्यथार्कबिम्बानि सुबहूनि घनोदरम्।। 18।।

She made disappear all those numerous Chakras in Her mouth, as if many solar orbs were disappearing into the midst of a cloud.

ततो जहासातिरुषा भीमं भैरवनादिनी।
कालीकरालवक्त्रान्तर्दुर्दर्शदशनोज्ज्वला।। 19।।

Then the '*Bhairavanadini-Kali*' roared frightfully and Her fearful teeth were shining within Her dreadful mouth. She laughed terribly in extreme fury and anger.

उत्थाय च महासिं हं देवी चण्डमधावत।
गृहीत्वा चास्य केशेषु शिरस्तेनासिनाच्छिनत्।। 20।।

The Devi took the big sword in Her hand and pronouncing '*Ham*' mystic sound rushed at *Chanda*—the Asura, siezed him by his hair and severed his head.

अथ मुण्डोऽभ्यधावत्तां दृष्ट्वा चण्डं निपातितम्।
तमप्यपातयद्भूमौ सा खड्गाभिहतं रुषा।। 21।।

Seeing *Chanda* laid down dead, *Munda* rushed at Her. Then Devi felled him also on the ground. Thus enraged and then struck him dead with Her sword.

हतशेषं ततः सैन्यं दृष्ट्वा चण्डं निपातितम्।
मुण्डं च सुमहावीर्यं दिशो भेजे भयातुरम्।। 22।।

On Seeing the vailent Chanda and Munda down dead, the rest of the army got too panicky with dread to flee in all the directions.

शिरश्चण्डस्य काली च गृहीत्वा मुण्डमेव च।
प्राह प्रचण्डाट्टहासमिश्रमभ्येत्य चण्डिकाम्।। 23।।

'*Kali*' held the heads of '*Chanda*' and '*Munda*' in Her hands, approached '*Chandika*' and said while making a loud laughter.

मया तवात्रोपहृतौ चण्डमुण्डौ महापशू।
युद्धयज्ञे स्वयं शुम्भं निशुम्भं च हनिष्यसि।। 24।।

"O Devi! I have brought you the offerings of heads of the two great animals in the form of Chanda and Munda. Now You shall Yourself slay *Shumbha* and *Nishumbha* in the *Yuddha Yajna*/the sacrificial battle."

ऋषिरुवाच।। 25।।

The Rishi Said :

तावानीतौ ततो दृष्ट्वा चण्डमुण्डौ महासुरौ।
उवाच कालीं कल्याणी ललितं चण्डिका वचः।। 26।।

There and then seeing Chanda and Munda—the great

Asuras, brought to Her, the *Kalyani* auspicious Chandika said to Kali in the sweet tone :

यस्माच्चण्डं च मुण्डं च गृहीत्वा त्वमुपागता।
चामुण्डेति ततो लोके ख्याता देवि भविष्यसि।। ॐ ।। 27 ।।

"O Devi! as You have brought Me holding both Chanda and Munda, so You shall be known with fame by the name 'Chamunda', in the universe". Om.

इति श्रीमार्कण्डेयपुराणे सावर्णिके मन्वन्तरे देवीमहात्म्ये
चण्डमुण्डवधो नाम सप्तमोऽध्यायः।। 7 ।।

The seventh chapter entitled 'slaying of Chanda and Munda' in the Devi Mahatmya, during the time span of Savarni— the Manu, occuring in the Markandeya Purana, is concluded.

उवाच 2, श्लोकः 25, एवम् 27, एवमादितः 439।।

Narration 2, shlokas 25, total 27, in all 439 shlokas.

अष्टमोऽध्यायः

EIGHTH CHAPTER

रक्तबीज-वध

Slaying of Raktabija

ध्यानम्

Meditation

ॐ अरुणां करुणातरङ्गिताक्षीं
धृतपाशाङ्कुशबाणचापहस्ताम्।
अणिमादिभिरावृतां मयूखै-
रहमित्येव विभावये भवानीम्।।

OM. I meditate upon *Bhavani,* who is enveloped with the perfections containing 'Animaa-adi/the Anima Siddhi etc. Her complexion is *Aruna*—the dawn like orange and red. Her eyes contain *Karuna*—compassion and holds '*Pasha*'—noose, '*Ankusha*'—goad, '*Bana*'—bows, '*Chapa*'—arrow, in Her hands.

ॐ ऋषिरुवाच।। 1।।

Om The Rishi Said :

चण्डे च निहते दैत्ये मुण्डे च विनिपातिते।
बहुलेषु च सैन्येषु क्षयितेष्वसुरेश्वरः।। 2।।

By killing Chanda and Munda Daityas and destroying of the large army, the Asura king....,

ततः कोपपराधीनचेताः शुम्भः प्रतापवान्।
उद्योगं सर्वसैन्यानां दैत्यानामादिदेश ह।। 3।।

...Shumbha got highly enraged and commanded the whole army battalions of the Daityas to go in for war.

अद्य सर्वबलैर्दैत्याः षडशीतिरुदायुधाः।
कम्बूनां चतुरशीतिर्निर्यान्तु स्वबलैर्वृताः।। 4।।

Today will go eighty-six generals of the '*Udayudha*' battalion of armed forces and eighty-four generals of the '*Kumbu*' armed force....,

कोटिवीर्याणि पञ्चाशदसुराणां कुलानि वै।
शतं कुलानि धौम्राणां निर्गच्छन्तु ममाज्ञया।। 5।।

...and also fifty Asura generals of '*Koti-virya*'—ten million force alongwith hundred Asura generals of '*Dhaumralochan*' army will march ahead by my orders.....,

कालका दौर्हृदा मौर्याः कालकेयास्तथासुराः।
युद्धाय सज्जा निर्यान्तु आज्ञया त्वरिता मम।। 6।।

.....and under my orders, '*Kalaka, Daurhrda, Maurya* and *Kalkeye*' Asuras will march forward immediately towards the great war.

इत्याज्ञाप्यासुरपतिः शुम्भो भैरवशासनः।
निर्जगाम महासैन्य सहस्त्रैर्बहुभिर्वृतः।। 7।।

Having issued such orders, Shumbha—the 'Asurapati'/Lord of Asuras, and being competent, tough and terrible ruler, marched forward and thus attended by thousands of large forces.

आयान्तं चण्डिका दृष्ट्वा तत्सैन्यमतिभीषणम्।
ज्यास्वनैः पूरयामास धरणीगगनान्तरम्।। 8।।

On seeing that highly terrible army marching towards Her, *Chandika* filled the space between the earth and the sky with the twang of Her bow-string.

ततः सिंहो महानादमतीव कृतवान् नृप।
घण्टास्वनेन तन्नादमम्बिका चोपबृंहयत्।। 9।।

O King! Then Her lion made a vehement loud roar, and Ambika created more strength in that roar with the clinging of Her own bell.

धनुर्ज्यासिंहघण्टानां नादापूरितदिङ्मुखा।
निनादैर्भीषणैः काली जिग्ये विस्तारितानना।। 10।।

The noise of Her bow-string, the roar of Her lion and the sound of Her bell and Her terrific roars, filled all the directions with terrible noise. Thus *Kali*, expanded Her mouth widely making the terrific sound.

तं निनादमुपश्रुत्य दैत्यसैन्यैश्चतुर्दिशम्।
देवी सिंहस्तथा काली सरोषैः परिवारिताः।। 11।।

On hearing that roar, all the infuriated Asura contingents surrounded the Devi Chandika, the lion and Kali, on all the four sides.

एतस्मिन्नन्तरे भूप विनाशाय सुरद्विषाम्।
भवायामरसिंहानामतिवीर्यबलान्विताः।। 12।।

At that time, O king, in order to vanquish the foes of the Devas and for their welfare, filled with vigour and strength....,

ब्रह्मेशगुहविष्णूनां तथेन्द्रस्य च शक्तयः।
शरीरेभ्यो विनिष्क्रम्य तद्रूपैश्चण्डिकां ययुः।। 13।।

....She issued forth the Shaktis from the bodies of *Brahma, Isha, Guha-Kartikeya, Vishnu, Indra* and other Devas with forms, they then went before *Chandika.*

यस्य देवस्य यद्रूपं यथाभूषणवाहनम्।
तद्वदेव हि तच्छक्तिरसुरान् योद्धुमाययौ।। 14।।

Whatever was the form of each Deva and whatever was his ornaments and vehicle, in that very form each *Shakti* marched ahead to make fight alongwith Chandika.

हंसयुक्तविमानाग्रे साक्षसूत्रकमण्डलुः।
आयाता ब्रह्मणः शक्तिर्ब्रह्माणी साभिधीयते।। 15।।

Brahma's Shakti was drawn by swans in a heavenly chariot, carrying '*Aksha-sutra*'—rosary and a Kamandalu—pot. She is called Brahmani.

माहेश्वरी वृषारूढा त्रिशूलवरधारिणी।
महाहिवलया प्राप्ता चन्द्ररेखाविभूषणा।। 16।।

Maheshvari arrived, being seated on a bull and holding a fine '*Trishula*'—trident, wearing bracelets of '*Mahanaga/Ahi*'—great cobras and adorned with the '*Chandrarekha*'—crescent on the moon.

कौमारी शक्तिहस्ता च मयूरवरवाहना।
योद्धुमभ्याययौ दैत्यानम्बिका गुहरूपिणी।। 17।।

Kaumari Ambika in the form of '*Guha*'—Kartikeya, holding Shakti missile in Her hand, riding on the best peacock, advanced to attack the 'Daityas'.

तथैव वैष्णवी शक्तिर्गरुडोपरि संस्थिता।
शङ्खचक्रगदाशार्ङ्गखड्गाहस्ताभ्युपाययौ।। 18।।

Likewise the Shakti of Vishnu came, who was seated on '*Garuda*'—eagle, holding *Shankha*—conch; *Gada*—Club; *Sharanga*—bow and *Khadga*—sword in Her hands.

यज्ञवाराहमतुलं रूपं या बिभ्रतो हरेः।
शक्तिः साप्याययौ तत्र वाराहीं बिभ्रती तनुम्।। 19।।

The Shakti of Hari, who took the imcomparable form of a Sacrificial Boar, also approached there in the '*Varahi*'—boar form.

नारसिंही नृसिंहस्य बिभ्रती सदृशं वपुः।
प्राप्ता तत्र सटाक्षेपक्षिप्तनक्षत्रसंहतिः।। 20।।

Narasimhi arrived there, assuming the body like that of *Narasimha*—the Man lion and was bringing down the '*Nakshatras*'—constellation by the toss of Her mane.

वज्रहस्ता तथैवैन्द्री गजराजोपरि स्थिता।
प्राप्ता सहस्रनयना यथा शक्रस्तथैव सा।। 21।।

The thousand eyed *Aindri* arrived, holding a '*Vajra*'—the thunderbolt in hand, was riding on the grand elephant just as '*Shakra*'—the Indra does.

ततः परिवृतस्ताभिरीशानो देवशक्तिभिः ।
हन्यन्तामसुराः शीघ्रं मम प्रीत्याऽऽह चण्डिकाम् ।। 22 ।।

Surrounded by the Shakti of the Devas, then *Ishana—Shiva* said to *Chandika* : 'Let the Asura be killed immediately by You for My gratification'.

ततो देवीशरीरात्तु विनिष्क्रान्तातिभीषणा ।
चण्डिकाशक्तिरत्युग्रा शिवाशतनिनादिनी ।। 23 ।।

Thereupon from the Devi's being sprung forth the Shakti of Chandika, who was most terrific, and extremely fierce. She was yelling like a hundred female jackals.

सा चाह धूम्रजटिलमीशानमपराजिता ।
दूत त्वं गच्छ भगवन् पार्श्वं शुम्भनिशुम्भयोः ।। 24 ।।

That '*Aparajita*'—invincible Shakti said to '*Dhumra-jatila-Ishan-Shiva* of dark coloured matted locks : "O Bhagvan! Go as *Duta*—ambassador to the presence of Shumbha and Nishumbha.

ब्रूहि शुम्भं निशुम्भं च दानवावतिगर्वितौ ।
ये चान्ये दानवास्तत्र युद्धाय समुपस्थिताः ।। 25 ।।

Tell those two proud Danvas—Shumbha and Nishumbha and other Danvas assembled there for battle.

त्रैलोक्यमिन्द्रो लभतां देवाः सन्तु हविर्भुजः ।
यूयं प्रयात पातालं यदि जीवितुमिच्छथ ।। 26 ।।

If you are interested in your life, then you go to the *Patala*—nether world and let Indra obtain the three worlds and let the Devas enjoy the oblations of '*Havi*'—sacrifices.

बलावलेपादथ चेद्भवन्तो युद्धकाङ्क्षिणः ।
तदागच्छत तृप्यन्तु मच्छिवाः पिशितेन वः ।। 27 ।।

If you are very anxious to make the battle, on the basis of the pride of strength, then come on and let my *Shivas* (Yoginis) be satisfied to the full with your raw flesh."

यतो नियुक्तो दौत्येन तया देव्या शिवः स्वयम्।
शिवदूतीति लोकेऽस्मिंस्ततः सा ख्यातिमागता।। 28।।

Since that Devi appointed Shiva himself as 'Duta', thereby She became renowned in this '*Loka*'—world as 'Shivaduti'.

तेऽपि श्रुत्वा वचो देव्याः शर्वाख्यातं महासुराः।
अमर्षापूरिता जग्मुर्यत्र कात्यायनी स्थिता।। 29।।

Those great Asuras also got enraged, on hearing such words as communicated by '*Sharva*'—Shiva. They were filled with great rage and advanced to the place where 'Katyayani' stood.

ततः प्रथममेवाग्रे शरशक्त्यृष्टिवृष्टिभिः।
ववर्षुरुद्धतामर्षास्तां देवीममरारयः।। 30।।

Then in the first instance, the enraged foes of the Devas, poured showers of '*Shara*'—arrows, '*Shakti*' and other 'Rishti' missiles etc. upon the Devi...,

सा च तान् प्रहितान् बाणाञ्छूलशक्तिपरश्वधान्।
चिच्छेद लीलयाऽऽध्मातधनुर्मुक्तैर्महेषुभिः।। 31।।

...then, She in a playful manner cut those '*Bana*', *Shakti* and '*Parshu*'—arrows, missiles and axes with the twang of Her full drawn bow, which were hurled by the *Asuras*.

तस्याग्रतस्तथा काली शूलपातविदारितान्।
खट्वाङ्गपोथितांश्चारीन् कुर्वती व्यचरत्तदा।। 32।।

The Kali, pierced the enemies to pieces and crushed them with her '*Shula*'—spear, '*Khatvanga*', missile bearing a staff carrying the skulls in front of him (Shumbha) and roamed in the battle-field.

कमण्डलुजलाक्षेपहतवीर्यान् हतौजसः।
ब्रह्माणी चाकरोच्छत्रून् येन येन स्म धावति।। 33।।

Wherever *Brahmani* ran, She made the enemies bereft of valour and strength, by sprinkling the water on the enemies from Her *Kamandalu* pot.

माहेश्वरी त्रिशूलेन तथा चक्रेण वैष्णवी।
दैत्याञ्जघान कौमारी तथा शक्त्यातिकोपना।। 34।।

Being in wrath, *Maheshvari* slew the Daityas with *Trishula*—trident; *Vaishanavi* with Her Chakra—discus, Kaumari with Her Shakti—missiles....,

ऐन्द्रीकुलिशपातेन शतशो दैत्यदानवाः।
पेतुर्विदारिताः पृथ्व्यां रुधिरौघप्रवर्षिणः।। 35।।

....*Aindri* with the Shakti of thunderbolt made Daityas and Danavas fell on the earth in hundreds and were torn into pieces, making streams of blood flowing out of them.

तुण्डप्रहारविध्वस्ता दंष्ट्राग्रक्षतवक्षसः।
वाराहमूर्त्या न्यपतंश्चक्रेण च विदारिताः।। 36।।

Varaha-Murti Shakti with blows of Her pig snout, wounded the Daityas in their chests, by Her foretusk and torn by Her '*Chakra*'—discus and felled them down.

नखैर्विदारितांश्चान्यान् भक्षयन्ती महासुरान्।
नारसिंही चचाराजौ नादापूर्णदिगम्बरा।। 37।।

Narasimhi roamed about in the battle-field making all the quarters and sky filled with the *Simhanada*—'Lion's roar'. She devoured the great Asuras by piercing them by Her claws.

चण्डाट्टहासैरसुराः शिवदूत्यभिदूषिताः।
पेतुः पृथिव्यां पतितांस्तांश्चखादाथ सा तदा।। 38।।

Many of the Asuras fell down on the earth, when being demoralised by the fierce laughter of *Shivaduti*, and ate them up who had fallen down, then...,

इति मातृगणं क्रुद्धं मर्दयन्तं महासुरान्।
दृष्ट्वाभ्युपायैर्विविधैर्नेशुर्देवारिसैनिकाः।। 39।।

....the army contingents of the Deva's foes took to their heels, when they witnessed the infuriated '*Matraganas*'—host of Mothers crushing the great Asuras by various means.

पलायनपरान् दृष्ट्वा दैत्यान् मातृगणार्दितान्।
योद्धुमभ्याययौ क्रुद्धो रक्तबीजो महासुरः।। 40।।

Raktabija—the great Asura got enraged, when he saw the Daitya suppressed by the 'Matraganas' and fleeing. He came forward to fight in violent anger.

रक्तबिन्दुर्यदा भूमौ पतत्यस्य शरीरतः।
समुत्पतति मेदिन्यां तत्प्रमाणस्तदासुरः।। 41।।

Whenever a drop of blood fell on the ground from his body, at that very moment was born a new great Asura of the same strength, from the earth.

युयुधे स गदापाणिरिन्द्रशक्त्या महासुरः।
ततश्चैन्द्री स्ववज्रेण रक्तबीजमताडयत्।। 42।।

When that great Asura fought with Shakti of Indra, taking '*Gada*'—club in his hand, then *Aindri* also struck *Raktabija* with Her own '*Vajra*'—thunderbolt.

कुलिशेनाहतस्याशु बहु सुस्राव शोणितम्।
समुत्तस्थुस्ततो योधास्तद्रूपास्तत्पराक्रमाः।। 43।।

Thus being wounded by the thunderbolt; blood flowed quickly and profusely from his body. From this blood sprung the valourous combatants of his form and strength.

यावन्तः पतितास्तस्य शरीराद्रक्तबिन्दवः।
तावन्तः पुरुषा जातास्तद्वीर्यबलविक्रमाः।। 44।।

As many as drops of blood fell from his body down, so many persons came into existence, of the same courage, strength and valour as he was.

ते चापि युयुधुस्तत्र पुरुषा रक्तसम्भवाः।
समं मातृभिरत्युग्रशस्त्रपातातिभीषणम्।। 45।।

Those persons, who sprung from his blood dreadfully fought

with the *Matris*—the manifestation of Divine Mothers in the battle-field, hurling the very dreadful and formidable missiles.

पुनश्च वज्रपातेन क्षतमस्य शिरो यदा।
ववाह रक्तं पुरुषास्ततो जाताः सहस्रशः।। 46।।

Again, his head was hit by the fall of *Vajra*—thunderbolt, his blood profusely flowed and person in thousands were born out of that blood.

वैष्णवी समरे चैनं चक्रेणाभिजघान ह।
गदया ताडयामास ऐन्द्री तमसुरेश्वरम्।। 47।।

'Vaishnavi Shakti' struck him with Her Chakra—discus in the battle-field and Aindri hit that Lord of Asuras with Her '*Gada*'—club.

वैष्णवीचक्रभिन्नस्य रुधिरस्रावसम्भवैः।
सहस्रशो जगद्व्याप्तं तत्प्रमाणैर्महासुरैः।। 48।।

The world was pervaded with the thousands of great Asuras of the same strength and stature of that great Asura's blood that flowed from him when he was hit by the *Chakra*—discus of Vaishnavi.

शक्त्या जघान कौमारी वाराही च तथासिना।
माहेश्वरी त्रिशूलेन रक्तबीजं महासुरम्।। 49।।

'*Kumari*' with her Shakti—missiles, '*Varahi*' with Her 'Asi'—sword, '*Maheshvari*' with *Trishula*—trident struck '*Raktabija*'—the great Asura...,

स चापि गदया दैत्यः सर्वा एवाहनत् पृथक्।
मातृः कोपसमाविष्टो रक्तबीजो महासुरः।। 50।।

and Raktabija the Daitya also filled with wrath, struck severally one and all the '*Matris*'—Mothers with his club.

तस्याहतस्य बहुधा शक्तिशूलादिभिर्भुवि।
पपात यो वै रक्तौघस्तेनासञ्छतशोऽसुराः।। 51।।

On receiving the multiple wounds from the '*Shaktis*' and '*Shulas*'—spears and other weapons, a stream of blood fell on the earth, thus generating the hundreds of Asuras into existence.

तैश्चासुरासृक्सम्भूतैरसुरैः सकलं जगत्।
व्याप्तमासीत्ततो देवा भयमाजग्मुरुत्तमम्।। 52।।

The whole world got pervaded by the Asuras, born from the blood of Raktabija and the Devas got dejected because of terror.

तान् विषण्णान् सुरान् दृष्ट्वा चण्डिका प्राह सत्वरा।
उवाच कालीं चामुण्डे विस्तीर्णं वदनं कुरु।। 53।।

Chandika laughed at seeing the plight of the Devas and spoke immediately to Kali : "O Chamunda, open out your mouth wide...,

मच्छस्त्रपातसम्भूतान् रक्तबिन्दून्महासुरान्।
रक्तबिन्दोः प्रतीच्छ त्वं वक्त्रेणानेन वेगिना।। 54।।

....and consume each drop of blood quickly and also the great Asuras born of the drops of that blood of (Raktabija), generated by the hit of the weapons.

भक्षयन्ती चर रणे तदुत्पन्नान्महासुरान्।
एवमेष क्षयं दैत्यः क्षीणरक्तो गमिष्यति।। 55।।

You roam about in the battle-field, devouring the great Asuras born from him. Thus this Daitya will be destroyed, with his blood emptied.

भक्ष्यमाणास्त्वया चोग्रा न चोत्पत्स्यन्ति चापरे।
इत्युक्त्वा तां ततो देवी शूलेनाभिजघान तम्।। 56।।

When you will devour all those dreadful Daityas, then other fierce Asuras will not be born. Having spoken such words, the Devi hit him (Raktabija) with Her '*Shula*'—spear.

मुखेन काली जगृहे रक्तबीजस्य शोणितम्।
ततोऽसावाजघानाथ गदया तत्र चण्डिकाम्।। 57।।

Kali consumed the whole blood of Raktabija with Her mouth, thereupon he struck *Chandika* with his club...,

न चास्या वेदनां चक्रे गदापातोऽल्पिकामपि।
तस्याहतस्य देहात्तु बहु सुस्राव शोणितम्।। 58।।

....but that blow of the club did not make any slightest pain. And from his trickle body flowed blood profusely..,

यतस्ततस्तद्वक्त्रेण चामुण्डा सम्प्रतीच्छति।
मुखे समुद्गता येऽस्या रक्तपातान्महासुराः।। 59।।

...which was swallowed by *Chamunda* in Her mouth alongwith those great Asuras, who sprang from the flow of blood of that great Asura...

तांश्चखादाथ चामुण्डा पपौ तस्य च शोणितम्।
देवी शूलेन वज्रेण बाणैरसिभिर्ऋष्टिभिः।। 60।।

...and all were devoured by Her. She drank the blood of (Raktabija) and then the Devi killed him with '*Shula*'—dart, '*Vajra*—thunderbolt, '*Bana*-arrows, '*Asi*'—sword and '*Rishti*' missile.

जघान रक्तबीजं तं चामुण्डापीतशोणितम्।
स पपात महीपृष्ठे शस्त्रसङ्घसमाहतः।। 61।।

When Chamunda went on drinking the blood of Raktabija and felling him down by blowing him with a multitude of weapons...,

नीरक्तश्च महीपाल रक्तबीजो महासुरः।
ततस्ते हर्षमतुलमवापुस्त्रिदशा नृप।। 62।।

...and that made Raktabija the great Asura bloodless. O King! Thereupon the Devas attained great joy.

तेषां मातृगणो जातो ननर्तासृङ्मदोद्धतः।। ॐ।। 63।।

The multitude of 'Matris'—the Divine Mothers being intoxicated with blood drunk from the oozing Daityas, danced. Om.

इति श्रीमार्कण्डेयपुराणे सावर्णिके मन्वन्तरे देवीमाहात्म्ये रक्तबीजवधो नामाष्टमोऽध्याय: ।। 8 ।।

The eighth chapter entitled *'The Slaying of Raktabija'* of the Devi Mahatamya in the Markandeya Purana, during the time span of Savarni—the Manu is concluded.

उवाच 1, अर्धश्श्लोक: 1, श्लोका: 61, एवम् 63, एवमादित: 502 ।।

Narration Mantras 1, half Shloka 1, Shloka 61 total 63, in all 502 Mantras.

नवमोऽध्यायः

NINTH CHAPTER

निशुम्भ-वध

Slaying of Nishumbha

ध्यानम्

Meditation

ॐ बन्धूककाञ्चननिभं रुचिराक्षमालां
पाशाङ्कुशौ च वरदां निजबाहुदण्डैः।
बिभ्राणमिन्दुशकलाभरणं त्रिनेत्र-
मर्धाम्बिकेशमनिशं वपुराश्रयामि ।।

I make obeisance to '*Ardha-ambikesh*'/*Ardha-Nareshwara* constantly. His golden complexion is that of '*Bandhuka*'—flower and colour mixed red and yellow'. He holds the beautiful '*Akshamala*'—rosary of Aksha-beads, '*Pasha*'—noose, '*Ankusha*'—goad and '*Varda*'—auspicious Mudra. He is three eyed and the half-moon is His ornament.

ॐ राजोवाच ।। 1 ।।

Om the King Said :

विचित्रमिदमाख्यातं भगवन् भवता मम।
देव्याश्चरितमाहात्म्यं रक्तबीजवधाश्रितम् ।। 2 ।।

"O Bhagvan, you have related to me, the wonderful Mahatmya of *Devi-Charitam* with regard to the slaying of 'Rakta-bija'.

भूयश्चेच्छाम्यहं श्रोतुं रक्तबीजे निपातिते।
चकार शुम्भो यत्कर्म निशुम्भश्चातिकोपनः ।। 3 ।।

I would like listening to, what the very angry *Shumbha* and *Nishumbha* did after Raktabija was killed".

ऋषिरुवाच।। 4।।

The Rishi Said :

चकार कोपमतुलं रक्तबीजे निपातिते।
शुम्भासुरो निशुम्भश्च हतेष्वन्येषु चाहवे।। 5।।

"There was no limit in the wrath of Shumbha and Nishumbha, after Raktabija was slain and other Asuras got killed in the battle.

हन्यमानं महासैन्यं विलोक्यामर्षमुद्वहन्।
अभ्यधावन्निशुम्भोऽथ मुख्ययासुरसेनया।। 6।।

Nishumbha got enraged and rushed forward with the chief of the Asura forces, on seeing his great army slaughtered.

तस्याग्रतस्तथा पृष्ठे पार्श्वयोश्च महासुराः।
संदष्टौष्ठपुटाः क्रुद्धा हन्तुं देवीमुपाययुः।। 7।।

The great Asuras were infront of him, behind him and on both sides of him, who got very enraged and were biting their lips and they marched ahead to slay the Devi.

आजगाम महावीर्यः शुम्भोऽपि स्वबलैर्वृतः।
निहन्तुं चण्डिकां कोपात्कृत्वा युद्धं तु मातृभिः।। 8।।

Mahavirya—the great valorous Shumbha also came forward alongwith his own troops to slay Chandika, after fighting with the '*Matris*'—the Divine Mothers.

ततो युद्धमतीवासीद्देव्या शुम्भनिशुम्भयोः।
शरवर्षमतीवोग्रं मेघयोरिव वर्षतोः।। 9।।

Then a great combat took place between the Devi and Shumbha-Nishumbha. Both of them showered clouds of arrows on Her, like thunder.

चिच्छेदास्ताञ्छरांस्ताभ्यां चण्डिका स्वशरोत्करैः।
ताडयामास चाङ्गेषु शस्त्रौघैरसुरेश्वरौ।। 10।।

Chandika pierced the arrows, shot by the two Asuras quickly with Her numerous arrows. She smote and hit those two lords of Asuras on their limbs with Her mass of weapons.

निशुम्भो निशितं खड्गं चर्म चादाय सुप्रभम्।
अताडयन्मूर्ध्नि सिंहं देव्या वाहनमुत्तमम्।। 11।।

Nishumbha struck the lion—vehicle of the Devi on the head, while holding a sharp sword and a shining shield.

ताडिते वाहने देवी क्षुरप्रेणासिमुत्तमम्।
निशुम्भस्याशु चिच्छेद चर्म चाप्यष्टचन्द्रकम्।। 12।।

On being lion struck, which is the vehicle of the Devi, She quickly cut off Nishumbha's superb sword with a sharp-edged arrow and also his shield on which were figured the '*Ashtachandrakam*'—decoration of eight moons.

छिन्ने चर्मणि खड्गे च शक्तिं चिक्षेप सोऽसुरः।
तामप्यस्य द्विधा चक्रे चक्रेणाभिमुखागताम्।। 13।।

When his shield was torn off and his sword was broken, then that Asura hurled the *Shakti*—missile; as the missile advanced towards the Devi, that too was split into two by Her *Chakra*—discus.

कोपाध्मातो निशुम्भोऽथ शूलं जग्राह दानवः।
आयातं मुष्टिपातेन देवी तच्चाप्यचूर्णयत्।। 14।।

Then *Nishumbha*—the *Danava* got swollen up with wrath, holding a '*Shula*'/dart, and when it approached near the Devi, She then crushed it with a blow of Her fist.

आविध्याथ गदां सोऽपि चिक्षेप चण्डिकां प्रति।
सापि देव्या त्रिशूलेन भिन्ना भस्मत्वमागता।। 15।।

Then he waved his *Gada*—club; and flung/threw it against Chandika, but it also was turned into ashes by the '*Trishula*'—trident of the Devi.

ततः परशुहस्तं तमायान्तं दैत्यपुङ्गवम्।
आहत्य देवी बाणौघैरपातयत भूतले।। 16।।

Then the Devi attacked the '*Daitya-pungavam*'—heroic Danava, who was advancing with a '*Parshu*'/axe in hand, and laid him low on the ground, with the arrows.

तस्मिन्निपतिते भूमौ निशुम्भे भीमविक्रमे।
भ्रातर्यतीव संक्रुद्धः प्रययौ हन्तुमम्बिकाम्।। 17।।

(Shumbha) got extremely infuriated and rushed ahead to slay Ambika, when he saw his brother Nishumbha of terrific strength, fallen on the ground...,

स रथस्थस्तथात्युच्चैर्गृहीतपरमायुधैः।
भुजैरष्टाभिरतुलैर्व्याप्याशेषं बभौ नभः।। 18।।

...he shone in the entire space, by pervading the sky; while standing on his chariot and holding all the excellent weapons in his incomparable eight arms.

तमायान्तं समालोक्य देवी शङ्खमवादयत्।
ज्याशब्दं चापि धनुषश्चकारातिव दुःसहम्।। 19।।

On seeing him approaching, the Devi blew Her '*Shankha*'/ conch and also made a twang of Her bow-string, which was extremely unbearable...,

पूरयामास ककुभो निजघण्टास्वनेन च।
समस्तदैत्यसैन्यानां तेजोवधविधायिना।। 20।।

...and filled all the directions with the ringing of Her bell, which destroyed the '*tejas*'—excellent strength of the army of the Daityas.

ततः सिंहो महानादैस्त्याजितेभमहामदैः।
पूरयामास गगनं गां तथैव दिशो दश।। 21।।

Then the lion's loud roar filled the earth and the ten quarters of the sky, which made the great elephants to give up their violent roars...

ततः काली समुत्पत्य गगनं क्ष्मामताडयत्।
कराभ्यां तन्निनादेन प्राक्स्वनास्ते तिरोहिताः।।22।।

...Kali then sprang upwards in the sky and hit the earth with both of Her hands This noise thus made all the previous sounds dull.

अट्टाट्टहासमशिवं शिवदूती चकार ह।
तैः शब्दैरसुरास्त्रेसुः शुम्भः कोपं परं ययौ ।। 23 ।।

Shivaduti made a maligning loud laughter at the Asuras and they got frightened by those sounds, but Shumbha got highly enraged.

दुरात्मंस्तिष्ठ तिष्ठेति व्याजहाराम्बिका यदा।
तदा जयेत्यभिहितं देवैराकाशसंस्थितैः ।। 24 ।।

As Ambika addressed to Shumbha : 'O, evil-natured one, stop, stop', thus the Devas stationed in the sky cheered up with the words : 'Be victorious'!

शुम्भेनागत्य या शक्तिर्मुक्ता ज्वालातिभीषणा।
आयान्ती वह्निकूटाभा सा निरस्ता महोल्कया ।। 25 ।।

Shumbha then targetted the Shakti—missile upon the Devi,—which was highly inflamable and shining like a mass of fire, but She—the Devi made it ineffective with Her '*Ulka*'—great fine-ball.

सिंहनादेन शुम्भस्य व्याप्तं लोकत्रयान्तरम्।
निर्घातनिःस्वनो घोरो जितवानवनीपते ।। 26 ।।

O king, at that time all the three worlds got pervaded by the lion-like roar of Shumbha. Its echo created dreadful thunder-clap, which silenced all other sounds.

शुम्भमुक्ताञ्छरान्देवी शुम्भस्तत्प्रहिताञ्छरान्।
चिच्छेद स्वशरैरुग्रैः शतशोऽथ सहस्रशः ।। 27 ।।

The Devi split the arrows shot by Shumbha and in return Shumbha also split the arrows shot by Her and pierced it in hundreds and thousands pieces.

ततः सा चण्डिका क्रुद्धा शूलेनाभिजघान तम्।
स तदाभिहतो भूमौ मूर्च्छितो निपपात ह ।। 28 ।।

She then got highly enraged and smote him with a 'Shula'/ dart. Thus wounded, he became unconscious and fell down on the ground.

ततो निशुम्भः सम्प्राप्य चेतनामात्तकार्मुकः।
आजघान शरैर्देवीं कालीं केसरिणं तथा।। 29।।

Then Nishumbha regained consciousness, siezed his bow and struck the Devi, Kali and the *Kesari*/lion with arrows.

पुनश्च कृत्वा बाहूनामयुतं दनुजेश्वरः।
चक्रायुधेन दितिजश्छादयामास चण्डिकाम्।। 30।।

Then the Lord of *Danujas*/Rakshasas putting forth great number of arms, covered Chandika with numberless discs.

ततो भगवती क्रुद्धा दुर्गा दुर्गार्तिनाशिनी।
चिच्छेद तानि चक्राणि स्वशरैः सायकांश्च तान्।। 31।।

Thus Durga Bhagavati, the destroyer of difficulties and afflictions, became enraged and pierced those *'Chakras'*/ discus and *'Saykas'*—the arrow fans with Her own *Sharas*/ arrows.

ततो निशुम्भो वेगेन गदामादाय चण्डिकाम्।
अभ्यधावत वै हन्तुं दैत्यसेनासमावृतः।। 32।।

Thereupon, Nishumbha, surrounded by the Daitya army, swiftly lifed his club, rushed at Chandika, to kill Her.

तस्यापतत एवाशु गदां चिच्छेद चण्डिका।
खड्गेन शितधारेण स च शूलं समाददे।। 33।।

As he was just approaching at Her, She with Her sharp edged sword pierced his club, he then took hold of a *'Shula'*—dart.

शूलहस्तं समायान्तं निशुम्भममरार्दनम्।
हृदि विव्याध शूलेन वेगाविद्धेन चण्डिका।। 34।।

Chandika on seeing Shumbha—the afflictor of the Devas advancing towards Her with a Shula/dart in his hand, She then pierced him in the heart with a swiftly hurled 'Shula'/ dart.

भिन्नस्य तस्य शूलेन हृदयान्निःसृतोऽपरः।
महाबलो महावीर्यस्तिष्ठेति पुरुषो वदन्।। 35।।

From his pierced heart, hit by the Shula—dart, instantly issued forth another person of great strength and great valour asking the Devi to 'stop' there.

तस्य निष्क्रामतो देवी प्रहस्य स्वनवत्ततः।
शिरश्चिच्छेद खड्गेन ततोऽसावपतद्भुवि।। 36।।

Then the Devi laughed at the issued forth person and severed him of his head, with Her sword. He then fell on the ground.

ततः सिंहश्चखादोग्रं दंष्ट्राक्षुण्णशिरोधरान्।
असुरांस्तांस्तथा काली शिवदूती तथापरान्।। 37।।

The lion then killed those Asuras, whose necks were crushed with his fierce teeth, thereupon Kali and Shivaduti killed others.

कौमारीशक्तिनिर्भिन्नाः केचिन्नेशुर्महासुराः।
ब्रह्माणीमन्त्रपूतेन तोयेनान्ये निराकृताः।। 38।।

Many of the great Asuras got perished, when being pierced through by the *Kaumari Shakti*—missile and others were repulsed/driven back by the sanctified water purified by Brahmani.

माहेश्वरीत्रिशूलेन भिन्नाः पेतुस्तथापरे।
वाराहीतुण्डघातेन केचिच्चूर्णीकृता भुवि।। 39।।

Pierced by the '*Trishula*'—trident of Maheshvari, many fell down. Some were reduced to powder on the ground by the blows from the *Varahi tunda*—the tusk snout of the Varahi.

खण्डं खण्डं च चक्रेण वैष्णव्या दानवाः कृताः।
वज्रेण चैन्द्रीहस्ताग्रविमुक्तेन तथापरे।। 40।।

Vaishnavi also cut many Danavas into pieces by Her *Chakra*—discus and others by the *Vajra*—the thunderbolt discharged from the palm of *Aindri*.

केचिद्विनेशुरसुराः केचिन्नष्टा महाहवात्।
भक्षिताश्चापरे कालीशिवदूतीमृगाधिपैः।। ॐ ।।41।।

Some of the Asuras perished, some fled from the battle-field and others were devoured by Kali, Shivaduti and '*Mrigaddhipa*'—the vehicle lion of the Devi.

इति श्रीमार्कण्डेयपुराणे सावर्णिके मन्वन्तरे देवीमाहात्म्ये निशुम्भवधो नाम नवमोऽध्यायः।। 9।।

The ninth chapter entitled 'The slaying of *Nishumbha*' in the Devi Mahatyma during the time span of Savarni—the Manu, occuring in the Markandeya Purana in concluded.

उवाच, 2, श्लोकाः 39, एवम् 41, एवमादितः 543।।

Narration 2, Shlokas 39, concluded 41 Shlokas in all 543 Shlokas

दशमोऽध्यायः

TENTH CHAPTER

शुम्भ-वध

Slaying of Shmbha

ध्यानम्

Meditation

ॐ उत्तप्तहेमरुचिरां रविचन्द्रवह्नि-
नेत्रां धनुश्शरयुताङ्कुशपाशशूलम्।
रम्यैर्भुजैश्च दधतीं शिवशक्तिरूपां
कामेश्वरीं हृदि भजामि धृतेन्दुलेखाम्।।

I meditate upon *Shiva-Shakti-Rupa-Kameshvari* in my heart. She is manifest in beautiful looks like that of heated gold. '*Ravi-Chandra-Vahni*'—the sun, moon and fire are Her three eyes. She holds '*Dhanusha-Shara-Ankusha-Pasha-Shulas*' / the bow, arrow, goad, noose and spear in Her beautiful hands.

ॐ ऋषिरुवाच।। 1।।

Om Rishi Said :

निशुम्भं निहतं दृष्ट्वा भ्रातरं प्राणसम्मितम्।
हन्यमानं बलं चैव शुम्भः क्रुद्धोऽब्रवीद्वचः।। 2।।

Seeing his dear brother Nishumbha, who was so dear to him as his own life, slain and his army being perished, Shumbha angrily said :

बलावलेपादुष्टे त्वं मा दुर्गे गर्वमावह।
अन्यासां बलमाश्रित्य युद्धयसे यातिमानिनी।। 3।।

"O Dushte Durge! Wicked Durga! Do not exhibit your pride as being puffed up with the pride of valour. You have become exceedingly haughty, but resorting to the strength of other women".

देव्युवाच।। 4।।

The Devi Said :

एकैवाहं जगत्यत्र द्वितीया का ममापरा।
पश्यैता दुष्ट मय्येव विशन्त्यो मद्विभूतयः।। 5।।

"I am quite alone in this world, who else is there except myself". "See; O *Dushta*—vile one! These are all My *Vibhutis*—manifestations of powers and entering into my Ownself".

ततः समस्तास्ता देव्यो ब्रह्माणीप्रमुखा लयम्।
तस्या देव्यास्तनौ जग्मुरेकैवासीत्तदाम्बिका।। 6।।

Then all those Devis, Brahmani and the rest, were absorbed in the body of the Devi, then alone Ambika remained.

देव्युवाच।। 7।।

The Devi Said :

अहं विभूत्या बहुभिरिह रूपैर्यदास्थिता।
तत्संहृतं मयैकैव तिष्ठाम्याजौ स्थिरो भव।। 8।।

"I had manifested here in numerous forms by My own Vibhuti—super creative power, then those have been withdrawn by Me and now I hereby stand alone, be ready to fight."

ऋषिरुवाच।। 9।।

The Rishi Said :

ततः प्रववृते युद्धं देव्याः शुम्भस्य चोभयोः।
पश्यतां सर्वदेवानामसुराणां च दारुणम्।। 10।।

"Then a fierceful battle took place between both Shumbha and the Devi, while all the Devas and Asuras looked on it.

शरवर्षैः शितैः शस्त्रैस्तथास्त्रैश्चैव दारुणैः ।
तयोर्युद्धमभूद्भूयः सर्वलोकभयङ्करम् ।। 11 ।।

All the worlds got frightened when the fight between them started again with showering of arrows, with sharp weapons and frightful missiles.

दिव्यान्यस्त्राणि शतशो मुमुचे यान्यथाम्बिका ।
बभञ्ज तानि दैत्येन्द्रस्तत्प्रतीघातकर्तृभिः ।। 12 ।।

All those divine missiles discharged by Ambika in hundreds were all repulsed by the *Daityendra*/Shumbha with anti-missile weapons.

मुक्तानि तेन चास्त्राणि दिव्यानि परमेश्वरी ।
बभञ्ज लीलयैवोग्रहुङ्कारोच्चारणादिभिः ।। 13 ।।

Parmeshvari—the Supreme Sovereign Devi also playfully broke the excellent divine missiles discharged by him, with the fierce sound of '*Hum*' and similar shouts.

ततः शरशतैर्देवीमाच्छादयत सोऽसुरः ।
सापि तत्कुपिता देवी धनुश्चिच्छेद चेषुभिः ।। 14 ।।

That Asura enveloped the Devi with hundreds of arrows; in return, the wrathful Devi also split his bow with Her arrows.

छिन्ने धनुषि दैत्येन्द्रस्तथा शक्तिमथाददे ।
चिच्छेद देवी चक्रेण तामप्यस्य करे स्थिताम् ।। 15 ।।

On being the bow pierced, the *Daitendra*/lord of the Anti divine forces *Shumbha* took up the Shakti—missile. The Devi (in return) split that, even it was in his hand.

ततः खड्गमुपादाय शतचन्द्रं च भानुमत् ।
अभ्यधावत्तदा देवीं दैत्यानामधिपेश्वरः ।। 16 ।।

Then the supreme lord of the *Daityas*—Shumbha took his bright sword which was like the Sun and the shield was bearing the images of a hundred Moons, rushed at the Devi at that time.

तस्यापतत एवाशु खड्गं चिच्छेद चण्डिका।
धनुर्मुक्तैः शितैर्बाणैश्चर्म चार्ककरामलम्।। 17।।

Chandika pierced his sword with sharp arrows, and also his shield which was as bright as the solar rays, as he rushed forward, he was shot by the Devi from Her bow....

हताश्वः स तदा दैत्यश्छिन्नधन्वा विसारथिः।
जग्राह मुद्गरं घोरमम्बिकानिधनोद्यतः।। 18।।

Then his horse and charioteer was slain, his bow was broken and then the Daitya took up his '*Mudgaram*'—terrible mace, and became ready to kill Ambika.

चिच्छेदापततस्तस्य मुद्गरं निशितैः शरैः।
तथापि सोऽभ्यधावत्तां मुष्टिमुद्यम्य वेगवान्।। 19।।

Seeing the mace reshuing towards Her, She split it with Her sharp arrows. Even then, he rushed swiftly, raising his fist towards Her.

स मुष्टिं पातयामास हृदये दैत्यपुङ्गवः।
देव्यास्तं चापि सा देवी तलेनोरस्यताडयत्।। 20।।

That '*Daitya pungavah*'—king Shumbha forced his fist down on the heart of the Devi and the Devi also smote him on his chest with Her palms.

तलप्रहाराभिहतो निपपात महीतले।
स दैत्यराजः सहसा पुनरेव तथोत्थितः।। 21।।

That *Daityaraja*—Shumbha fell down on the earth, when he was wounded by the blow of Her palm, but he rose up again immediately.

उत्पत्य च प्रगृह्योच्चैर्देवीं गगनमास्थितः।
तत्रापि सा निराधारा युयुधे तेन चण्डिका।। 22।।

Then he sprang up and siezed the Devi and stood mounted up in the sky. There also Chandika fought with him lonely without any support.

नियुद्धं खे तदा दैत्यश्चण्डिका च परस्परम्।
चक्रतुः प्रथमं सिद्धमुनिविस्मयकारकम्।। 23।।

Then the Daitya and Chandika fought with each other in the sky, as it had never been before. It brought surprise to the *Siddhas*—the perfect sages and *Munis*—the celebrated ascetics.

ततो नियुद्धं सुचिरं कृत्वा तेनाम्बिका सह।
उत्पात्य भ्रामयामास चिक्षेप धरणीतले।। 24।।

Ambika had a close fight with him for a pretty long time and then lifted him up, whirled him around and threw him down on the earth.

स क्षिप्तो धरणीं प्राप्य मुष्टिमुद्यम्य वेगितः।
अभ्यधावत दुष्टात्मा चण्डिकानिधनेच्छया।। 25।।

Flung thus that evil-natured reached the earth and then raised his fist. He swiftly rushed ahead with a will to kill Chandika.

तमायान्तं ततो देवी सर्वदैत्यजनेश्वरम्।
जगत्यां पातयामास भित्त्वा शूलेन वक्षसि।। 26।।

Seeing the supreme lord of Daityas approaching Her, the Devi pierced him on his chest, with a '*Shula*'—dart, and threw him down on the earth.

स गतासुः पपातोर्व्यां देवीशूलाग्रविक्षतः।
चालयन् सकलां पृथ्वीं साब्धिद्वीपां सपर्वताम्।। 27।।

He fell down dead lifeless, when got pierced by the pointed '*Shula*'—the dart of the Devi. The whole earth was shaken with its seas, islands and mountains.

ततः प्रसन्नमखिलं हते तस्मिन् दुरात्मनि।
जगत्स्वास्थ्यमतीवाप निर्मलं चाभवन्नभः।। 28।।

On being that *Duratman*—anti divine Shumbha slain, the whole world heaved a sigh of relief, regained perfect peace and the sky grew clear.

उत्पातमेघाः सोल्का ये प्रागासंस्ते शमं ययुः।
सरितो मार्गवाहिन्यस्तथासंस्तत्र पातिते।। 29।।

Flaming clouds and the *'Ulkas'*/falling stars-meteors that were being witnessed before, became tranquil and subsided. The rivers kept within their courses when that (Shumbha) was killed there.

ततो देवगणाः सर्वे हर्षनिर्भरमानसाः।
बभूवुर्निहते तस्मिन् गन्धर्वा ललितं जगुः।। 30।।

When he had been slain, then all the Devas attained a great joy in their minds and the *Gandharvas*—celestial singers sang sweetly.

अवादयंस्तथैवान्ये ननृतुश्चाप्सरोगणाः।
ववुः पुण्यास्तथा वाताः सुप्रभोऽभूद्दिवाकरः।। 31।।

Others played sweet tunes, and *Apsaras*/the nymph folk danced. Likewise the favourable winds blew and the Sun shone very brilliantly.

जज्वलुश्चाग्नयःशान्ताः शान्ता दिग्जनितस्वनाः।। ॐ।। 32।।

The sacred Fire again inflammed and blazed. The strange sounds that had risen in different quartess, became tranquil".

इति श्रीमार्कण्डेयपुराणे सावर्णिके मन्वन्तरे देवीमाहात्म्ये
शुम्भवधो नाम दशमोऽध्यायः।। 10।।

The tenth chapter entitled 'The slaying of *Shumbha*' in the Devi Mahatmya during the lifetime of Savarni—the Manu, occuring in the Markandeya Purana is concluded.

उवाच 4, अर्धश्लोकः 1, श्लोकाः 27, एवम् 32, एवमादितः 575।।

Narration 4, half Shloka, 1 Shlokas 27, total 32, in all 575 Shlokas.

एकादशोऽध्यायः

ELEVENTH CHAPTER

देवताओं द्वारा देवी की स्तुति तथा देवी द्वारा देवताओं को वरदान

(Laudation by the Devas to Devi Narayani and Bestowing upon them with Boons)

ध्यानम्

Meditation

ॐ बालरविद्युतिमिन्दुकिरीटां तुङ्गकुचां नयनत्रययुक्ताम्।
स्मेरमुखीं वरदाङ्कुशपाशाभीतिकरां प्रभजे भुवनेशीम्।।

OM. I meditate upon Bhuvaneshvari, whose radiance is that of the early mornign sun, wearing the crown of the moon on Her head. She has three eyes and with Her breasts up. Her face is ever-smiling and holds '*Varda*'—missiles, '*Ankusha*'—goad, '*Pasha*'—noose and '*Abhaya-mudra*' in Her hands.

ॐ ऋषिरुवाच।। 1।।

Om Rishi Said :

देव्या हते तत्र महासुरेन्द्रे
सेन्द्राः सुरा वह्निपुरोगमास्ताम्।
कात्यायनीं तुष्टुवुरिष्टलाभाद्
विकाशिवक्त्राब्ज विकाशिताशाः।। 2।।

The great lord of Asuras being slain by the Devi, Indra and other Devas led by Agni offered their '*Stuti*'—laudation of the *Devi Katyayani*. Since their objects were fulfilled and their cheerful faces were illumining all the quarters.

देवि प्रपन्नार्तिहरे प्रसीद
प्रसीद मातर्जगतोऽखिलस्य।
प्रसीद विश्वेश्वरि पाहि विश्वं
त्वमीश्वरी देवि चराचरस्य।। 3।।

O Devi! Be gracious, You remove the sufferings'. Be auspicious, O Mother of the entire world! You be pleased and protect the universe! O *Vishveshvari*—the sovereign supreme! You are O Devi, verily, the *Ishvari*—the ruler of all what is animate and inanimate!

आधारभूता जगतस्त्वमेका
महीस्वरूपेण यतः स्थितासि।
अपां स्वरूपस्थितया त्वयैत-
दाप्यायते कृत्स्नमलङ्घ्यवीर्ये।। 4।।

You are the only foundation of this world, because You exist in the form of 'Mahi'—the earth. By You alone, this universe has the feeling of satisfaction, as You exist in the shape of water. O Devi, You are of tremendous valour!

त्वं वैष्णवी शक्तिरनन्तवीर्या
विश्वस्य बीजं परमासि माया।
सम्मोहितं देवि समस्तमेतत्
त्वं वै प्रसन्ना भुवि मुक्तिहेतुः।। 5।।

You are the *Vaishnavi Shakti*—the power of Vishnu and have the infinite strength. You are the seed of the Universe and the Primordial Maya. By You alone, this whole existence has been put into an illusion. O Devi, If You become gracious, You become the cause of 'Mukti'—final beatitude of this world!

विद्याः समस्तास्तव देवि भेदाः
स्त्रियः समस्ताः सकला जगत्सु।
त्वयैकया पूरितमम्बयैतत्
का ते स्तुतिः स्तव्यपरा परोक्तिः।। 6।।

O Devi, all the branches of knowledge are Your aspects, so are all women in the world. O Ambika—the Universal Mother, by You alone this universe is enveloped. What praise thus can be for You in the nature of being '*Paravak*'—transcendent speech and beyond the words of Stuti.

सर्वभूता यदा देवी स्वर्गमुक्तिप्रदायिनी।
त्वं स्तुता स्तुतये का वा भवन्तु परमोक्तयः ।। 7 ।।

O Devi, what words are left, however excellent be the praise to You, when You have been lauded as the embodiment of all beings. You are the bestower of '*Svarga*'—heavenly enjoyment and '*Mukti*'—liberation!

सर्वस्य बुद्धिरूपेण जनस्य हृदि संस्थिते।
स्वर्गापवर्गदे देवि नारायणि नमोऽस्तु ते।। 8।।

Namaskar be to You O Devi *Narayani*! O You abide in the form of intellct in the hearts of all the beings and You bestow '*Svarga-apavarga*'—both higher enjoyment and final liberation!

कलाकाष्ठादिरूपेण परिणामप्रदायिनि।
विश्वस्योपरतौ शक्ते नारायणि नमोऽस्तु ते।। 9।।

Namaskar be to You O Devi Narayani who abides, in 'Kala'—minutest unit of time '*Kashthadi*'—1/30th of *Kala* and other divisions of time; and who brings about change in things and have the potency to destroy the universe!

सर्वमङ्गलमङ्गल्ये शिवे सर्वार्थसाधिके।
शरण्ये त्र्यम्बके गौरि नारायणि नमोऽस्तु ते।। 10।।

Namaskar be to You, O Devi, Narayani! You O Shiva—the auspicious Devi. You are the good; above all good and carry out every object with perfection. You the giver of refuge and You are three eyed Gauri!

सृष्टिस्थितिविनाशानां शक्तिभूते सनातनि।
गुणाश्रये गुणमये नारायणि नमोऽस्तु ते।। 11।।

Namaskar be to You, O Devi Narayani! You are '*Sanatani*'—the eternal one. You alone have the power of creation, preservatoin and destruction. You hold all the '*gunas*'—qualities in You. You are the embodiment of all the gunas—attributes.

शरणागतदीनार्तपरित्राणपरायणे ।
सर्वस्यार्तिहरे देवि नारायणि नमोऽस्तुते।। 12।।

Namaskar be to You, O Devi Narayani! O You are intent on saving those persons, who take refuge under You. You remove the sufferings of all those, who are dejected and distressed!

हंसयुक्तविमानस्थे ब्रह्माणीरूपधारिणी।
कौशाम्भःक्षरिके देवि नारायणि नमोऽस्तु ते।। 13।।

Namaskar be to You, O Devi Narayani! You ride in the celestial chariot yoked with swans and assuming the form of Brahmani. O Devi, You sprinkle water with *Kusha* grass!.

त्रिशूलचन्द्राहिधरे महावृषभवाहिनि।
माहेश्वरीस्वरूपेण नारायणि नमोऽस्तु ते।। 14।।

Namaskar be to You, O Devi Narayani! O You are who ride on a big bull and hold *Trishula*—trident, *Chandra*—the moon and Ahi—the serpent and have the form of *Maheshvari*!

मयूरकुक्कुटवृते महाशक्तिधरेऽनघे।
कौमारीरूपसंस्थाने नारायणि नमोऽस्तु ते।। 15।।

Namaskar be to You, O Devi Narayani! O You are surrounded by peacock and cock and bear *Mahashakti*—the great Shakti missile. O You take the form of *Kaumari*, and are '*Anagha*'/sinless.

शङ्खचक्रगदाशार्ङ्गगृहीतपरमायुधे ।
प्रसीद वैष्णवीरूपे नारायणि नमोऽस्तु ते।। 16।।

Namaskar be to You, O Devi Narayani! O You are who holds conch, discus, club and bow and take the form of *Vaishnavi*.

गृहीतोग्रमहाचक्रे दंष्ट्रोद्धृतवसुंधरे।
वराहरूपिणि शिवे नारायणि नमोऽस्तु ते।। 17।।

Namaskar be to You, O Devi Narayani! O You hold a huge formidable disc and uplift the earth with Your tusk and take the form of *Varaha*—the boar.

नृसिंहरूपेणोग्रेण हन्तुं दैत्यान् कृतोद्यमे।
त्रैलोक्यत्राणसहिते नारायणि नमोऽस्तु ते।। 18।।

Namaskar be to You, O Devi Narayani! You are who possesses the benevolence of saving the three worlds, and put forth Your violent efforts to slay the Daityas by assuming the form of Narsimha.

किरीटिनि महावज्र सहस्रनयनोज्ज्वले।
वृत्रप्राणहरे चैन्द्रि नारायणि नमोऽस्तु ते।। 19।।

Namaskar be to You, O Devi Narayani! You are who has taken away the life of Vrtrasura. You hold a diadem and a great thunderbolt dazzling with a thousand eyes by assuming the form of Aindri.

शिवदूतीस्वरूपेण हतदैत्यमहाबले।
घोररूपे महारावे नारायणि नमोऽस्तु ते।। 20।।

Namaskar be to You, O Devi Narayani! You are who is with terrible form, terrific loud throat and who slew the mighty force of Daityas assuming the form of *Shivaduti*.

दंष्ट्राकरालवदने शिरोमालाविभूषणे।
चामुण्डे मुण्डमथने नारायणि नमोऽस्तु ते।। 21।।

Namaskar be to You, O Devi Narayani! You are who has a terrible face with tusks and is adorned with a garland of heads. Verily, you are *Chamunda*—the slayer of *Munda*.

लक्ष्मि लज्जे महाविद्ये श्रद्धे पुष्टिस्वधे ध्रुवे।
महारात्रि महाऽविद्ये नारायणि नमोऽस्तु ते।। 22।।

Namaskar be to You, O Devi Narayani! You are verily to

manifest as '*Lakshmi*'—good fortune, '*Lajja*'—modesty, '*Mahavidya*'—great knowledge, '*Shradha*'—faith, '*Pusthi*'—nourishment and '*Svadha*'—the oblation to the manes, '*Dhurva*'—immovable, '*Maharatri*'—great Night and '*Mahamaya*'—great illusion.

मेधे सरस्वति वरे भूति बाभ्रवि तामसि।
नियते त्वं प्रसीदेशे नारायणि नमोऽस्तु ते।। 23।।

Namaskar be to You, O Devi Narayani! You are verily, *Sarasvati*—the intellect united with Supreme Mother, '*Vara*'—the auspicious one, '*Bhuti*'—prosperity, '*Babhravi*'—of the dark brown colour, '*Gauri*'—of the white complexion, '*Tamasi*'—of the great innertia, '*Mahakali*'—the Supreme Mother, and '*Niyati*'—the fate. Be pleased, O Sovereign Mother!

सर्वस्वरूपे सर्वेशे सर्वशक्तिसमन्विते।
भयेभ्यस्त्राहि नो देवि दुर्गे देवि नमोऽस्तु ते।। 24।।

Namaskar be to You, O Devi! You are '*Sarva-Svarupa*'—the formatoin of all that exits, '*Sarvesha*'—the master sovereign of all, '*Sarvashakti'-Samanvita*'—accompanied by all the *Shaktis*. O Devi! May you protect us from fear!

एतत्ते वदनं सौम्यं लोचनत्रयभूषितम्।
पातु नः सर्वभीतिभ्यः कात्यायनि नमोऽस्तुते।। 25।।

Namaskar be to You, O *Devi Katyayani*—the daughter of Katyayan Rishi! May your benign face adorned with triple eyes guard us from all the malign forces!

ज्वालाकरालमत्युग्रमशेषासुरसूदनम् ।
त्रिशूलं पातु नो भीतेर्भद्रकालि नमोऽस्तु ते।। 26।।

Namaskar be to You, O Devi, O *Bhadrakali*! May You protect us with '*Trishula*'—the trident from the fear and terror, as that missile is terrible with flames, exceedingly sharp edged and destroyer of all the *Asuras*—anti-divine forces!

हिनस्ति दैत्यतेजांसि स्वनेनापूर्य या जगत्।
सा घण्टा पातु नो देवि पापेभ्योऽनः सुतानिव।। 27।।

O Devi! May that '*Ghanta*'—the bell protect us from the evil, which fills the world with its terrible sound destroying the prowess and valour of the Asuras! May it protect like a Mother to her children!

असुरासृग्वसापङ्कचर्चितस्ते करोज्ज्वलः।
शुभाय खड्गो भवतु चण्डिके त्वां नता वयम्।। 28।।

O Chandika! May Your sword soiled and greased with the oozing blood and marrow of the Asuras and radiating with rays, be for our welfare and betterment! O Devi! We bow down to you.

रोगानशेषानपहंसि तुष्टा
रुष्टा तु कामान् सकलानभीष्टान्।
त्वामाश्रितानां न विपन्नराणां
त्वामाश्रिता ह्याश्रयतां प्रयान्ति।। 29।।

When You get pleased, You destroy all the ailments and when You become angry, You destroy all the desires being longed for. Whosoever depends upon You, is not subjected to any calamity. Those who depend upon You and resort to You, become source of refuge to others.

एतत्कृतं यत्कदनं त्वयाद्य
धर्मद्विषां देवि महासुराणाम्।
रूपैरनेकैर्बहुधाऽऽत्ममूर्तिं
कृत्वाम्बिके तत्प्रकरोति कान्या।। 30।।

O Devi Ambika! None has the potential to do that work, which You did in slaughtering the great Asuras immediately. You made Your form manifold variously, to slay those opposite forces of *Dharma*—righteousness, as they hate Dharma.

विद्यासु शास्त्रेषु विवेकदीपे-
ष्वाद्येषु वाक्येषु च का त्वदन्या।
ममत्वगर्तेऽतिमहान्धकारे
विभ्रामयत्येतदतीव विश्वम्।। 31।।

You alone have been glorified in the branches of '*Vidya*'—Supreme knowledge, '*Shastras*'—the illumining scriptures and the '*Adi-Vakyas*—the Primal Vedic mantras, that light the lamps of '*Viveka*'—discrimination and wisdom. You alone cause this universe to move, in whirls of dense darkness and in the depths of attachment of 'me' and 'mine'.

रक्षांसि यत्रोग्रविषाश्च नागा
यत्रारयो दस्युबलानि यत्र।
दावानलो यत्र तथाब्धिमध्ये
तत्र स्थिता त्वं परिपासि विश्वम्।। 32।।

Where there exist, dreadful virulent poisonous snakes; where there are foes and the huge force of robbers; where there is wild fire and in being amidst the sea; there You stand and save the universe from disaster.

विश्वेश्वरि त्वं परिपासि विश्वं
विश्वात्मिका धारयसीति विश्वम्।
विश्वेशवन्द्या भवती भवन्ति
विश्वाश्रया ये त्वयि भक्तिनम्राः।। 33।।

O Supreme Sovereign of the universe! You protect the universe. You support and make the universe stable, as being the very self of it. You are worthy to be adored even by *Vishvesha*—the Supreme Lord of the Universe. Those who bow at Your feet with reverence, they verily, become the refuge of the universe.

देवि प्रसीद परिपालय नोऽरिभीते-
र्नित्यं यथासुरवधादधुनैव सद्यः।
पापानि सर्वजगतां प्रशमं नयाशु
उत्पातपाकजनितांश्च महोपसर्गान्।। 34।।

O Devi! Be pleased and protect us always from the fear of our foes, as You have just saved us by slaying the Asuras. Destroy the sins committed in the whole universe and the great calamities which have sprung from the maturing of malign omens.

प्रणतानां प्रसीद त्वं देवि विश्वार्तिहारिणि।
त्रैलोक्यवासिनामीड्ये लोकानां वरदा भव।। 35।।

O Devi! You are the destroyer of the afflictions and distress of the universe. Be gracious to those who bow to you. May You be '*Varda*'—the bestower of the boons to the worlds, as you are worthy of adoration by the inhabitants of Triloki—the triple world!

देव्युवाच।। 36।।
The Devi Said :

वरदाहं सुरगणा वरं यन्मनसेच्छथ।
तं वृणुध्वं प्रयच्छामि जगतामुपकारकम्।। 37।।

O, the host of Suras! I shall grant the boon whatsoever you desire in your minds. You choose that one. I shall give it to you for the benefit of the world".

देवा ऊचुः।। 38।।
The Devatas Said :

सर्वाबाधाप्रशमनं त्रैलोक्यस्याखिलेश्वरि।
एवमेव त्वया कार्यमस्मद्वैरिविनाशनम्।। 39।।

O Sovereign of all the worlds! You must destroy all our enemies and all the afflictions of the three-worlds, in the same manner as You did.

देव्युवाच।। 40।।
The Devi Said :

वैवस्वतेऽन्तरे प्राप्ते अष्टाविंशतिमे युगे।
शुम्भो निशुम्भश्चैवान्यावुत्पत्स्येते महासुरौ।। 41।।

The two great Asuras Shumbha and Nishumbha will be born in the life cycle of (seventh) 'Vaivasvata' Manu, at the approaching of the twenty eighth Yuga.

नन्दगोपगृहे जाता यशोदागर्भसम्भवा।
ततस्तौ नाशयिष्यामि विन्ध्याचलनिवासिनी।। 42।।

I will be born from the womb of *Yashoda*, in the home of *Nandagopa*—cowherd Nanda and will be dwelling in the Vindhya hills. Then I shall slay them both.

पुनरप्यतिरौद्रेण रूपेण पृथिवीतले।
अवतीर्य हनिष्यामि वैप्रचित्तांस्तु दानवान्।। 43।।

Again, I shall descend and take birth on earth in the most terrible form and shall slay the Danvas, who have descended from *Vaiprachitta* clan of Asuras.

भक्षयन्त्याश्च तानुग्रान् वैप्रचित्तान्महासुरान्।
रक्ता दन्ता भविष्यन्ति दाडिमीकुसुमोपमाः।। 44।।

My teeth will become red like the pomegranate flower, when I shall devour those great Vaiprachitta clan of Asuras.

ततो मां देवताः स्वर्गे मर्त्यलोके च मानवाः।
स्तुवन्तो व्याहरिष्यन्ति सततं रक्तदन्तिकाम्।। 45।।

Then the Devas in the *Svarga*—heaven and men on the mortal world/earth planet will therefore, praise Me and shall, speak of Me always as *Raktadantika*—the Devi with red teeth.

भूयश्च शतवार्षिक्यामनावृष्ट्यामनम्भसि।
मुनिभिः संस्तुता भूमौ सम्भविष्याम्ययोनिजा।। 46।।

And again, when for the hundred years there will be no rains on account of drought, thus I shall be praised by the Munis. I shall again descend on earth, without being born of a womb.

ततः शतेन नेत्राणां निरीक्षिष्यामि यन्मुनीन्।
कीर्तयिष्यन्ति मनुजाः शताक्षीमिति मां ततः।। 47।।

Then I shall look upon the Munis with my hundred eyes. I shall be adored then as *Shatakshi*—the Mother divinity with hundred eyes, by the mankind—the descendants of Manu.

ततोऽहमखिलं लोकमात्मदेहसमुद्भवैः।
भरिष्यामि सुराः शाकैरावृष्टेः प्राणधारकैः।। 48।।

O Suras! At that time I shall sustain the whole world with self-grown vegetables, born out of my Own cosmic principle of Self, till rains fall.

शाकम्भरीति विख्यातिं तदा यास्माम्यहं भुवि।
तत्रैव च वधिढयामि दुर्गमाख्यं महासुरम्।। 49।।

By doing this good to the world, I shall be renowned in the world as '*Shakambhari*'. I shall slay the great *Asura Durgama* in that incarnation.

दुर्गा देवीति विख्यातं तन्मे नाम भविष्यति।
पुनश्चाहं यदा भीमं रूपं कृत्वा हिमाचले।। 50।।

Then I shall verily, get the famous name of **Durga Devi—the Mother Durga**. Again manifesting in a terrible form, on the mountain '*Himalaya*'—the abode of snow.....

रक्षांसि भक्षयिष्यामि मुनीनां त्राणकारणात्।
तदा मां मुनयः सर्वे स्तोष्यन्त्यानम्रमूर्तयः।। 51।।

....thus I shall destroy and devour the *Rakshasas* for the protection of the *Munis*—sages. Then all the Munis, will pay their obeisance by kneeling down and praise me....

भीमा देवीति विख्यातं तन्मे नाम भविष्यति।
यदारुणाख्यस्त्रैलोक्ये महाबाधां करिष्यति।। 52।।

...and I shall be having the celebrated name of Bhimadevi, when the great *Aruna* will create havoc in *Triloki*—the triple world....,

तदाहं भ्रामरं रूपं कृत्वाऽसंख्येयषट्पदम्।
त्रैलोक्यस्य हितार्थाय वधिष्यामि महासुरम्।। 53।।

..then I shall asume the form of cluster of numberless bees. I shall then slay great Asura for the good and welfare of the triple world.

भ्रामरीति च मां लोकास्तदा स्तोष्यन्ति सर्वतः।
इत्थं यदा यदा बाधा दानवोत्था भविष्यति ।। 54 ।।

I shall be lauded as *Brahmari* everywhere by all the human beings. Thus, whenever havoc will be created by the *Danavas...,*

तदा तदावतीर्याहं करिष्याम्यरिसंक्षयम्।। ॐ ।। 55 ।।

...then I shall incarnete My being for the destruction of the foes. OM.

इति श्रीमार्कण्डेयपुराणे सावर्णिके मन्वन्तरे देवीमाहात्म्ये
देव्याः स्तुतिर्नामैकादशोऽध्यायः ।। 11 ।।

The eleventh chapter entitled '*Devi-Stuti*' hymn to Narayani Devi of the Devi Mahatmya during the time span of Savarni—the Manu, occuring in the Shri Markandeya Purana, is concluded.

उवाच 4, अर्धश्लोकः 1, श्लोकाः 50, एवम् 55,
एवमादितः ।। 630 ।।

Narration 4 Mantra, half Shloka 1, Shloka : 50, Total 55 Shlokas, total in all 630.

द्वादशोऽध्याय:

TWELFTH CHAPTER

देवी-चरित्रों के पाठ का महात्म्य

Glory of the Recitation of Devi-Charitra

ध्यानम्

Meditation

ॐ विद्युद्दामसमप्रभां मृगपतिस्कन्धस्थितां भीषणां
कन्याभिः करवालखेटविलसद्धस्ताभिरासेविताम्।
हस्तैश्चक्रगदासिखेटविशिखांश्चापं गुणं तर्जनीं
बिभ्राणामनलात्मिकां शशिधरां दुर्गां त्रिनेत्रां भजे।।

I meditate upon the **Trinetra Durga**—Divine Mother Durga having three eyes. Her being is illumined like the lightening. She is seated on the shoulders of lion and looks very terrific. Many divine girls are attending to Her with handling swords and shields in their hands. She holds '*Chakra*'—discus, sword, shield, arrow, bow and '*Tarjani*' mudra' in Her hands. Her *Svarupa*—innate form is of *Agni*—the fire element. She holds the lunar crown on Her forehead.

ॐ देव्युवाच।। 1।।

Om Devi Said :

एभिः स्तवैश्च मां नित्यं स्तोष्यते यः समाहितः।
तस्याहं सकलां बाधां नाशयिष्याम्यसंशयम्।। 2।।

Whosoever praises Me constantly with full concentration with those 'Stavas'/lauds, I shall without any doubt put an end to his all troubles.

मधुकैटभनाशं च महिषासुरघातनम्।
कीर्तयिष्यन्ति ये तद्वद् वधं शुम्भनिशुम्भयोः ।।3।।

....and those who shall make recitation of the destruction of 'Madhu-Kaitabha' and the killing of Mahishasura and likewise the slaying of 'Shumbha-Nishumbha'....,

अष्टम्यां च चतुर्दश्यां नवम्यां चैकचेतसः।
श्रोष्यन्ति चैव ये भक्त्या मम माहात्म्यमुत्तमम्।। 4।।

......and those also ,who listen to my 'Mahatmyam'—the glory of Mine actions on the eighth, fourteenth and ninth *Tithi*—days of the fortnight with single minded concentration....,

न तेषां दुष्कृतं किञ्चिद् दुष्कृतोत्था न चापदः।
भविष्यति न दारिद्र्यं न चैवेष्टवियोजनम्।। 5।।

...to them, nothing untoward shall befall. Neither misfortunes will take place, which could arise out of ill-happenings. They shall neither be subjected to any poverty nor will be separated from their kiths and kins.

शत्रुतो न भयं तस्य दस्युतो वा न राजतः।
न शस्त्रानलतोयौघात्कदाचित्सम्भविष्यति।। 6।।

He will not be put to any fear from foes, robbers and not even from kings, and not from weapons, fire and floods.

तस्मान्ममैतन्माहात्म्यं पठितव्यं समाहितैः।
श्रोतव्यं च सदा भक्त्या परं स्वस्त्ययनं हि तत्।। 7।।

Hence this 'Mahatmya'/Mine glory must be chanted by the devotees with concentrated mind and also to be listened to with devotion. It is verily, the Supreme way to welfare.

उपसर्गानशेषांस्तु महामारीसमुद्भवान्।
तथा त्रिविधमुत्पातं माहात्म्यं शमयेन्मम।। 8।।

This 'Glory of Mine' will eradicate all sufferings casued by Mahamari/epidemics and other calamities, alongwith three-fold confusions/nuisances.

यत्रैतत्पठ्यते सम्यङ्नित्यमायतने मम।
सदा न तद्विमोक्ष्यामि सांनिध्यं तत्र मे स्थितम्।। 9।।

I shall never leave that place where this 'Glory of Mine' is chanted everyday, I will never forsake and my constant presene is there.

बलिप्रदाने पूजायामग्निकार्ये महोत्सवे।
सर्वं ममैतच्चरितमुच्चार्यं श्राव्यमेव च।। 10।।

At the time of '*Bali*'/sacrifice, during '*Puja*'/worship '*Agni Karya*'/rituals with fire and on great festivals, all this *Mahatmyam*—Divine Glory must be chanted and listened to.

जानताऽजानता वापि बलिपूजां तथा कृताम्।
प्रतीच्छिष्याम्यहं प्रीत्या वह्निहोमं तथा कृतम्।। 11।।

I shall accept with love the offerings, worship and the '*Vahni-homa*'—sacrifices offered in fire for Me likewise, whether they are done with proper knowledge or not.

शरत्काले महापूजा क्रियते या च वार्षिकी।
तस्यां ममैतन्माहात्म्यं श्रुत्वा भक्तिसमन्वितः।। 12।।

During the autumnal *Mahapuja* or annually in the beginning of year (*Navaratra* days), when Puja is performed, the man hearing my '*Mahatmyam*' with devotion and concentration...,

सर्वाबाधाविनिर्मुक्तो धनधान्यसुतान्वितः।
मनुष्यो मत्प्रसादेन भविष्यति न संशयः।। 13।।

..will be freed from all troubles and be blessed with wealth, food grains and progeny through My grace. There is no doubt about it.

श्रुत्वा ममैतन्माहात्म्यं तथा चोत्पत्तयः शुभाः।
पराक्रमं च युद्धेषु जायते निर्भयः पुमान्।। 14।।

Hearing this Divine glory, and the auspicious incarnations of Mine and My prowess in battles, the man (devotee) becomes fearless.

रिपवः संक्षयं यान्ति कल्याणं चोपपद्यते।
नन्दते च कुलं पुंसां माहात्म्यं मम शृण्वताम्।। 15।।

Those men who listen to my 'Mahatmya', obtain the rejoices of their families. Their enemies get destroyed and are blessed with '*Kalyana*'—welfare/prosperity/excellence.

शान्तिकर्मणि सर्वत्र तथा दुःस्वप्नदर्शने।
ग्रहपीडासु चोग्रासु माहात्म्यं शृणुयान्मम।। 16।।

Let the devotee listen to my 'Mahatmyam' everywhere, at the '*Shanti-Karmas*'—propitiatory ceremony, on seeing a bad dream and great eventualities arising due to planetary positions.

उपसर्गाः शमं यान्ति ग्रहपीडाश्च दारुणाः।
दुःस्वप्नं च नृभिर्दृष्टं सुस्वप्नमुपजायते।। 17।।

Troubles subside, also the dreadful planetary influences subside. The bad dream seen by man turns into favourable dream.

बालग्रहाभिभूतानां बालानां शान्तिकारकम्।
संघातभेदे च नृणां मैत्रीकरणमुत्तमम्।। 18।।

It destroys the evil influence of 'Balagraha'/'siezure of children over children and creates peacefulness in them. It is the best means of creating friendship among men, when split occur in their relationship.

दुर्वृत्तानामशेषाणां बलहानिकरं परम्।
रक्षोभूतपिशाचानां पठनादेव नाशनम्।। 19।।

It destroys the strength of evil-doers most effectively of all men. By its mere chanting the 'Rakshasas'/demons, 'Bhutas'/ ghosts '*Pishachas*'/ogresses do perish.

सर्वं ममैतन्माहात्म्यं मम सन्निधिकारकम्।
पशुपुष्पार्घ्यधूपैश्च गन्धदीपैस्तथोत्तमैः।। 20।।

The entire '*Mahatmya*' of Mine draws one very close to Me.

By means of '*Pashu*'—animal for sacrifices, '*Pushpa*'—flowers, '*Dhupa*—incenses, '*Arghya*—flowers and rice mixed, '*Gandha*—scents and perfumes '*Dhipa*' ghee lamps of the best varieties....,

विप्राणां भोजनैर्होमैः प्रोक्षणीयैरहर्निशम्।
अन्यैश्च विविधैर्भोगैः प्रदानैर्वत्सरेण या।। 21।।

and by feeding *Vipras*—the well versed in the Vedic tradition, *Homa*—offerings through *Yajnas*, '*Prokshaniya*' / Sacramental sprinkling of water. Also by other offerings and gifts, by worshipping for full one year....,

प्रीतिर्मे क्रियते सास्मिन् सकृत्सुचरिते श्रुते।
श्रुतं हरति पापानि तथाऽऽरोग्यं प्रयच्छति।। 22।।

...the same satisfaction I get, when My Charitam—the Divine Story of Mine is listened to with devotion. The chanting and listening to My Mahatmya removes sins and grants sound health......,

रक्षां करोति भूतेभ्यो जन्मनां कीर्तनं मम।
युद्धेषु चरितं यन्मे दुष्टदैत्यनिबर्हणम्।। 23।।

.....it affords protection from evil spirits, by singing of My manifestations. If My exploits of slaying of wicked 'Daityas' during battles are .....,

तस्मिञ्छ्रुते वैरिकृतं भयं पुंसां न जायते।
युष्माभिः स्तुतयो याश्च याश्च ब्रह्मर्षिभिः कृताः।। 24।।

...listened to, they then do not experience any fear from enemies. O Devas ! The hymns uttered by you and by the '*Brahma Rishis*'......,

ब्रह्मणा च कृतास्तास्तु प्रयच्छन्ति शुभां मतिम्।
अरण्ये प्रान्तरे वापि दावाग्निपरिवारितः।। 25।।

......along with those others made by Brahma give auspiciousness in mind and thought. In the dense forests, lonely spots or the places surrounded by wild fire.....,

दस्युभिर्वा वृतः शून्ये गृहीतो वापि शत्रुभिः।
सिंहव्याघ्रानुयातो वा वने वा वनहस्तिभिः ।। 26 ।।

....and who is surrounded by robbers or else caught by the enemies in a desolate place, or in a jungle pursued by lion, tiger or by wild elephants....,

राज्ञा क्रुद्धेन चाज्ञप्तो वध्यो बन्धगतोऽपि वा।
आघूर्णितो वा वातेन स्थितः पोते महार्णवे ।। 27 ।।

... or who is under orders of the wrathful king to be executed or imprisoned, or caught in a boat tossed by the winds in the big and vast oceans.....,

पतत्सु चापि शस्त्रेषु संग्रामे भृशदारुणे।
सर्वाबाधासु घोरासु वेदनाभ्यर्दितोऽपि वा ।। 28 ।।

.....or who is in most terrible battle and facing the deadly weapons; or in the midst of terible problems or who is subjected to pain....,

स्मरन्ममैतच्चरितं नरो मुच्येत संकटात्।
मम प्रभावात्सिंहाद्या दस्यवो वैरिणस्तथा ।। 29 ।।

...such a person remembering my 'Charitam' is saved from his trobules. By my power, animals like lions etc., robbers and enemies...,

दूरादेव पलायन्ते स्मरतश्चरितं मम ।। 30 ।।

...flee from the far distance from him who remembers my *Charitam*—the story of my manifestation.

ऋषिरुवाच ।। 31 ।।

The Rishi Said :

इत्युक्त्वा सा भगवती चण्डिका चण्डविक्रमा ।। 32 ।।

"Saying so, She the Chandi of the great and ferrocious spirit, having full of effulgence.....

पश्यतामेव देवानां तत्रैवान्तरधीयत।
तेऽपि देवा निरातङ्काः स्वाधिकारान् यथा पुरा ।। 33 ।।

....vanished Itself there, even when all the Devas were gazing at Her. The Devas also assumed and enjoyed their power, after being rid of the terror of the Danavas....,

यज्ञभागभुजः सर्वे चक्रुर्विनिहतारयः।
दैत्याश्च देव्या निहते शुम्भे देवरिपौ युधि।। 34।।

......and participated in their share of '*Yajnyas*'—sacrifices. They retained their authority as before, when Shumbha—the enemy of Devas was killed by the Devi in the battle.....,

जगद्विध्वंसिनि तस्मिन् महोग्रेऽतुलविक्रमे।
निशुम्भे च महावीर्ये शेषाः पातालमाययुः।। 35।।

....who brought ruin to the world. Like him Nishumbha was unparalled in prowess and was also killed by the Devi. The remaining Asuras entered '*Patala*'—the Nether worlds".

एवं भगवती देवी सा नित्यापि पुनः पुनः।
सम्भूय कुरुते भूप जगतः परिपालनम्।। 36।।

Thus O king! The Bhagavati Devi, although She is eternal, manifests again and again for the protection of the world.

तयैतन्मोह्यते विश्वं सैव विश्वं प्रसूयते।
सा याचिता च विज्ञानं तुष्टा ऋद्धिं प्रयच्छति।। 37।।

It is She, who deludes this unvierse and it is She verily, ,who creates this universe. She when entreated properly grants '*Vijnan*'—Supreme knowlege and when propitiated, bestows '*Riddhi*'—prosperity.

व्याप्तं तयैतत्सकलं ब्रह्माण्डं मनुजेश्वर।
महाकाल्या महाकाले महामारीस्वरूपया।। 38।।

O sovereign among kings! By Her, this entire *Brahmanda*—universe in macro or Brahma's egg is pervaded and verily, She as *Mahakali* assumes the form of *Mahamari*, at the time of the great destruction.

सैव काले महामारी सैव सृष्टिर्भवत्यजा।
स्थितिं करोति भूतानां सैव काले सनातनी।। 39।।

She undoubtedly, assumes the form of 'Mahamari'—Great Death at the proper time. And She becomes this '*Srishti*'—creation, though unborn She is. She is '*Snatani*'—eternal Being Herself and sustains the creation at the appropriate time.

भवकाले नृणां सैव लक्ष्मीर्वृद्धिप्रदा गृहे।
सैवाभावे तथाऽलक्ष्मीर्विनाशायोपजायते।। 40।।

During the time of good fortune, She is verily, *Lakshmi*, for men granting growth and prosperity in their homes, and at the time of misfortunes, She herself become *Alakshmi* and brings about ruin and destruction.

स्तुता सम्पूजिता पुष्पैर्धूपगन्धादिभिस्तथा।
ददाति वित्तं पुत्रांश्च मतिं धर्मे गतिं शुभाम्।। ॐ ।। 41।।

Adored and properly worshipped with '*Pushpas*'—flowers, '*Dhupa*'—fragrance, '*Gandha*'—incense; She bestows wealth, sons/progeny and pure mind to be directed towards *Dharma*—righteousness. Om.

इति श्रीमार्कण्डेयपुराणे सावर्णिके मन्वन्तरे देवी माहात्म्ये
फलस्तुतिर्नाम द्वादशोऽध्यायः।। 12।।

The twelfth chapter entitled 'Phala-Stuti' hymn in the Markandeya Purana of the Devi Mahatmya occuring during the time span of *Savarni*—the Manu, is concluded.

उवाच 2, अर्धश्लोकौ 2, श्लोकाः 37, एवम् 41, एवमादितः 671।।

Narration 2, half Shlokas 2, Sholkas 37, in this chapter 41, total 671.

त्रयोदशोऽध्यायः

THIRTEENTH CHAPTER

सुरथ और वैश्य को देवी का वरदान

(Devi's Boon to Suratha and Vaishya)

ध्यानम्

Meditation

ॐ बालार्कमण्डलाभासां चतुर्बाहुं त्रिलोचनाम्।
पाशाङ्कुशवराभीतिर्धारयन्तीं शिवां भजे॥

I meditate upon Shiva, who has assumed the form of the Sun, at the time of early dawn. She has four arms and three eyes. She holds 'Pasha'—noose, 'Ankusha'—goad, 'Vara' and 'Abhaya'—the two 'Mudras'—of bestowing boon and boldness.

ॐ ऋषिरुवाच॥ 1॥

Om the Rishi Said :

एतत्ते कथितं भूप देवीमाहात्म्यमुत्तमम्।
एवंप्रभावा सा देवी ययेदं धार्यते जगत्॥ 2॥

O King ! I have narrated to you this grand 'Mahatmya'—glory of the Divine Mother Devi. The Devi is endowed with such glory, by whom this world is upheld and sustained.

विद्या तथैव क्रियते भगवद्विष्णुमायया।
तया त्वमेष वैश्यश्च तथैवान्ये विवेकिनः॥ 3॥

Vidya—the knowledge is conferred upon by Her through the '*Yoga-Maya*' of Bhagvan Vishnu. By Her, this *Vaishya*—

the merchant and other *Vivekin*—the men of discrimination...,

मोह्यन्ते मोहिताश्चैव मोहमेष्यन्ति चापरे।
तामुपैहि महाराज शरणं परमेश्वरीम्।। 4।।

...are being deluded and were deluded before. Many others will be deluded in the future. So O King! Take refuge in Her, who is *Parmeshvari*—the Supreme Sovereign authority, par excellence.

आराधिता सैव नृणां भोगस्वर्गापवर्गदा।। 5।।

Verily, She bestows on men '*Bhoga*'—enjoyments, Svarga—heaven and *Apavarga*—final release from the transmigration of soul, when worshipped.

मार्कण्डेय उवाच।। 6।।

Markandeya Said

इति तस्य वचः श्रुत्वा सुरथः स नराधिपः।। 7।।

"Hearing his words, Suratha the king of the subjects....,

प्रणिपत्य महाभागं तमृषिं शंसितव्रतम्।
निर्विण्णोऽतिममत्वेन राज्यापहरणेन च।। 8।।

.....paid obeisance to that great Rishi. Suratha had become despondent, consequent upon his over attachment and the loss of his kingdom.

जगाम सद्यस्तपसे स च वैश्यो महामुने।
संदर्शनार्थमम्बाया नदीपुलिनसंस्थितः।। 9।।

O *Mahamuni*—the Great sage ! 'He took to severe penances and thereby started 'Tapas'—austerities, along with '*Samadhi*—the Vaishya'. Both of them stationed themselves on the bank of the river to obtain the Divine vision of *Amba*—the Mother creatrix.

स च वैश्यस्तपस्तेपे देवीसूक्तं परं जपन्।
तौ तस्मिन् पुलिने देव्याः कृत्वा मूर्तिं महीमयीम्।। 10।।

He and Vaishya performed the 'Tapas', reciting the Devi-Suktam' for 'Japam'. Both of them made the Murti/image of Devi—the Divine Mother out of clay on the banks of the river....,

अर्हणां चक्रतुस्तस्याः पुष्पधूपाग्नितर्पणैः।
निराहारौ यताहारौ तन्मनस्कौ समाहितौ॥ 11॥

...and worshipped Her in the image with '*Pushpa*'—flowers, '*Dhupa*'—incense, 'Agni *Homa*'—the rituals with fire, '*Tarpanam*'—offerings of water, restraining and abstaining from food, they kept their minds concentrated with single minded devotion.

ददतुस्तौ बलिं चैव निजगात्रासृगुक्षितम्।
एवं समाराधयतोस्त्रिभिर्वर्षैर्यतात्मनोः॥ 12॥

Both of them offered '*Bali*'—sacrifices to Devi dipped in the blood drawn from their own bodies, for three years constantly exercising self-control and self-will.

परितुष्टा जगद्धात्री प्रत्यक्षं प्राह चण्डिका॥ 13॥

Jagaddhatri—the sustainer of the worlds, who is verily *Chandika* got highly pleased, appeared before them and spoke :

देव्युवाच॥ 14॥

The Devi Said :

यत्प्रार्थ्यते त्वया भूप त्वया च कुलनन्दन।
मत्तस्तत्प्राप्यतां सर्वं परितुष्टा ददामि तत्॥ 15॥

O King (Raja Suratha) whatever is prayed for by you—and O *Kulanandana*—the delight of your family (Samadhi Vaishya), whatever you long for, receive that from me. I am highly pleased. I bestow all that to both of you".

मार्कण्डेय उवाच।। 16।।

Markandeya Said :

ततो वव्रे नृपो राज्यमविभ्रंश्यन्यजन्मनि।
अत्रैव च निजं राज्यं हतशत्रुबलं बलात्।। 17।।

Then the King chose a kingdom, which would be imperishable even in future life and in this life his own kingdom would be taken back by destroying the armies of his enemies.

सोऽपि वैश्यस्ततो ज्ञानं वव्रे निर्विण्णमानसः।
ममेत्यहमिति प्राज्ञः सङ्गविच्युतिकारकम्।। 18।।

Being very wise, Vaishya's mind was full of dispassion and opted for *Jnanam*/Supreme knowledge which gives release from the attachment of 'I and mine'.

देव्युवाच।। 19।।

The Devi Said :

स्वल्पैरहोभिर्नृपते स्वं राज्यं प्राप्स्यते भवान्।। 20।।

"O king, you will get your own kingdom, during a period of few days...,

हत्वा रिपूनस्खलितं तव तत्र भविष्यति।। 21।।

.....after slaying your foes, the kingdom will not slip away from you any more.

मृतश्च भूयः सम्प्राप्य जन्म देवाद्विवस्वतः।। 22।।

And when you are dead, you shall again be born from the Sun God—*Vivasvat*....,

सावर्णिको नाम मनुर्भवान् भुवि भविष्यति।। 23।।

..and shall have status of '*Manu*' on earth by the name of '*Savarni*'.

वैश्यवर्य त्वया यश्च वरोऽस्मत्तोऽभिवाञ्छितः।। 24।।

O the best amongst Vaishyas, I grant the boon to you, which you have desired from Me and longed for....,

तं प्रयच्छामि संसिद्धयै तव ज्ञानं भविष्यति ।। 25 ।।

...I shall confer that to you. You will be blessed with the Jnanam—Supreme knowledge for supreme perfection.

मार्कण्डेय उवाच ।। 26 ।।

Markandeya Said :

इति दत्त्वा तयोर्देवी यथाभिलषितं वरम् ।। 27 ।।

Having thus granted them '*Vara*'—the boons of their choice, the Devi....,

बभूवान्तर्हिता सद्यो भक्त्या ताभ्यामभिष्टुता ।
एवं देव्या वरं लब्ध्वा सुरथः क्षत्रियर्षभः ।। 28 ।।

....thus immediately disappeared forthwith, as they were paying their obeisance with devotion to Her. Thus Suratha, the best of the Kshatriyas having got the boon from the Devi...,

सूर्याज्जन्म समासाद्य सावर्णिर्भविता मनुः ।। 29 ।।

.....shall obtain a new birth through Surya—the Sun god. And shall become Manu named Savarni.

एवं दव्या वरं लब्ध्वा सुरथः क्षत्रियर्षभः ।
सूर्याज्जन्म समासाद्य सावर्णिर्भविता मनुः ।। क्लीं ॐ ।।

Thus Suratha—the best of the Kshatriyas having got the boon from the Devi shall obtain a new birth through Surya, and will become Manu to be named Savarni. KLIM OM

इति श्रीमार्कण्डेयपुराणे सावर्णिके मन्वन्तरे देवीमाहात्म्ये
सुरथ-वैश्ययोर्वर-प्रदानं नाम त्रयोदशोऽध्यायः ।। 13 ।।

The thirteenth chapter entitled '*Suratha-Vaishya yor-Vara-Paradanam*—the bestowing of boons to Suratha and Vaishya in the *Devi Mahatmya* of the *Markandeya Purana*, occuring during the period of Savarni—the Manu is concluded.

उवाच 6, अर्द्धश्लोकाः 11, श्लोकाः 12, एवम् 29, एवमादितः 700 ।।

Narration 6, half Shlokas 11, Shlokas 12, total 29 in this chapter total in all 700 Shlokas.

समस्ता उवाचमन्त्राः 57, अर्द्धश्लोकाः 42, श्लोकाः 535, अवदानानि ।। 66 ।।

उपसंहार

EPILOGUE

The Viniyoga-Nyasa-Dhyanam are to be performed in the same procedure as has been done earlier before the recitation/Homa of the Sapta Shati Patham.

विनियोगः

While pouring water recite the Viniyoga Mantra.

श्रीगणपतिर्जयति। ॐ अस्य श्रीनवार्णमन्त्रस्य ब्रह्मविष्णुरुद्रा ऋषयः, गायत्र्युष्णिगनुष्टुभश्छन्दांसि, श्रीमहाकालीमहालक्ष्मीमहा-सरस्वत्यो देवताः, ऐं बीजम्, ह्रीं शक्तिः, क्लीं कीलकम्, श्रीमहाकालीमहालक्ष्मीमहासरस्वतीप्रीत्यर्थे जपे विनियोगः।

ऋष्यादिन्यासः

Perform the Rishi Adi Nyasa

ब्रह्मविष्णुरुद्रऋषिभ्यो नमः, शिरसि। गायत्र्युष्णिगनुष्टुप्छन्दोभ्यो नमः, मुखे। महाकालीमहालक्ष्मीमहासरस्वतीदेवताभ्यो नमः, हृदि। ऐं बीजाय नमः, गुह्ये। ह्रीं शक्तये नमः, पादयोः। क्लीं कीलकाय नमः, नाभौ।

ॐ ऐं ह्रीं क्लीं चामुण्डायै विच्चे- इति मूलेन करौ संशोध्य-

करन्यासः

Perform the Kara Nyasa

ॐ ऐं अङ्गुष्ठाभ्यां नमः। ॐ ह्रीं तर्जनीभ्यां नमः। ॐ क्लीं मध्यमाभ्यां नमः। ॐ चामुण्डायै अनामिकाभ्यां नमः। ॐ ऐं ह्रीं क्लीं चामुण्डायै विच्चे करतलकरपृष्ठाभ्यां नमः।

हृदयादिन्यासः

Perform the Hridaya Adi Nayasa

ॐ ऐं हृदयाय नमः। ॐ ह्रीं शिरसे स्वाहा। ॐ क्लीं शिखायै वषट्। ॐ चामुण्डायै कवचाय हुम्। ॐ विच्चे नेत्रत्रयाय वौषट्। ॐ ऐं ह्रीं क्लीं चामुण्डायै विच्चे अस्त्राय फट्।

अक्षरन्यासः

Perform the Akshara Nyasa.

ॐ ऐं नमः, शिखायाम्। ॐ ह्रीं नमः, दक्षिणनेत्रे। ॐ क्लीं नमः, वामनेत्रे। ॐ चां नमः, दक्षिणकर्णे। ॐ मुं नमः, वामकर्णे। ॐ डां नमः, दक्षिणनासापुटे। ॐ यैं नमः, वामनासापुटे। ॐ विं नमः, मुखे। ॐ च्चें नमः, गुह्ये।

'एवं विन्यास्याष्टवारं मूलेन व्यापकं कुर्यात्'

After the 'Akshara Nyasa' feel the pulsation of the Navarana Mantra eight times in your body, from Head to the Feet, by touching them with your both hands.

दिङ्न्यासः

Perform the Dik Nyasa.

ॐ ऐं प्राच्यै नमः। ॐ ऐं आग्नेय्यै नमः। ॐ ह्रीं दक्षिणायै नमः। ॐ ह्रीं नैर्ऋत्यै नमः। ॐ क्लीं प्रतीच्यै नमः। ॐ क्लीं वायव्यै नमः। ॐ चामुण्डायै उदीच्यै नमः। ॐ चामुण्डायै ऐशान्यै नमः। ॐ ऐं ह्रीं क्लीं चामुण्डायै विच्चे ऊर्ध्वायै नमः। ॐ ऐं ह्रीं क्लीं चामुण्डायै विच्चे भूम्यै नमः।

ध्यानम्

Recite and meditate upon Mahakali.

खड्गं चक्रगदेषु चापपरिघाञ्छूलं भुशुण्डीं शिरः
शङ्खं संदधतीं करैस्त्रिनयनां सर्वाङ्गभूषावृताम्।

नीलाश्मद्युतिमास्यपाददशकां सेवे महाकालिकां
यामस्तौत्स्वपिते हरौ कमलजो हन्तुं मधुं कैटभम्।। 1।।

Recite and Meditate upon Mahalakshmi.

अक्षस्त्रक्परशुं गदेषुकुलिशं पद्मं धनुः कुण्डिकां
दण्डं शक्तिमसिं च चर्म जलजं घण्टां सुराभाजनम्।
शूलं पाशसुदर्शने च दधतीं हस्तैः प्रसन्नाननां
सेवे सैरिभमर्दिनीमिह महालक्ष्मीं सरोजस्थिताम्।। 2।।

Recite and Meditate upon Mahasaraswati.

घण्टाशूलहलानि शङ्खमुसले चक्रं धनुः सायकं
हस्ताब्जैर्दधतीं घनान्तविलसच्छीतांशुतुल्यप्रभाम्।
गौरीदेहसमुद्भवां त्रिजगतामाधारभूतां महा-
पूर्वामत्र सरस्वतीमनुभजे शुम्भादिदैत्यार्दिनीम्।। 3।।

Pay your obeisance to the Akshamala

ऐं ह्रीं अक्षमालिकायै नमः

Perform the Japam of Navarana Mantra 108 times.

ॐ ऐं ह्रीं क्लीं चामुण्डायै विच्चे।

Give your obeisance to Devi for attaining the mertis and for removing the obstacles during the Japa times.

Recite :

ॐ मां माले महामाये सर्वशक्तिस्वरूपिणि।
चतुर्वर्गस्त्वयि न्यस्तस्तस्मान्मे सिद्धिदा भव।।

ॐ अविघ्नं कुरु माले त्वं गृह्णामि दक्षिणे करे।
जपकाले च सिद्ध्यर्थं प्रसीद मम सिद्धये।।

ॐ अक्षमालाधिपतये सुसिद्धिं देहि देहि सर्वमन्त्रार्थसाधिनि साधय साधय सर्वसिद्धिं परिकल्पय परिकल्पय मे स्वाहा।

Dedicate the Japam to the Devi.

गुह्यातिगुह्यगोप्त्री त्वं गृहाणास्मत्कृतं जपम्।
सिद्धिर्भवतु मे देवि त्वत्प्रसादान्महेश्वरि।।

करन्यासः

Perform Kara Naysa.

ॐ ह्रीं अङ्गुष्ठाभ्यां नमः। ॐ चं तर्जनीभ्यां नमः। ॐ डिं मध्यमाभ्यां नमः। ॐ कां अनामिकाभ्यां नमः। ॐ यैं कनिष्ठिकाभ्यां नमः। ॐ ह्रीं चण्डिकायै करतलकरपृष्ठाभ्यां नमः।

Perform Hridaya—Adi Nyasa

ॐ खड्गिनी शूलिनी घोरा गदिनी चक्रिणी तथा।
शङ्खिनी चापिनी बाणभुशुण्डीपरिघायुधा।। हृदयाय नमः।
ॐ शूलेन पाहि नो देवि पाहि खड्गेन चाम्बिके।
घण्टास्वनेन नः पाहि चापज्यानिःस्वनेन च।। शिरसे स्वाहा।
ॐ प्राच्यां रक्ष प्रतीच्यां च चण्डिके रक्ष दक्षिणे।
भ्रामणेनात्मशूलस्य उत्तरास्यां तथेश्वरि।। शिखायै वषट्।
ॐ सौम्यानि यानि रूपाणि त्रैलोक्ये विचरन्ति ते।
यानि चात्यर्थघोराणि तै रक्षास्मांस्तथा भुवम्।। कवचाय हुम्।
ॐ खड्गशूलगदादीनि यानि चास्त्राणि तेऽम्बिके।
करपल्लवसङ्गीनि तैरस्मान् रक्ष सर्वतः।। नेत्रयाय वौषट्।
ॐ सर्वस्वरूपे सर्वेशे सर्वशक्तिसमन्विते।
भयेभ्यस्त्राहि नो देवि दुर्गे देवि नमोऽस्तु ते।। अस्त्राय फट्।

ध्यानम्

Recite the Shloka and Medidate upon Shri Durga.

ॐ विद्युद्दामसमप्रभां मृगपतिस्कन्धस्थितां भीषणां
कन्याभिः करवालखेटविलसद्धस्ताभिरासेविताम्।
हस्तैश्चक्रगदासिखेटविशिखांश्चापं गुणं तर्जनीं
बिभ्राणामनलात्मिकां शशिधरां दुर्गां त्रिनेत्रां भजे।।

I meditate upon *Trinetra Durga*—Divine Mother Durga having three eyes. Her being is illumined like the lightening. She is seated on the shoulders of lion and looks very terrific. Many divine girls are attending to Her, with handling swords and shields in their hands. She holds '*Chakra*'—discus, sword, shield, arrow, bow and '*Tarjani mudra*' in Her hands. Her '*Svarupa*'—innate form is of '*Agni*'—the fire element. She holds the lunar crown on Her forehead.

ऋग्वेदोक्त देवीसूक्तम्

Recite the Rigvedic Devisuktam alongwith Viniyoga.

ॐ अहमित्यष्टर्चस्य सूक्तस्य वागाम्भृणी ऋषिः, सच्चित्सुखात्मकः सर्वगतः परमात्मा देवता, द्वितीयाया ऋचो जगती, शिष्टानां त्रिष्टुप् छन्दः, देवीमाहात्म्यपाठे विनियोगः।

OM! Vagambhrini is the Rishi of the eight Suktas. The Devata is Parmataman, who is *Sat-Chit-Sukh-Atmaka* (truth, consciousness and the innate nature of higher bliss. Second Mantra is of *Jagati Chhanda* and rest are of Kali *Trishtup Chhanda*/Metre. The application of the Suktam is in the recitation of the *Devi Mahatmya Patham.*

ध्यानम्

ॐ सिंहस्था शशिशेखरा मरकतप्रख्यैश्चतुर्भिर्भुजैः
शङ्खं चक्रधनुःशरांश्च दधती नेत्रैस्त्रिभिः शोभिता।
आमुक्ताङ्गदहारकङ्कणरणत्काञ्चीरणन्नूपुरा
दुर्गा दुर्गतिहारिणी भवतु नो रत्नोल्लसत्कुण्डला॥

May Durga Bhagvati remove all our obstacles! She is seated on the back of the lion. Her forehead is decorated with the crown of the moon which is effulgent and lustrous like 'Markata' jewel. She holds conch, discus, bow and arrow. Her three eyes are very inspiring. She is adorned with different ornaments like bracelet, necklace, girdle which give a lustre all around. She is adorned with ear-rings decorated with jewels.

देवीसूक्तम्

Devi Suktam

ॐ अहं रुद्रेभिर्वसुभिश्चराम्यहमादित्यैरुत विश्वदेवैः।
अहं मित्रावरुणोभा बिभर्म्यहमिन्द्राग्नी अहमश्विनोभा।। 1।।

I associate with all the men of learning called as Vasu—the young preceptors and Aditya—the highly acclaimed preceptors. I am the support of all manifestations what is known as nature. Also I support the Sun, Ocean, Fire, Lightning and the Ashvinis—the twin divine physicians.

अहं सोममाहनसं बिभर्म्यहं त्वष्टारमुत पूषणं भगम्।
अहं दधामि द्रविणं हविष्मते सुप्राव्ये यजमानाय सुन्वते।। 2।।

I support the herbs which are for destroying the enemies. I support the Moon and the strength giving food and riches. I bestow upon wealth to the institutor of worship with the offerings of the Homa and I deserve careful protection to perform good and noble deeds with selflessness.

अहं राष्ट्री संगमनी वसूनां चिकितुषी प्रथमायज्ञियानाम्।
तां मा देवा व्यदधुः पुरुत्रा भूरिस्थात्रां भूर्य्यावेशयन्तीम्।। 3।।

I am the Sovereign Mother of the manifestation, who collects treasures. I am complete and full wisdom. I am 'Vak' first among those who deserve reverence. Thus the learned people honour me in all the situations and in numerous functions.

मया सो अन्नमत्ति यो विपश्यति यः
प्राणिति य ईं शृणोत्युक्तम्।
अमन्तवो मां त उप क्षियन्ति श्रुधि
श्रुत श्रद्धिवं ते वदामि।। 4।।

Though I am alone but I am with all. Whosoever eats food is all because of me. It is through me that one sees, breaths, hears and speaks. Those who are ignorant of me are to perish. May all hear, one and all listen to me! I tell you the truth and you have to accept it.

अहमेव स्वयमिदं वदामि जुष्टं
देवेभिरुत मानुषेभिः।
यं कामये तं तमुग्रं कृणोमि
तं ब्रह्माणं तमृषिं तं सुमेधाम्।। 5 ।।

Verily, I declare the truth myself, which is approached by men and the Divine ones. I make them formidable, who may be a sage, a seer and wise, whomsoever I choose.

अहं रुद्राय धनुरा तनोमि ब्रह्मद्विषे शरवे हन्तवा उ।
अहं जनाय समदं कृणोम्यहंद्यावापृथिवी आविवेश।। 6 ।।

I bend the bow of the absolute lord so that his arrow may strike and destroy enemy of those, who are learned and pious devotees. I wage war against the hostile forces. I pervade in heaven and earth.

अहं सुवे पितरमस्य मूर्धन्मम
योनिरप्स्वन्तः समुद्रे।
ततो वि तिष्ठे भुवनानु विश्वो-
तामूं द्यां वर्ष्मणोप स्पृशामि।। 7 ।।

I create the Father sky at the summit of this world, who is the Supreme authority. Under the Supreme authority of the Lord in the form of oceans, I create life and water in the form of intellect. It is because of me that everything exits. I pervade the whole universe and I touch the heaven with my own manifested glory.

अहमेव वात इव प्रवाम्यारभमाणा भुवनानि विश्वा।
परो दिवा पर एना पृथिव्यैतावती महिना संबभूव।। 8 ।।

Whenever, I make the start of this Universe with Primal cause then I move in this universe like air without getting any influence from any source. I do act upon working with my own free-will. I transcend both the earth and the sky. I attained this Glory because of my innate nature.

अथ तन्त्रोक्तं देवीसूक्तम्

Recite the Tantrik Devi Suktam.

नमो देव्यै महादेव्यै शिवायै सततं नमः।
नमः प्रकृत्यै भद्रायै नियताः प्रणताः स्म ताम्।। 1।।

रौद्रायै नमो नित्यायै गौर्यै धात्र्यै नमो नमः।
ज्योत्स्नायै चेन्दुरूपिण्यै सुखायै सततं नमः।। 2।।

कल्याण्यै प्रणतां वृद्ध्यै सिद्ध्यै कुर्मो नमो नमः।
नैर्ऋत्यै भूभृतां लक्ष्म्यै शर्वाण्यै ते नमो नमः।। 3।।

दुर्गायै दुर्गपारायै सारायै सर्वकारिण्यै।
ख्यात्यै तथैव कृष्णायै धूम्रायै सततं नमः।। 4।।

अतिसौम्यातिरौद्रायै नतास्तस्यै नमो नमः।
नमो जगत्प्रतिष्ठायै देव्यै कृत्यै नमो नमः।। 5।।

या देवी सर्वभूतेषु विष्णुमायेति शब्दिता।
नमस्तस्यै नमस्तस्यै नमस्तस्यै नमो नमः।। 6।।

या देवी सर्वभूतेषु चेतनेत्यभिधीयते।
नमस्तस्यै नमस्तस्यै नमस्तस्यै नमो नमः।। 7।।

या देवी सर्वभूतेषु बुद्धिरूपेण संस्थिता।
नमस्तस्यै नमस्तस्यै नमस्तस्यै नमो नमः।। 8।।

या देवी सर्वभूतेषु निद्रारूपेण संस्थिता।
नमस्तस्यै नमस्तस्यै नमस्तस्यै नमो नमः।। 9।।

या देवी सर्वभूतेषु क्षुधारूपेण संस्थिता।
नमस्तस्यै नमस्तस्यै नमस्तस्यै नमो नमः।। 10।।

या देवी सर्वभूतेषुच्छायारूपेण संस्थिता।
नमस्तस्यै नमस्तस्यै नमस्तस्यै नमो नमः।। 11।।

या देवी सर्वभूतेष शक्तिरूपेण संस्थिता।
नमस्तस्यै नमस्तस्यै नमस्तस्यै नमो नमः।। 12।।

या देवी सर्वभूतेषु तृष्णारूपेण संस्थिता।
नमस्तस्यै नमस्तस्यै नमस्तस्यै नमो नमः।। 13।।

या देवी सर्वभूतेषु क्षान्तिरूपेण संस्थिता।
नमस्तस्यै नमस्तस्यै नमस्तस्यै नमो नमः।। 14।।

या देवी सर्वभूतेषु जातिरूपेण संस्थिता।
नमस्तस्यै नमस्तस्यै नमस्तस्यै नमो नमः।। 15।।

या देवी सर्वभूतेषु लज्जारूपेण संस्थिता।
नमस्तस्यै नमस्तस्यै नमस्तस्यै नमो नमः।। 16।।

या देवी सर्वभूतेषु शान्तिरूपेण संस्थिता।
नमस्तस्यै नमस्तस्यै नमस्तस्यै नमो नमः।। 17।।

या दवी सर्वभूतेषु श्रद्धारूपेण संस्थिता।
नमस्तस्यै नमस्तस्यै नमस्तस्यै नमो नमः।। 18।।

या देवी सर्वभूतेषु कान्तिरूपेण संस्थिता।
नमस्तस्यै नमस्तस्यै नमस्तस्यै नमो नमः।। 19।।

या देवी सर्वभूतेषु लक्ष्मीरूपेण संस्थिता।
नमस्तस्यै नमस्तस्यै नमस्तस्यै नमो नमः।। 20।।

या देवी सर्वभूतेषु वृत्तिरूपेण संस्थिता।
नमस्तस्यै नमस्तस्यै नमस्तस्यै नमो नमः।। 21।।

या देवी सर्वभूतेषु स्मृतिरूपेण संस्थिता।
नमस्तस्यै नमस्तस्यै नमस्तस्यै नमो नमः।। 22।।

या देवी सर्वभूतेषु दयारूपेण संस्थिता।
नमस्तस्यै नमस्तस्यै नमस्तस्यै नमो नमः।। 23।।

या देवी सर्वभूतेषु तुष्टिरूपेण संस्थिता।
नमस्तस्यै नमस्तस्यै नमस्तस्यै नमो नमः।। 24।।

या देवी सर्वभूतेषु मातृरूपेण संस्थिता।
नमस्तस्यै नमस्तस्यै नमस्तस्यै नमो नमः।। 25।।

या देवी सर्वभूतेषु भ्रान्तिरूपेण संस्थिता।
नमस्तस्यै नमस्तस्यै नमस्तस्यै नमो नमः।। 26।।

इन्द्रियाणामधिष्ठात्री भूतानां चाखिलेषु या।
भूतेषु सततं तस्यै व्याप्तिदेव्यै नमो नमः।। 27।।

चितिरूपेण या कृत्स्नमेतद्व्याप्य स्थिता जगत्।
नमस्तस्यै नमस्तस्यै नमस्तस्यै नमो नमः।। 28।।

स्तुता सुरैः पूर्वमभीष्टसंश्रया-
त्तथा सुरेन्द्रेण दिनेषु सेविता।
करोतु सा नः शुभहेतुरीश्वरी
शुभानि भद्राण्यभिहन्तु चापदः।। 29।।

या साम्प्रतं चोद्धतदैत्यतापितै-
रस्माभिरीशा च सुरैर्नमस्यते।
या च स्मृता तत्क्षणमेव हन्ति नः
सर्वापदो भक्तिविनम्रमूर्तिभिः।। 30।।

The Translation of the Tantrik Ratri Suktam is given in the fifth chapter from Shloka number 9 to 82.

अथ प्राधानिकं रहस्यम्

The Primal Secret

Perform the *Viniyoga* of the *Triple Rahasyam* viz. the *Pradhanikam-Vaikritikam-Murti Rahasyam,* by reciting the *Viniyoga Mantra* and pouring water from the right hand on the Copper pot.

ॐ अस्य श्रीसप्तशतीरहस्यत्रयस्य नारायण ऋषिरनुष्टुप्छन्दः, महाकालीमहालक्ष्मीमहासरस्वत्यो देवता यथोक्तफलावाप्त्यर्थं जपे विनियोगः।

Om *Narayan* is the *Rishi,* Anushtup is the *Chhanda*—metre, *Mahakali, Mahalakshmi, Mahasarasvati* are the Devatas of the Traya—three *Shri Sapta Shati Rahasyas*—secrets. Its *Viniyoga*—the application is to attain the fruits of eternity/high merits as said in this scripture.

राजोवाच

The King Said :

भगवन्नवतारा मे चण्डिकायास्त्वयोदिताः।
ऐतेषां प्रकृतिं ब्रह्मन् प्रधानं वक्तुमर्हसि।। 1।।

O Gracious Rishi! You have narrated me the episode of the incarnations of Shri Chandika. O Brahman! Please be gracious enough to reveal me the mystry behind the *Pradhanika Rahasyam.*

आराध्यं यन्मया देव्याः स्वरूपं येन च द्विज।
विधिना ब्रूहि सकलं यथावत्प्रणतस्य मे।। 2।।

O great *Dvija*/Brahmin! I make prostration before you. Be gracious enough to reveal me about the methodology to be undertaken with respect to the Devi's worship. Do please tell me in its right perspective.

ऋषिरुवाच

The Rishi Said

इदं रहस्यं परममनाख्येयं प्रचक्षते।
भक्तोऽसीति न मे किञ्चित्तवावाच्यं नराधिप।। 3।।

O king! This is highly occult and mystic. It need not to be disclosed. But since you are my devotee, I cannot avoid you.

सर्वस्याद्या महालक्ष्मीस्त्रिगुणा परमेश्वरी।
लक्ष्यालक्ष्यस्वरूपा सा व्याप्य कृत्स्नं व्यवस्थिता।। 4।।

Mahalakshmi is the Primal cause of this universe. She is *Trigunamayi Parmeshvari*—the Supreme Sovereign Mother with triple attributes. She is manifest in the universe, with Her immanent and transcendent nature.

मातुलुङ्गं गदां खेटं पानपात्रं च बिभ्रती।
नागं लिङ्गं च योनिं च बिभ्रती नृप मूर्धनि।। 5।।

O King! She holds *Matulunga* flower, mace, shield and a casket containing betel leaves, in Her four hands. Also She is adorned with a Naga/cobra; *Lingam* and *Yoni*/the symbols of *Purusha* and *Prakriti* (the male and female characteristics) on Her forehead.

तप्तकाञ्चनवर्णाभा तप्तकाञ्चनभूषणा।
शून्यं तदखिलं स्वेन पूरयामास तेजसा।। 6।।

Her looks are lustrous like pure gold and Her ornaments are of the pure gold. She has filled the void with the lustrous looks, which She posseses.

शून्यं तदखिलं लोकं विलोक्य परमेश्वरी।
बभार परमं रूपं तमसा केवलेन हि।। 7।।

On seeing the void/nothingness of the universe, She

assumed another form with Her *Tamas* quality, which was excellently superb.

सा भिन्नाञ्जनसंकाशा दंष्ट्राङ्कितवरानना।
विशाललोचना नारी बभूव तनुमध्यमा।। 8।।

That form took the manifestation of a woman, whose appearance was nothing but the jet black like '*Kajal*'—collyrium and Her luminous face was with the strong set of teeth. Her eyes were large and Her waist was slim.

खड्गपात्रशिरः खेटैरलंकृतचतुर्भुजा।
कबन्धहारं शिरसा बिभ्राणा हि शिरःस्त्रजम्।। 9।।

She was holding shield, sword, cup and severed head in Her four hands. Her breast was adorned with the garland of human trunks and forehead with severed heads.

सा प्रोवाच महालक्ष्मीं तामसी प्रमदोत्तमा।
नाम कर्म च मे मातर्देहि तुल्यं नमो नमः।। 10।।

Thus incarnated the best among the women folk, She the *Tamasi Devi* addressed to *Mahalakshmi*—'O Mata—the Mother Supreme! My obeisance be to you. Do please tell me my name and the action to be performed by me.

तां प्रोवाच महालक्ष्मीस्तामसीं प्रमदोत्तमाम्।
ददामि तव नामानि यानि कर्माणि तानि ते।। 11।।

Then Mahalakshmi said to Tamasi Devi—the highly intoxicated but the excellent one among women folk "'I am giving you the name and the actions you need to perform.

महामाया महाकाली महामारी क्षुधा तृषा।
निद्रा तृष्णा चैकवीरा कालरात्रिर्दुरत्यया।। 12।।

Mahamaya, Mahakali, Mahamari, Kshuda, Trisha, Nidra, Trishna, Ekvira, Kalaratri and Duratyaya....

इमानि तव नामानि प्रतिपाद्यानि कर्मभिः।
एभिः कर्माणि ते ज्ञात्वा योऽधीते सोऽश्नुते सुखम्।। 13।।

are Your Names, which will be appropriate according to Your deeds and actions. Whosoever, reads and recites Your *Patham*, fully knowing its appropriation, will get contentment and happiness".

तामित्युक्त्वा महालक्ष्मीः स्वरूपमपरं नृप।
सत्त्वाख्येनातिशुद्धेन गुणेनेन्दुप्रभं दधौ।। 14।।

So said these words to Mahakali, O King! Mahalakshmi assumed/incarnated the second form through Pure Sattva—the innate nature, which was crystal clear like the moon.

अक्षमालाङ्कुशधरा वीणापुस्तकधारिणी।
सा बभूव वरा नारी नामान्यस्यै च सा ददौ।। 15।।

She, the Excellent Mother possessed *Akshamala*—the garland of Rudraksha beads, goad, Vina and a book in Her hands and was given the Names by *Mahalakshmi* as....,

महाविद्या महावाणी भारती वाक् सरस्वती।
आर्या ब्राह्मी कामधेनुर्वेदगर्भा च धीश्वरी।। 16।।

....*Mahavidya, Mahavani, Bharati, Vak, Saraswati, Arya, Brahmi, Kamadhenu, Vedagarbha* and *Dhishwari*.

अथोवाच महालक्ष्मीर्महाकालीं सरस्वतीम्।
युवां जनयतां देव्यौ मिथुने स्वानुरूपतः।। 17।।

Thereafter *Mahalakshmi* addressed to Mahakali and Mahasarasvati : "O Devis! You create the pairs according to your names and attributes."

इत्युक्त्वा ते महालक्ष्मीः ससर्ज मिथुनं स्वयम्।
हिरण्यगर्भौ रुचिरौ स्त्रीपुंसौ कमलासनौ।। 18।।

Saying so, Mahalakshmi Herself created a pair of male and female with Name and Form. Both of them being lovely and beautiful, were filled with the Divine knowledge of *Hiranyagarbha* (Golden fetus womb), seated on the lotus.

ब्रह्मन् विधे विरिञ्चेति धातरित्याह तं नरम्।
श्रीः पद्मे कमले लक्ष्मीत्याह माता च तां स्त्रियम्।। 19।।

Then Mahalakshmi addressed to *Purusha*—Male incarnation : 'Vidhi, Viranchi, Dhata' and 'Shri, Padma, Kamala, Lakshmi' etc. to the Female incarnation.

महाकाली भारती च मिथुने सृजतः सह।
एतयोरपि रूपाणि नामानि च वदामि ते।। 20।।

Then *Mahakali* and *Bharti / Saraswati* created a pair separately. I am also conveying you their names and forms.

नीलकण्ठं रक्तबाहुं श्वेताङ्गं चन्द्रशेखरम्।
जनयामास पुरुषं महाकाली सितां स्त्रियम्।। 21।।

Mahakali created the Purusha having a blue spot in his throat region and having red arms, white complexion and crown of the moon on his forehead. Also She created the woman with the excellent fair colour.

स रुद्रः शंकरः स्थाणुः कपर्दी च त्रिलोचनः।
त्रयी विद्या कामधेनुः सा स्त्री भाषाक्षरा स्वरा।। 22।।

That Purusha was named having the excellence of *Sthanu, Kapardi* and *Trilochana*, the female was named as *Trayi, Vidya, Kamadhenu, Bhasha, Akshara* and *Svara*.

सरस्वती स्त्रियं गौरीं कृष्णं च पुरुषं नृप।
जनयामास नामानि तयोरपि वदामि ते।। 23।।

O King! Saraswati created Gauri—the grand fair woman and the dark coloured Purusha—the male incarnation. I am telling you the Names of those incarnation.

विष्णुः कृष्णो हृषीकेशो वासुदेवो जनार्दनः।
उमा गौरी सती चण्डी सुन्दरी सुभगा शिवा।। 24।।

"The Purusha was adored as *Vishnu, Krishna, Hrishikesha, Vasudeva* and *Janardana* and the Female as *Uma, Gauri, Sati, Chandi, Sundari, Subhaga* and *Shiva*.

एवं युवतयः सद्यः पुरुषत्वं प्रपेदिरे।
चक्षुष्मन्तो नु पश्यन्ति नेतरेऽतद्विदो जनाः।। 25।।

Thus all the three Yuvatis—young females instantly attained the Male forms. This transformation can be known only to Chakshumanta—the *Jnanis*/men of Divine knowledge/ realisation and not by others lacking that knowledge.

ब्रह्मणे प्रददौ पत्नीं महालक्ष्मीर्नृप त्रयीम्।
रुद्राय गौरीं वरदां वासुदेवाय च श्रियम्।। 26।।

O King! Mahalakshmi offered Saraswati—with the Triple knowledge of the Vedas, i.e. of (*Parmatman, Jivatman* and *Prakriti*) to Brahma as his consort; *Gauri*—the bestower of boons to Rudra and Shri/Lakshmi to Bhagavan Vishnu.

स्वरया सह सम्भूय विरिञ्चोऽण्डमजीजनत्।
बिभेद भगवान् रुद्रस्तद् गौर्या सह वीर्यवान्।। 27।।

Brahma created *Brahmanda*—the Universal egg through Saraswati and the Powerful Rudra pierced it with the help of Gauri.

अण्डमध्ये प्रधानादि कार्यजातमभून्नृप।
महाभूतात्मकं सर्वं जगत्स्थावरजङ्गमम्।। 28।।

O King! With that cosmic egg, *Pradhana*—primal force etc. viz. *Mahat-tattva* with the *Pancha Mahabhutas* manifested in the animate and inanimate form in the Universe.

पुपोष पालयामास तल्लक्ष्म्या सह केशवः।
संजहार जगत्सर्वं सह गौर्या महेश्वरः।। 29।।

After this process, *Keshva* (Vishnu) through the affiliation of Lakshmi sustained this Universe and at the time of Pralaya—the final dissolution, *Maheshwara* with *Gauri* annihilated this Universe.

महालक्ष्मीर्महाराज सर्वसत्त्वमयीश्वरी।
निराकारा च साकारा सैव नानाभिधानभृत्।। 30।।

O King! Mahalakshmi alone is the Sovereign Supreme Mother—creatrix of all the existence. She is both with form and formless, thus assuming various forms.

नामान्तरैर्निरूप्यैषा नाम्ना नान्येन केनचित्।। ॐ ।। 31 ।।

Mahalakashmi cannot be visualised / attained only with One name and form, but with various expositions of Names and Forms (as Mahalakshmi is vast and infinite).

इति प्राधानिकं रहस्यं सम्पूर्णम्

Here, concludes the Primal Secret.

अथ वैकृतिकं रहस्यम्

THE SECRET OF MUTATION/MODIFICATION

ऋषिरुवाच

The Rishi Said :

ॐ त्रिगुणा तामसी देवी सात्त्विकी या त्रिधोदिता।
सा शर्वा चण्डिका दुर्गा भद्रा भगवतीर्यते।। 1।।

Om. Verily, She is *Sharva, Chandika, Durga, Bhadra, Bhagavati* and with other such Names, as has been said of the *Triguna-Tamsi* with the Triple nature by the *Devi Sattviki* (Mahalakshmi).

योगनिद्रा हरेरुक्ता महाकाली तमोगुणा।
मधुकैटभनाशार्थं यां तुष्टावाम्बुजासनः।। 2।।

Mahakali is the *Yoga-nidra*/mystic sleep of Hari (Vishnu), and is of the Tamas nature. She was adored by (Brahma), seated on the navel lotus of *Shri Hari* for killing Madhu and Kaitabha Rakshaas.

दशवक्त्रा दशभुजा दशपादाञ्जनप्रभा।
विशालया राजमाना त्रिंशल्लोचनमालया।। 3।।

She is having ten faces, ten arms and ten feet. She is jet black like *Kajal*—black ointment, and looking exceedingly excellent with the garland layer of thirty eyes.

स्फुरद्दशनदंष्ट्रा सा भीमरूपापि भूमिप।
रूपसौभाग्यकान्तीनां सा प्रतिष्ठा महाश्रियः।। 4।।

O King! Her teeth and jaws are trickling. Though She is with ferocious looks, yet She is the Supreme store-house of grace, auspiciousness, lustre and prosperity.

खड्गबाणगदाशूलचक्रशङ्खभुशुण्डिभृत्।
परिघं कार्मुकं शीर्षं निश्च्योतद्रुधिरं दधौ।। 5।।

She holds sword, arrow, mace, spear, discus, conch, *Bhushundi*, *Parigha*, bow and skull, through which blood is eternally oozing out...,

एषा सा वैष्णवी माया महाकाली दुरत्यया।
आराधिता वशीकुर्यात् पूजाकर्तुश्चराचरम्।। 6।।

...so is the Mahakali—the Eternal Maya of Shri Vishnu. When adored and worshipped, She blesses devotees with the force of keeping the static and dynamic world at the will of devotees.

सर्वदेवशरीरेभ्यो याऽऽविर्भूतामितप्रभा।
त्रिगुणा सा महालक्ष्मीः साक्षान्महिषमर्दिनी।। 7।।

She is verily, Mahalakshmi with infinite lustre, who got incarnated from the beings of all the Devatas. She is adored as Triple Natured Prakriti, who is the slayer of Mahishasura.

श्वेतानना नीलभुजा सुश्वेतस्तनमण्डला।
रक्तमध्या रक्तपादा नीलजङ्घोरुरुन्मदा।। 8।।

Her face is extremely fair; arms are dark blue, white is the breast, waist and feet are red, thighs and calf—muscles are of dark blue colour. She is ever excited.

सुचित्रजघना चित्रमाल्याम्बरविभूषणा।
चित्रानुलेपना कान्तिरूपसौभाग्यशालिनी।। 9।।

She is adorned with multicoloured garments in Her upper waist, thus looks extremely beautiful and wonderful. Her looks are of lustre, beauty and giver of prosperity.

अष्टादशभुजा पूज्या सा सहस्रभुजा सती।
आयुधान्यत्र वक्ष्यन्ते दक्षिणाधःकरक्रमात्।। 10।।

Though She is having thousands of arms, yet She is to be worshipped with eighteen arms alone. Now, a description is given about the garments, which is covered underneath Her left and right hands.

अक्षमाला च कमलं बाणोऽसिः कुलिशं गदा।
चक्रं त्रिशूलं परशुः शङ्खो घण्टा च पाशकः।। 11।।

She is armed with Akshamala, lotus, arrow, sword, thunderbolt, mace, discus, trident, axe, conch, bell, noose...

शक्तिर्दण्डश्चर्म चापं पानपात्रं कमण्डलुः।
अलंकृतभुजामेभिरायुधैः कमलासनाम्।। 12।।

..Shakti, staff/stick, shield, bow, casket of betel leaf and pot which give splendour to Her arms. She is seated on the throne of lotus.

सर्वदेवमयीमीशां महालक्ष्मीमिमां नृप।
पूजयेत्सर्वलोकानां स देवानां प्रभुर्भवेत्।। 13।।

She is All Divinity, Supreme Sovereignity. Whosoever worships such Mahalakshmi attains the sovereignity over all the Devas and the world.

गौरीदेहात्समुद्भूता या सत्त्वैकगुणाश्रया।
साक्षात्सरस्वती प्रोक्ता शुम्भासुरनिबर्हिणी।। 14।।

She is said to be Saraswati of the Sattva nature who has come out from the very being of *Gauri/Parvati*, and has verily, killed the Asura Shumbha.

दधौ चाष्टभुजा बाणमुसले शूलचक्रभृत्।
शङ्खं घण्टां लाङ्गलं च कार्मुकं वसुधाधिप।। 15।।

O King! She is having eight arms and holds arrow, pestle, spear, discus, conch, bell, plough and bow...,

एषा सम्पूजिता भक्त्या सर्वज्ञत्वं प्रयच्छति।
निशुम्भमथिनी देवी शुम्भासुरनिबर्हिणी।। 16।।

...She is Devi (Saraswati), the giver of all wisdom and

knowledge, when worshipped with devotion, who has killed Shumbha and annihilated Nishumbha.

इत्युक्तानि स्वरूपाणि मूर्तीनां तव पार्थिव।
उपासनं जगन्मातु पृथगासां निशामय।। 17।।

O King! I have narrated you the very form of the Three Murtis (triple manifestation of Devi). Now listen to, how are they to be worshipped, separately.

महालक्ष्मीर्यदा पूज्या महाकाली सरस्वती।
दक्षिणोत्तरयोः पूज्ये पृष्ठातो मिथुनत्रयम्।। 18।।

Install Mahalakshmi in the centre, when you have to worship Her. Establish *Mahakali* and *Mahasaraswati* in Her south and north side respectively. In the back, all the three *Yugal Devatas* (pair divinities), should be adored and worshipped.

विरञ्चिः स्वरया मध्ये रुद्रो गौर्या च दक्षिणे।
वामे लक्ष्म्या हृषीकेषः पुरतो देवतात्रयम्।। 19।।

Just in the central back of Mahalakshmi, Brahma with Saraswati to be worshipped. In the right, Rudra with Gauri and in the left *Vishnu / Hrishikesha* with *Lakshmi* to be adored. The Three Devi-Devatas are also to be worshipped in front of Mahalakshmi.

अष्टादशभुजा मध्ये वामे चास्या दशानना।
दक्षिणेऽष्टभुजा लक्ष्मीर्महतीति समर्चयेत्।। 20।।

Ashtadashabhuja Lakshmi' with eighteen arms in the centre, *Dashanana / Mahakali* with ten faces in the left and in the right *Ashtabhuja Mahasaraswati* with eight arms is to be worshipped before Mahalakshmi.

अष्टादशभुजा चैषा यदा पूज्या नराधिप।
दशानना चाष्टभुजा दक्षिणोत्तरयोस्तदा।। 21।।

O King! When *Ashtadashbhuja*-Devi with eighteen arms is invoked, then Dashanana with ten faces and *Ashtabhuja*—Devi with eight faces are to be adored in the directions of South and North respectively...,

कालमृत्यू च सम्पूज्यौ सर्वारिष्टप्रशान्तये।
यदा चाष्टभुजा पूज्या शुम्भासुरनिबर्हिणी।। 22।।

....*Kala Mrityu* (Time and Death) is to be worshiped for warding off all the obstacles, the Ashtabuja is to be worshipped, who is the killer of Shumbha Asura.

नवास्याः शक्तयः पूज्यास्तदा रुद्रविनायकौ।
नमो देव्या इति स्तोत्रैर्महालक्ष्मीं समर्चयेत।। 23।।

Nine Shaktis are to be worshipped alongwith Rudra and Ganesha. Mahalakshmi is invoked with the *Namo Devi...*, *mantra.*

अवतारत्रयार्चायां स्तोत्रमन्त्रास्तदाश्रयाः।
अष्टादशभुजा चैषा पूज्या महिषमर्दिनी।। 24।।

All the *Stotras* and *Mantras* need to be recited regarding their three incarnations. Ashtadashabhuja Devi is the Supreme among all, as She is the slayer of Mahishasura.

महालक्ष्मीर्महाकाली सैव प्रोक्ता सरस्वती।
ईश्वरी पुण्यपापानां सर्वलोकमहेश्वरी।। 25।।

She is Mahakali, Mahalakshmi and Mahasaraswati. She is Ishvari—the Sovereign Supreme authority and the source of all the *Punyas-Papas* (virtues and sins).

महिषान्तकरी येन पूजिता स जगत्प्रभुः।
पूजयेज्जगतां धात्रीं चण्डिकां भक्तवत्सलाम्।। 26।।

Verily, he is the master of the Universe, who adores Mahalakshmi with great devotion, Who has slain Mahishasura, so do adore and worship the Great Chandika, She is Bhaktavatsala—very dear to the devotees. She is the sustainer of the Universe.

अर्घ्यादिभिरलंकारैर्गन्धपुष्पैस्तथाक्षतैः।
धूपैर्दीपैश्च नैवेद्यैर्नानाभक्ष्यसमन्वितैः।। 27।।

With water oblations, ornaments, scents, flowers, rice,

incense, lamp and with different types of eatables, She is to be worshipped.

रुधिराक्तेन बलिना मांसेन सुरया नृप।
(बलिमांसादिपूजेयं विप्रवर्ज्या मयेरिता।।
तेषां किल सुरामांसैर्नोक्ता पूजा नृप क्वचित्।)
प्रणामाचमनीयेन चन्दनेन सुगन्धिना।। 28।।

The killing of animals and wine is also used in the worship, (but not recommended for the Brahmins, as there is no such scriptural injuction). They need to worship through *Pranayama, Achamana, Chandana* and with fragrances only...,

सकर्पूरैश्च ताम्बूलैर्भक्तिभावसमन्वितैः।
वामभागेऽग्रतो देव्याश्छिन्नशीर्षं महासुरम्।। 29।।

...also with camphor and *Tambul*, with devotion and surrender before Devi. In the left side of the Devi *Mahishasura*—the Asura of great prowess, with slain head should be worshipped....

पूजयेन्महिषं येन प्राप्तं सायुज्यमीशया।
दक्षिणे पुरतः सिंहं समग्रं धर्ममीश्वरम्।। 30।।

.....as Mahisha also attained identity with the Devi. *Singha*—Lion should be worshipped in the right side of the Devi, who is the symbol of coordination and Dharma...,

वाहनं पूजयेद्देव्या धृतं येन चराचरम्।
कुर्याच्च स्तवनं धीमांस्तस्या एकाग्रमानसः।। 31।।

....as being the vehicle of Devi. It is Devi who holds this static and dynamic world. She is to be adored with single pointed concentration, devotion, by the men with intellect.

ततः कृताञ्जलिर्भूत्वा स्तुवीत चरितैरिमैः।
एकेन वा मध्यमेन नैकेनेतरयोरिह।। 32।।

Then with folded hands, Devi is to be adored with all the three episodes. If a devotee wants to worship with single episode, he should thus worship with the middle episode only, and not from the first or third.

चरितार्धं तु न जपेज्जपञ्छिद्रमवाप्नुयात्।
प्रदक्षिणानमस्कारान् कृत्वा मूर्ध्नि कृताञ्जलिः ।। 33 ।।

Half of the episode should not be recited as it creates *Chhidra* / perforation. *Pradakshina* and *Namaskar* (circumambulation and prostration) with folded hands...,

क्षमापयेज्जगद्धात्रीं मुहुर्मुहुरतन्द्रितः।
प्रतिश्लोकं च जुहुयात्पायसं तिलसर्पिषा ।। 34 ।।

...to be made with attentive mind at every moment, begging for forgivingness before the Jagat *Dhatri*. *Payasam / Kshira* to be mixed with *tils*—sesame and *Sarpisha*—clarified butter and each *Sholka* to be recited....

जुहुयात्स्तोत्रमन्त्रैर्वा चण्डिकायै शुभं हविः।
भूयो नामपदैर्देवीं पूजयेत्सुसमाहितः ।। 35 ।।

.....for *Havih Homa*, or with *Stotras* which occur in the text of Shri Chandi. After Homa, *Nama-Mantras* of Devi to be recited with single mindedness / full concentration.

प्रयतः प्राञ्जलिः प्रह्वः प्रणम्यारोप्य चात्मनि।
सुचिरं भावयेदीशां चण्डिकां तन्मयो भवेत् ।। 36 ।।

Then prostrate before the Devi, keeping the mind and sense organs under control and concentrate on the Devi for the considerable period of time.

एवं यः पूजयेद्भक्त्या प्रत्यहं परमेश्वरीम्।
भुक्त्वा भोगान् यथाकामं देवीसायुज्यमाप्नुयात् ।। 37 ।।

Whosoever, worships the *Parmeshwari* under discipline, attains the identity with the Devi, after enjoying all the merits of life.

यो न पूजयते नित्यं चण्डिकां भक्तवत्सलाम्।
भस्मीकृत्यास्य पुण्यानि निर्दहेत्परमेश्वरी ।। 38 ।।

Those who do not worship Chandika regularly, who is *Bhaktavatsala*—the Loving/Adorable Mother of the devotees, thus She reduces their merits to ashes.

तस्मात्पूजय भूपाल सर्वलोकमहेश्वरीम्।
यथोक्तेन विधानेन चण्डिकां सुखमाप्स्यसि॥39॥

Therefore, O King! Make an obeisance to Chandika, who is the Sovereign Supreme Mother of the Universe. Thus you will attain peace, pleasure/prosperity, as described and prescribed in the Sacred text.

इति वैकृतिकं रहस्यं सम्पूर्णम्

Here, the Secret of Mutation/Modification is concluded.

अथ मूर्तिरहस्यम्

THE SECRET OF FORM

ऋषिरुवाच

The Rishi Said :

ॐ नन्दा भगवती नाम या भवष्यिति नन्दजा।
स्तुता सा पूजिता भक्त्या वशीकुर्याज्जगत्त्रयम्।। 1 ।।

O King! *Nanda Devi,* to be born from Nanda, keeps the triple world under the control of the Devotee, if She is adored and worshipped with all devotion and dedication.

कनकोत्तमकान्तिः सा सुकान्तिकनकाम्बरा।
देवी कनकवर्णाभा कनकोमत्तमभूषणा।। 2 ।।

Her lustrous limbs are but the very luminous shine of the gold. Her garments are beautiful and of golden colour. Her hue is that of gold and is adorned with the golden ornaments.

कमलाङ्कुशपाशाब्जैरलंकृतचतुर्भुजा ।
इन्दिरा कमला लक्ष्मीः सा श्री रुक्माम्बुजासना।। 3 ।।

Her four arms are adorned with lotus, goad, noose and conch. She is embodiment of *Indira, Kamala, Lakshmi, Shri* and *Rukam-ambuja-asana* (having Her seat on the golden throne of lotus.

या रक्तदन्तिका नाम देवी प्रोक्ता मयानघ।
तस्याः स्वरूपं वक्ष्याणि शृणु सर्वभयापहम्।। 4 ।।

O pious King! Listen to me. At the outset, I gave you the names of *Ruktadantika,* I will give you Devi's description of Her being. She removes all the obstacles.

रक्ताम्बरा रक्तवर्णा रक्तसर्वाङ्गभूषणा।
रक्तायुधा रक्तनेत्रा रक्तकेशातिभीषणा।। 5।।

She is adorned with red garments. Her hue is also red and all the ornaments of the libms are also red. All Her missiles are red. Her eyes are red. Her hair of the head is also red....,

रक्ततीक्ष्णनखा रक्तदशना रक्तदन्तिका।
पतिं नारीवानुरक्ता देवी भक्तं भजेज्जनम्।। 6।।

Her sharp nails are also red. Her teeth are red, so She is *Raktadantika*. As a wife is devoted/attached to her husband, so the devotees is to be dedicated to Devi who is Supreme Mother.

वसुधेव विशाला सा सुमेरुयुगलस्तनी।
दीर्घौ लम्बावतिस्थूलौ तावतीव मनोहरौ।। 7।।

Raktadantika resembles like Mother earth in volume. Both of Her breasts are resembling like the mountain Sumeru, as being long, wide, gross ad superb.

कर्कशावतिकान्तौ तौ सर्वानन्दपयोनिधी।
भक्तान् सम्पाययेद्देवी सर्वकामदुघौ स्तनौ।। 8।।

Though stiff, yet those are beautiful and are the oceans of bliss. She makes drink the milk of Her breasts to Her devotees, which fulfills all their desires.

खड्गं पात्रं च मुसलं लाङ्गलं च बिभर्ति सा।
आख्याता रक्तचामुण्डा देवी योगेश्वरीति च।। 9।।

She holds sword, casket of betel leaf, pestle/pounder and plough. She is verily *Raktachamunda* and *Yogeshwari*.

अनया व्याप्तमखिलं जगत्स्थावरजङ्गमम्।
इमां यः पूजयेद्भक्त्या स व्याप्नोति चराचरम्।। 10।।

The whole universe of animate and inanimate existence is manifested in Her. Whosoever worships the *Raktadantika* Devi with full devotion, he also gets vast and comprehensive view/higher knowledge of the universe.

(भुक्त्वा भोगान् यथाकामं देवीसायुज्यमाप्नुयात्।)

(He attains the identity with Devi, after enjoying all the merits in the world).

अधीते य इमं नित्यं रक्तदन्त्या वपुःस्तवम्।
तं सा परिचरेद्देवी पतिं प्रियमिवाङ्गना।। 11।।

Whosoever recites the Stuti of Raktadantika daily, the Devi will keep vigil on him with affectoin for his safety, just like a chaste woman is always at the service of her husband.

शाकम्भरी नीलवर्णा नीलोत्पलविलोचना।
गम्भीरनाभिस्त्रिवलीविभूषिततनूदरी।। 12।।

The hue of Shakambhari Devi is blue. Her eyes are like blue lotus. Her navel is descended and Her abdomen with *Trivali*—the triple skin fold is very slim.

सुकर्कशसमोत्तुङ्गवृत्तपीनघनस्तनी ।
मुष्टिं शिलीमुखापूर्णं कमलं कमलालया।। 13।।

Both of Her breasts are stiff, of the same dimension, upright, well rounded, gross and properly close to each other. She holds beautiful lotus in Her fist and Her abode is the lotus.

पुष्पपल्लवमूलादिफलाढ्यं शाकसञ्चयम्।
काम्यानन्तरसैर्युक्तं क्षुत्तृणमृत्युभयापहम्।। 14।।

She is of the botanical life, which is of flowers, tender leaves, roots and fruits, providing juices which keeps away from hunger, thirst, death and oldage...,

कार्मुकं च स्फुरत्कान्ति बिभ्रती परमेश्वरी।
शाकम्भरी शताक्षी सा सैव दुर्गा प्रकीर्तिता।। 15।।

...and thus She is the Parmeshwari. She holds shining and lustrous bow in Her hands. She is *Shakambhari, Shatakshi*—having hundred eyes. Verily, She is said to be Durga....

विशोका दुष्टदमनी शमनी दुरितापदाम्।
उमा गौरी सती चण्डी कालिका सा च पार्वती।। 16।।

...She is *Vishoka, Dushtadamani, Shamani* and *Duritapaadam,* (who removes all the miseries), annihilates the wicked, brings peace, and removes all the obstacles. She is *Uma, Gauri, Sati, Chandi, Kalika* and *Parvati.*

शाकम्भरीं स्तुवन् ध्यायञ्जपन् सम्पूजयन्नमन्।
अक्षय्यमश्नुते शीघ्रमन्नपानामृतं फलम्।। 17।।

Whosoever, meditates upon *Shakambhari* and performs Japam and prostrates before Her, adores Her; He attains the nectar of eternal bliss alongwith foods and drinks.

भीमापि नीलवर्णा सा दंष्ट्रादशनभासुरा।
विशाललोचना नारी वृत्तपीनपयोधरा।। 18।।

Bhima Devi is also of blue colour. Her jaws and teeth are shining and bright. Large are Her eyes. Feminine are Her looks and breasts are properly rounded and stiff.

चन्द्राहासं च डमरुं शिरः पात्रं च बिभ्रती।
एकवीरा कालरात्रिः सैवोक्ता कामदा स्तुता।। 19।।

She holds *Chandrahasa* sword, *Damru,* a skull and casket of betel leaves in Her hands. She is *Ekavira, Kalaratri* and *Kamada* and is worshipped with such Names.

तेजोमण्डलदुर्धषा भ्रामरी चित्रकान्तिभृत्।
चित्रानुलेपना देवी चित्राभरणभूषिता।। 20।।

The lustre of Bhrahmari Devi is superb and of multicolours. Her looks are multifarious and so are Her garments of different colours. She is adorned with wonderful ornaments.

चित्रभ्रमरपाणिः सा महामारीति गीयते।
इत्येता मूर्तयो देव्या याः ख्याता वसुधाधिप।। 21।।

Her attributes are sung in the form of being *Chitra-Bhramara-Pani* (holding multiformed bees in Her hands) and *Mahamari*/dreadful fatal diseases, plague etc. and such other Names. O King! These are the *Moortis*/divine formations of the Devi.

जगन्मातुश्चण्डिकायाः कीर्तिताः कामधेनवः।
इदं रहस्यं परमं न वाच्यं कस्यचित्त्वया।। 22।।

She is *Kamadhenu*, the giver of plenty fulfilling all the wishes/desires as She is the Universal Mother *Chandika*. "You should not give this secret to anybody, as it is highly occult/mystic.

व्याख्यानं दिव्यमूर्तिनामभीष्टफलदायकम्।
तस्मात् सर्वप्रयत्नेन देवीं जप निरन्तरम्।। 23।।

The episode of the Divine *Murtis* give the desired fruits. Hence, you need to devote yourself earnestly in the meditation of the Devi.

सपतजन्मार्जितैर्घोरैर्ब्रह्महत्यासमैरपि ।
पाठमात्रेण मन्त्राणां मुच्यते सर्वकिल्बिषैः।। 24।।

It is only through the recitation of the *Sapta Shati Mantra*, a man afflicted with the *Brahmahatya*/killing of Brahman like heinous sins since past seven births, gets freed from that sin.

देव्या ध्यानं मया ख्यातं गुह्याद् गुह्यतरं महत्।
तस्मात् सर्वप्रयत्नेन सर्वकामफलप्रदम्।। 25।।

I have with all earnestness and care revealed you the Secret *Dhyanam* of the Devi which is the giver/bestower of all auspiciousness.

(एतस्यास्त्वं प्रसादेन सर्वमान्यो भविष्यसि।
सर्वरूपमयी देवी सर्वं देवीमयं जगत्।
अतोऽहं विश्वरूपां तां नमामि परमेश्वरीम्।)

(You will thus regain all recognitions through Her grace. The Devi is All Form, the whole world is the manifestation of that Devi. So I make prostration before the Universal Mother, who is the whole universe in Herself)."

इति मूर्तिरहस्यं सम्पूर्णम्

Thus the Secret of Murti is concluded.

After concluding all the three Rahasyam, make a prayer to Shri Durga and recite.

क्षमा-प्रार्थना

PARDON PRAYER

अपराधसहस्राणि क्रियन्तेऽहर्निशं मया।
दासोऽयमिति मां मत्वा क्षमस्व परमेश्वरि।। 1।।

O Parmeshvari! the Sovereign Supreme Mother! I do commit thousands of sins day in and day out. Do forgive me considering me as your servant.

आवाहनं न जानामि न जानामि विसर्जनम्।
पूजां चैव न जानामि क्षम्यतां परमेश्वरि।। 2।।

I do not know how to invoke you, nor do I know how to bid You farewell. Nor I know Puja/worhsip. Please forgive me O Parmeshwari!

मन्त्रहीनं क्रियाहीनं भक्तिहीनं सुरेश्वरि।
यत्पूजितं मया देवि परिपूर्णं तदस्तु मे।। 3।।

I do not know what Mantra is. Neither I know its Kriya/ procedure. Nor I have devotion. In whatsoever manner, I have worshipped you, may that be whole and perfect! O Mother Sureshwari, You are the Mother of the Devas....

अपराधशतं कृत्वाजगदम्बेति चोच्चरेत्।
यां गतिं समवाप्नोति न तां ब्रह्मादयः सुराः।। 4।।

...whosoever surrenders before You and utters Jagadamba/ the Mother of the Universe, after committing hundreds of sins, he also attains that state, which is not accessible even to Brahma and other Devatas.

सापराधोऽस्मि शरणं प्राप्तस्त्वां जगदम्बिके।
इदानीमनुकम्प्योऽहं यथेच्छसि तथा कुरु।। 5।।

O Jagadamba! I have committed sins, but have surrended

before You, I need to be pardoned. Do whatever You deem right.

अज्ञानाद्विस्मृतेर्भ्रान्त्या यन्न्यूनमधिकं कृतम्।
तत्सर्वं क्षम्यतां देवि प्रसीद परमेश्वरि।। 6।।

O Parmeshvari! Little or more whatever I have done, due to forgetfulness, ignorance, or because of the intellectual illusion, please waive them all off. And be pleased with me!

कामेश्वरि जगन्मातः सच्चिदानन्दविग्रहे।
गृहाणार्चामिमां प्रीत्या प्रसीद परमेश्वरि।। 7।।

O Satchitananda! Truth, consciousnesss and bliss you are! You are Kameshvari and Jagadmata. Accept my worship with affection and be pleased with me!

गुह्यातिगुह्यगोप्त्री त्वं गृहाणास्मत्कृतं जपम्।
सिद्धिर्भवतु मे देवि त्वत्प्रसादात्सुरेश्वरि।। 8।

O Devi! O Sureshvari! You are the protection of everything which is of utmost secret. Please accept the Japam, which I offer to You. May I get perfection through your grace.

।। श्रीदुर्गार्पणमस्तु।।

May my prayer be dedicated to Shri Durga!

सिद्धकुंजिकास्तोत्रम्

Siddha-Kunjika-Stotram

शिव उवाच

Shiva Said :

श्रृणु देवि प्रवक्ष्यामि कुञ्जिकास्तोत्रमुत्तमम्।
येन मन्त्रप्रभावेण चण्डीजापः शुभो भवेत्।। 1।।

Listen, O Devi, to the Kunjika stotram, which in highly proficient/excellent! The Japam of Chandi becomes auspicious, with the effects of this Stotra mantras.

न कवचं नार्गलास्तोत्रं कीलकं न रहस्यकम्।
न सूक्तं नापि ध्यानं च न न्यासो न च वार्चनम्।। 2।।

There is no need of *Kavacham, Argala, Kilkam, Rahasyam, Suktam, Dyanam, Nyasa* and of *Archanam*.

कुञ्जिकापाठमात्रेण दुर्गापाठफलं लभेत्।
अति गुह्यतरं देवि देवानामपि दुर्लभम्।। 3।।

Kunjka Patha gives the merits of the *Durga Patham*. It is highly mystic and inaccessible to the *Devas* as well.

गोपनीयं प्रयत्नेन स्वयोनिरिव पार्वति।
मारणं मोहनं वश्यं स्तम्भनोच्चाटनादिकम्।
पाठमात्रेण संसिद्ध्येत् कुञ्जिकास्तोत्रमुत्तमम्।।4।।

O *Parvati*! Keep this Stotra hidden with efforts as you do keep your *Yoni*—the feminine part hidden. This highly proficient *Kunjika-Stotram* is accomplished and wards off untimely death hypnotics, physical handicaps etc.

अथ मन्त्रः

The Mantra

ॐ ऐं ह्रीं क्लीं चामुण्डायै विच्चे।। ॐ ग्लौं हुं क्लीं जूं सः ज्वालय ज्वालय ज्वल ज्वल प्रज्वल प्रज्वल ऐं ह्रीं क्लीं चामुण्डायै विच्चे ज्वल हं सं लं क्षं फट् स्वाहा।

"Aum Aim Hrim Klim Chamundayai Vichche. Aum Glaum Hum Klim Jum Sah Jwalaya Jwalaya Jwala Jwala Prajwala Prajwala Aim Hrim Klim Chamundayai Vichche Jwala Ham Sam Lam Ksham Phat Svaha!"

।। इति मन्त्रः ।।

(Mantra is concluded)

नमस्ते रुद्ररूपिण्यै नमस्ते मधुमर्दिनि।
नमः कैटभहारिण्यै नमस्ते महिषार्दिनि।। 1।।
नमस्ते शुम्भहन्त्र्यै च निशुम्भासुरघातिनि।। 2।।
जाग्रतं हि महादेवि जपं सिद्धं कुरुष्व मे।
ऐंकारी सृष्टिरूपायै ह्रींकारी प्रतिपालिका।। 3।।
क्लींकारी कामरूपिण्यै बीजरूपे नमोऽस्तु ते।
चामुण्डा चण्डघाती च यैकारी वरदायिनी।। 4।।
विच्चे चाभयदा नित्यं नमस्ते मन्त्ररूपिणि।। 5।।
धां धीं धूं धूर्जटेः पत्नी वां वीं वूं वागधीश्वरी।
क्रां क्रीं क्रूं कालिका देवि शां शीं शूं में शुभं कुरु।।6।।
हुं हुं हुंकाररूपिण्यै जं जं जं जम्भनादिनी।
भ्रां भ्रीं भ्रूं भैरवी भद्रे भवान्यै ते नमो नमः।। 7।।
अं कं चं टं तं पं यं शं वीं दुं ऐं वीं हं क्षं
धिजाग्रं धिजाग्रं त्रोटय त्रोटय दीप्तं कुरु कुरु स्वाहा।।
पां पीं पूं पार्वती पूर्णा खां खीं खूं खेचरी तथा।। 8।।
सां सीं सूं सप्तशती देव्या मन्त्रसिद्धिं कुरुष्व मे।।
इदं तु कुञ्जिकास्तोत्रं मन्त्रजागर्तिहेतवे।

अभक्ते नैव दातव्यं गोपितं रक्ष पार्वति।।
यस्तु कुञ्जिकया देवि हीनां सप्तशतीं पठेत्।
न तस्य जायते सिद्धिररण्ये रोदनं यथा।।
इति श्रीरुद्रयामले गौरीतन्त्रे शिवपार्वतीसंवादे
कुञ्जिकास्तोत्रं सम्पूर्णम्।
।। ॐ तत्सत्।।

Thus the Kunjika Stotram is here concluded
Om Tat Sat
(The translation is not given, as it is Matrika explanation of Phoneme, related to the Varna Mala, being highly occult and secret)

Note :
For the Readers/Devotees

1. *Siddha-Kunjika-Stotram* is a dialogue between *Shiva* and the *Devi,* who gives Her, the secrets of the *Chandi Japam.* In this mystic *Stotram*' there is no *Kavacham,* no *Argala,* no *Kilakam,* no *Rahasyam,* no *Suktam,* no *Dhyanam,* no *Nyasam* and no *Archanam,* which has been earlier recommended in the procedure of the *Durga Sapta Shati Patham/Homa.* It is highly occult and highly secret.
2. The mantra is the extension of the *Navarna Mantra* and the *Stuti*/ laudation is for *Rudrarupini-Madhumardini-Kaitabhharini, Mahishardini, Shumbhahantri and Nishumbhaghatini.*
3. The *Navarana Mantra* has been explained in Shloka no. 3,4 and 5 by *Shiva* Himself. The sacred *Matrikas* are highly potent and based on the *Tantras* narrated from Sholka no. 6 and onwards.
4. This *Stotram* should not be given to the unworthy but recommended for the devotees who recite the *Saptashati Patham,* as the recitation of the *Siddha Kunjika Stotram* gives more potency/efficacy in the accomplishment of the *Sapta Shati Patham.*

अथ देव्यपराधक्षमापनस्तोत्रम्

ATHA DEVYAPRADHAKSHAMAPANA STOTRAM

The Pardoning Stotram/Laudation to Devi for Apradha/Misdoings.

न मन्त्रं नो यन्त्रं तदपि च न जाने स्तुतिमहो
न चाह्वानं ध्यानं तदपि च न जाने स्तुतिकथाः।
न जाने मुद्रास्ते तदपि च न जाने विलपनं
परं जाने मातस्त्वदनुसरणं क्लेशहरणम्।। 1।।

O Mother Creatrix! Neither I am conversant with Mantra, nor with the Yantra. I am ignorant of doing the proper Stuti/ laudation and of your scriptural story. I am unaware of your Dhyāna/meditation with determination and know not how to invite Thee. Fully ignorant of your Mudras/physical settings, and know not what and how to propitiate Thee. But O Mother! I do know how to follow Thine Supreme self, which removes all the misfortunes and miseries.

विधेरज्ञानेन द्रविणविरहेणालसतया
विधेयाशक्यत्वात्तव चरणयोर्या च्युतिरभूत्।
तदेतत् क्षन्तव्यं जननि सकलोद्धारिणि शिवे
कुपुत्रो जायेत क्वचिदपि कुमाता न भवति।। 2।।

O Mother Creatrix! Procedure, I do not know, how to undertake, I am helpless and innately lazy, to perform the Puja/worship. Do please pardon me, as I could not follow and adore Thy foot steps. A son can possibly be born usually a stray boy, but not the mother at all.

पृथिव्यां पुत्रास्ते जननि बहवः सन्ति सरलाः
परं तेषां मध्ये विरलतरलोऽहं तव सुतः।

मदीयोऽयं त्यागः समुचितमिदं नो तव शिवे
कुपुत्रो जायेत क्वचिदपि कुमाता न भवति।। 3।।

O Mother Supreme! Many are Thy sons with simplicity and nobility on the earth planet, but I am a prodigal and untoward one of all the progeny. I have been deserted one, who do not behave. O Mother Shiva—the Benign Mother! Mother can never be the wrong one, but unworthy son is possibly born.

जगन्मातर्मातस्तव चरणसेवा न रचिता
न वा दत्तं देवि द्रविणमपि भूयस्तव मया।
तथापि त्वं स्नेहं मयि निरुपमं यत्प्रकुरुषे
कुपुत्रो जायेत क्वचिदपि कुमाता न भवति।। 4।।

O Universal Mother! Neither I did adore/worship Thy feet, nor I surrendered all the riches at Thy feet..., still Thou showereth Thine grace upon me, because, an unworthy son can be born, but least the Mother.

परित्यक्ता देवा विविधविधसेवाकुलतया
मया पञ्चाशीतेरधिकमपनीते तु वयसि।
इदानीं चेन्मातस्तव यदि कृपा नापि भविता
निरालम्बो लम्बोदरजननि कं यामि शरणम्।। 5।।

O the Mother of Ganesha! I did spend more than eighty five years of my life in propitiating the other Devas with different methods/procedures, thus deserted, I do not expect any favour from them. At this critical period of life, to whom should I pay my obeisance, save but Thine feet.

श्वपाको जल्पाको भवति मधुपाकोपमगिरा
निरातङ्को रङ्को विहरति चिरं कोटिकनकैः।
तवापर्णे कर्णे विशति मनुवर्णे फलमिदं
जनः को जानीते जननि जपनीयं जपविधौ।। 6।।

O mother Aparna/not taking a leaf even! If even a phoneme of your Mantra is heard per chance, surely and instantly a foolish dog eater also is graced with Thy compassion, to become evolved, a poorer man gets abundant wealth/riches to sustain the life with grandeur and luxury, then why not a devotee, who is ever absorbed in the methodological Japam—the incantation of Thy name.

चिताभस्मालेपो गरलमशनं दिक्पटधरो
जटाधारी कण्ठे भुजगपतिहारी पशुपतिः।
कपाली भूतेशो भजति जगदीशैकपदवीं
भवानि त्वत्पाणिग्रहणपरिपाटीफलमिदम्।। 7।।

O Bhavani—the Mother of Sustenance! He who smears his body with the ashes of cremation; He who takes poison as food, He who is without any garment to cover the body, He Who holds Vasuki serpent in His throat, He Who holds the head skull as a pot, to Him, who is Bhutesha/ lord of the animate beings and Pashupati/the lord of creation is verily adored as Jagadisha/the lord of universe. All this is so auspicious O Mother! Because Thou has given Thine hand to him, which is Panigrihana.

न मोक्षस्याकाङ्क्षा भवविभववाञ्छापि च न मे
न विज्ञानापेक्षा शशिमुखि सुखेच्छापि न पुनः।
अतस्त्वां संयाचे जननि जननं यातु मम वै
मृडानी रुद्राणी शिव शिव भवानीति जपतः।। 8।।

I have no desire to attain liberation/beatitude/the release from the cycle of birth and death, nor do I long for the worldly riches, aspire I do not for the gnostic self, and not determined to be in peace, but I should always be in constant recitation of Mridāni, Rudrani, Shiva, Shiva Bhavani etc.

नाराधितासि विधिना विविधोपचारैः
किं रुक्षचिन्तनपरैर्न कृतं वचोभिः।
श्यामे त्वमेव यदि किञ्चन मय्यनाथे
धत्से कृपामुचितमम्ब परं तवैव।। 9।।

O Mother Shyama! I could not accomplish Thy worship with the essentials of Aradhana Devotion. Neither was I with the soft tone, nor could I abstain myself from wrong things, still Thou art kind enough to grace me, as I am helpless. Thou alone grant Kripa/mercy. Thou, art the embodiment of compassion to bless me, even I am unworthy child/son.

आपत्सु मग्नः स्मरणं त्वदीयं
करोमि दुर्गे करुणार्णवेशि।
नैतच्छठत्वं मम भावयेथाः
क्षुधातृषार्ता जननीं स्मरन्ति।। 10।।

O Mother Durga! O Compassionate Mother! Being caught in the whirlpool of miseries. I invoke you. Do not consider O Mother, that my deceit..., always a child calls, to the mother when subjected to the pangs of thirst and hunger.]

जगदम्ब विचित्रमत्र किं
परिपूर्णा करुणास्ति चेन्मयि।
अपराधपरम्परापरं
न हि माता समुपेक्षते सुतम्।। 11।।

O Mother of the universe! There is no wonder, that Thine grace envelops me around. The child commits mistakes over mistakes, still the Mother does not desert him.

मत्समः पातकी नास्ति पापघ्नी त्वत्समा न हि।
एवं ज्ञात्वा महादेवी यथायोग्यं तथा कुरु।। 12।।

O Mother Mahadevi! None aheads me in the sins and none equals Thine nature to remove the stains of sins. Being considerate do whatever deems good for me.

इति श्रीशङ्कराचार्यविरचितं देव्यपराधक्षमापनस्तोत्रं
सम्पूर्णम्।

The Devi Aparadha Khamapana Stotram written by
Shri Shankaracharya is concluded.

THE MARKANDEYA PURANA

Markandeya Rishi has narrated a beautiful Purana in a very lucid manner describing the Divine Mother as the Supreme Mother of all the manifestation. Worship of the Divine as Durga is its theme in particular, but the other contents deal with the general characterization of creation, intermediate creation, divine dynasties and patriarches, manvantars and genealogy of the kings, as the norms stand for a Mahapurana :

सर्गश्च प्रतिसर्गश्च वंशोमन्वंतराणि च।
वंशानुचरितं चैव पुराणं पञ्चलक्ष्णम्।।

A Purana is defined as a scripture with five characteristics viz. *Sarga*—creation, *Prati-sarga*—dissolution and recreation, *Vamsha*—genealogies of Divine persons, *Manvantara*—age of *Manu's*, *Vamshanucharita*—geneologies of kings.

The Mahapuranas are eighteen in number :

ब्राह्मं पाद्मं वैष्णवं च शैवं भागवतं तथा।
तथान्यन्नारदीयं च मार्कण्डेयं च सप्तमं।।
आग्नेयमष्टकं प्रोक्तं भविष्यन्नवमं तथा।
दशमं ब्रह्मवैवर्त्तं लिङ्गमेकादशं तथा।।
वाराहं द्वादशं प्रोक्तं स्कान्दं चात्र त्रयोदशं।
चतुर्दशं वामनं च कौर्मं पञ्चदशं तथा।।
मात्स्यं च गारुडं चैव ब्रह्माण्डाष्टादशं तथा।।

1. Brahma 2. Padma 3. Vishnu 4. Shiva 5. Bhagavatam 6. Nardiya 7. Markandeya 8. Agni 9. Bhavishya 10. Brahmavaivarta 11. Linga 12. Varaha 13. Skanda

14. Vamana 15. Kurma 16. Matsya 17. Garuda 18. Brahmanda Purana, are the 18 puranas.

The Markandeya Purana is seventh in the line of Puranas. All the Puranas trace their origin to the Vedic period. So is the case with the Markandeya. This is the excellent and intriguing work of the Rishi, as the subject matter is a nice exposition of a dialogue between Jaimini and Rishi Markandeya which forms the very source of the Purana. The presentation of the dialogue is physical in nature and psychological in theme. 'Why, how and when' thought process occurs in the mind of Jaimini about the curse inflicted on Vapu–a celestial nymph by Durvasa Rishi. It forms the bed-rock of this Purana. It has branched off in various details, stories and parables intervowen together with the fabric of action on the loom of destiny. The birth of four Chātaka birds–all the embodiments of Dharma signify birth, action, rebirth in a cyclic form, as the very concept of 'Samsara'—the world. The sufferings of Harishchandra along with his queen and their son is the story of destination, put forth by the sage Vishwamitra, in order to testify Harishchandras' word of truth. The scenes of hell and the suffering in the hell as a punishment which reflects action and its corresponding reaction. The Alarak's episode deals with the transmigration of soul, followed by the birth of Dattatreya/the Trinity in unified body with triple heads reflecting the power of creation, sustenance and dissolution/merger. The episode of Nagakumars, speak of the relationship between the humans and the Nagas of the nether worlds. The obligation of Shrāddha, an oblation to the Pitris/manes/deceased person reflect a close relationship between the dead and the living.

The Shraddha makes us learn the Gotra system to trace our genealogy to the Rishis. The way is meditation and goal is Yoga, which forms the very basis of ancient psychology to attain the highest, however abstract it could be, is also dealt in the Purana. The episode of Madalsa also finds a beautiful place in this Purana.

The beauty of the Purana is in its narrative power. The spiritual philosophy lies in a long conversation between Markandeya–the Rishi and Kraushtaki describing the secrets of creation, time the eternal, time the serial with respect to Brahma's life duration, the formation of application of the 'Varnashrama Dharma', the genealogy of the Svayambhu Manu, the progeny of 'Daksha Prajapati'-the lord of creation, the description of Jambudvipa–the central earth region of the earth planet, including the description of the rivers, mountains, hills and the birth of Ganga–the sacred of all the rivers, significance of 'Kimpurusha', its relationship with Kubera, the incarnation of Kurma Avatara, the manifestation of Sravochisha and Svārochisha Manus, the description of eight Nidhi–treasures in observance of the Padmini Vidya, the birth of Tamas, Raivata, Chakshu, Vaivasvat and Savarnika Manus and their life span as Manus. All these episodes work as a preamble to the Devi-Mahatmya covering 13 chapters in 700 shlokas. Later covering the detailed description of Manu from 8th to the 13th Manu. The essence of Surya, the birth and glory of Surya as detailed in the Rajyavardhana's episode, followed by the episodes of Dishta's son Nabhaga, the slaying of Kujrimbha by Vatsapri and his marrying queen Mudawati. The stories of Kshupa, Vivimsha, Khaninetra, Karandhama, Avikshita Maruta, king Narishyanta and Dama find place in this Purana, which covers all the essential components of a Purana. The Purana is concluded by its Mahatmya/glorification of the Devi. Devi Mahatmya is the integral portion of the Markandeya Purana. It has given the concept of Motherhood in its exalted form. It is revered as the very fountain head of the Shakti tradition in India. This wonderful sacred text is philosophic in theme, mystic in language, ritualistic in approach and Yogic in practice. All phases of the cycles of the universe are attributed to the activities of Devi Mahamaya. Devi is the life-urge.

श्रीदेवीजी की आरती

जगजननी जय! जय!! (मा! जगजननी जय ! जय !!)
भयहारिणि, भवतारिणि, भवभामिनि जय! जय!! जग०

O *Jaga-Jannani*—the universal Mother! *Jaya*—Victory to thee O Mother of the Universe! Victory be to Thee and Thee! Thou art *Bhaya-harini*—remover of all threats and dreads, *Bhavatarini*—the Mother, who makes the devotees cross the transmigratory world, *Bhava-bhamini*—the Mother, who is the consort of Shiva in the benign form of *Bhava*—the existent one. *Jaya, Jaya*—Victory to the universal Mother!

तू ही सत-चित-सुखमय शुद्ध ब्रह्मरूपा।
सत्य सनातन सुन्दर पर-शिव सूर-भूपा।। 1 ।। जगजननी०

Thou art *Sat-Chit*—truth-consciousness, *Sukhamaya*—the embodiment of higher pleasure and *Shuddha Brahma Svarupa*-the very innate nature and form of Pure absolute Reality-Thou art *Satya*—Truth, Sanatana *Sundara*—Eternal beauty, *Para*—transcendent and the Supreme Queen of Shiva and of *Suras*—Devatas. *Jaya, Jaya*—Victory to the Universal Mother.

आदि अनादि अनामय अविचल अविनाशी।
अमल अनन्त अगोचर अज आनँदराशी।। 2 ।। जगजननी०

Thou art Adi and Anadi—the beginning and beyond beginning *Anamaya*—without any disease and afflictions, *Avichala*—static, without being moved and *Avinashi*—ever existent, without any dissolution. Thou art *Amala*—without any pollution, *Ananta*—Infinite, *Agochara*—invisible in form, Aja without any birth and *Ananda rashi*—the embodiment of absolute bliss. *Jaya, Jaya*—victory to the universal Mother

The tradition in India is to recite the Devi Arti in the native language, by performing Arti—the waiving of the Ghee Dipaks, Dhupa, Agarbatti in the manner of mass prayer.

अविकारी, अघहारी, अकल, कलाधारी।
कर्त्ता विधि, भर्त्ता हरि, हर सँहारकारी।। 3 ।। जगजननी०

Thou art *Avikari*/without any change and mutation, *Aghahari*—the destroyer of all sins, *Akala* and *Kala dhari*/without digits and the possessor of digits or forms. Thou art *Karta Vidhi-Bharta Hari-Hara-Sanghara Kari*—the source of creation, sustenance and destruction. *Jaya, Jaya*/victory to the universal Mother!

तू विधिवधू, रमा, तु उमा, महामाया।
मूल प्रकृति विद्या तू, तु जननी, जाया।। 4 ।। जगजननी०

Thou art *Vidhi-Vadhu/Brahmani*—the consort of Brahma the creator, *Rama/Lakshmi*. Thou art *Uma*—the daughter of *Himalaya, Mahamaya*—the cosmic illusion. Thou art *Moola Prakriti*—Primordial nature, *Vidya*/eternal knowledge. Thou art *Janani*—the Mother and *Jaya*—the Life partner. *Jaya, Jaya*—victory to Thee O Mother of the Universe.

राम, कृष्ण तू, सीता, व्रजरानी राधा।
तू वाञ्छकल्पद्रुम, हारिणि सब बाधा।। 5 ।। जगजननी०

Thou art *Sri Rama* and *Sri Krishna*, and *Sita-Vraja Rani Radha* Thou art *Vanchha-Kalpa-druma*—the celestial tree, the giver of all the desired things, and the destroyer of all the problems, obstacles. *Jaya, Jaya*—Victory to Thee, O Mother of the Universe.

दश विद्या, नव दुर्गा, नानाशस्त्रकरा।
अष्टमातृका, योगिनि, नव नव रूप धरा।। 6 ।। जगजननी०

Thou art Dasha *Vidya*—the great Ten Mothers, *Nava Durga*—the Nine Devis with different missiles, and *Ashta Matrika*—the very source of Eight Mothers. Thou art *Yogini*—ever absorbed in *Yoga* with ever fresh and new formations. *Jaya, Jaya*—Victory to thee, O Mother of the Universe.

तू परधामनिवासिनि, महाविलासिनि तू।
तू ही श्मशानविहारिणि, ताण्डवलासिनि तू।। 7 ।। जगजननी०

Thou abide in *Paradhama*—the transcendental realm and state, Maha *Vilasini*—the great enjoyer Thou art. Thou maketh movement in *Shamshanas*—the cremation grounds. Thou rejoiceth at the frentic death Tandava dance. *Jaya, Jaya*—Victory to thee, O Mother of the Universe.

सुर-मुनि-मोहिनि सौम्या तू शोभाऽऽधारा।
विवसन विकट-सरूपा, प्रलयमयी धारा।। 8।। जगजननी०

Thou art the *Saumya*—the beautiful and superb. *Suras* and *Munis* get *Moha*—intoxicated by Thyself. Thou art *Mohini*-Thou art the fundamental of all what is *Shobha*—the grandeur. Thou art with *Vikata Saroopa*—the frightening from. Thou art the *Dhara*/flow of *Pralaya*—the whole destruction/dissolution. *Jaya, Jaya*—Victory to thee, O Mother of the Universe.

तू ही स्नेह-सुधामयि, तू अति गरलमना।
रत्नविभूषित तू ही, तू ही अस्थितना।। 9।। जगजननी०

Thou art *Sneha Sudha*—filled with affectionate nectar and Thou art the source of *Garala*—the poison. Thou art adorned with *Ratna*—Jewels, also Thou art *Asthitana*—in the skeleton form. *Jaya, Jaya*—Victory to thee, O Mother of the Universe.

मूलाधारनिवासिनि, इहपर-सिद्धिप्रदे।
कालातीता काली, कमले तू वरदे।। 10।। जगजननी०

Thou abide in the *Yogic Mooladhara*, and great *Siddhi*—Perfection, here and hereafter. Thou art *Kamala / Lakshmi* and *Kali*, who transcends time. Grant us *Vara*—boons. Jaya, *Jaya*—Victory to thee, O Mother of the Universe.

शक्ति शक्तिधर तू ही नित्य अभेदमयी।
भेदप्रदर्शिनि वाणी विमले! वेदत्रयी।। 11।। जगजननी०

Thou art *Shakti*/the eternal energy and *Shakti* dhara, who keeps *Shakti* in his own being. Thou art *Nitya*—the eternal, *Abhedamayi*—without any dualism. Thou art Vimla—*Sarasvati, Vani*—Sound, which differentiates. Thous art the personification of *Veda Trayi*—the *Rik-Yajur* and *SamaVeda*. *Jaya, Jaya*—Victory to thee, O Mother of the Universe.

हम अति दीन दुखी मा! विपत-जाल घेरे।
हैं कपूत अति कपटी, पर बालक तेरे।। 12।। जगजननी०

O Mother! We are in misfortune and in suffering caught in the net of misfortunes. We are unworthy sons, we are deceitful but we are Thine Children. *Jaya, Jaya*—Victory to thee, O Mother of the Universe.

निज स्वभाववश जननी! दयादृष्टि कीजै।
करुणा कर करुणामयि! चरण-शरण दीजै।। 13।। जग०

O *Janani*—the Mother! All because of your kind nature, do keepeth the compassionate vigil on us. Thou art *Karunamayi*—the affectionrtely kind Mother! Bestow upon us the getting of grace under Thine feet. Jaya, Jaya/Victory to thee, O Mother of the Universe.

Recite the Vedic Shanti Mantra

ॐ द्यौ शान्तिरन्तरिक्षꣳ शान्तिः पृथिवी शान्तिरापः शान्तिरोषधयः शान्तिः। वनस्पतयः शान्तिर्विश्वेदेवाः शान्तिर्ब्रह्म शान्तिः सर्वꣳ शान्तिः शान्तिरेव शान्तिः सा मा शान्तिरेधि।

यजुर्वेद 36/17

May peace be in heaven, in sky and on earth! May peace be in the water resources and in the *herbs*—botanical world! May peace be around the *Vishva Devas*—the Cosmic forces! May there be peace in the *Brahamanda*—Universe! May there be peace anywhere and extended everywhere! May there be peace and peace alone! May peace come to me!

ॐशान्तिः शान्तिः शान्तिः
Aum Shantih Shantih Shantih
ॐ Peace-Peace-Peace

GLOSSARY

अंश-Amsha—a fraction, portion, part there of.

अक्षत-Akshata—unhurt, uninjured, complete, whole grain without any breakage, used as an article of Puja / worship to Devi during Homa.

अक्षोट-Akshota—a walnut, symbolises four Vedas, as having four seed segments in the walnut. Usually put in the Puja kalasha, according to the Kashmir Puja system.

अग्नि-Agni—sacred fire, a Vedic deity, Agni Homa is the integral part of the Saptashati Homa. Agni Samidha must be of non-fruit bearing tree, dried and seasoned, must be of the size of palm or even size.

अच्युत-Achyuta—firm and not fallen, epithet of Vishnu.

अथ Atha—sign of auspiciousness, to here/now, अ A is immutable syllable, is auspiciousness, a protection and preservation.

अथर्वन्-Atharvan—the name of Rishi, Atharva Veda is the fourth Veda.

अदृश्य-Adrishya—unnoticable, undetected, unseen, invisible.

अध्यात्म-Adhyatma—pertaining to self, supreme self transcending physical life.

अनाहार-Anahara—abstaining from food, as was done by Suratha Raja and Samadhi Vaishya, for being in communion with Devi.

अनुभव-Anubhava—direct realisation, knowledge derived from personal observation or experiment established by experience.

अनुष्टुभ छन्द-**Anushtubha Chandaḥ**—a Vedic metre consisting of four Padas/lines of 8 syllables each, and each shloka consists of 32 syllables.

अनुष्ठानं-**Anushthananm**—doing, performance, and undertaking a religious rite/homa/patha/ recitation.

अन्नमय कोष-**Annamaya kosha**—the gross material body made of food, which is the fifth and the last wrapper of the soul, anything having the material substance. Anna is food. Food is existence.

अपमृत्यु-**Apamritu**—death caused by accidents, natural upheavels, snake bites etc., premature death caused by any negligence.

अपराजिता-**Aparajita**—unconquered, name of Durga, to be worshipped on the Vijayadashmi day, one day after the autumnal Durga Puja is over.

अपराध-**Aparadha**—an offence, a crime, a fault committed. Aparadha kshamapana, requesting for pardoning of the offences, faults during Puja/Homa/Parayana-recitation etc.

अपान-**Apana**—breathing out, Apana is followed by Prana, one of the five vital breaths in the body.

अभय मुद्रा-**Abhaya Mudra**—the position of the fingers and hand, practised in devotion and a signet of security.

अमर-**Amar**—Immortal, Divinity, Devatas, undying Amaradhipati-Indra, the lord of heaven. Amartva-Immortality, the sons of Aditi are Adityas, all of them are Amar/immortal.

अम्बु-**Ambu**—water, same as अप:, Ambuja-lotus Ambunidhi-treasure of waters i.e. ocean.

अरविन्द-**Arvinda**—lotus, arrows of Kamadeva, pronounced as Aurobindo in Bengali. Sri Aurobindo wrote Savitri, to highlight Indian womanhood and made the Vedic prayer Tamsor mā jyotir gamaya, possible through the wit and wisdom of Savitri, to bring back her husband Satyavan back to life.

अर्चना-**Archana**—reverence, respect for the deities, an integral part of Puja, in the Pancha Deva Puja.

अर्थ-**Artha**—is an object, purpose, end and aim, the Anushtham stands for Dharma, Artha, Kāma and Moksha.

अलक्ष्मी:-**Alakshmi**—evil, torture, misfortune, poverty when Mahamaya does not bless, she comes in the form of Alaksmi, as does happen with the Asuras.

अवरोह-**Avaroha**—to descend, a yogic term, music, the descending scale of musical notes.

अश्व-**Ashva**—a horse, a symbolical expression for the number seven, Ashvārohi—mounted on the horses during the battle between Asuras and Devi.

अष्टमी-**Ashtami**—the eight tithi, Durgashtami, the eight tithi of the lunar fortnight in the month of Chaitra and Ashvini.

आ-Ā

आकाश-**Akasha**—the sky, the ether, considered as the 5th element, viz. Prithvi/earth, Vayu/air, Agni/fire, Salila/water and Akasha/ether.

आख्यानं-**Akhyānam**—a speech, declaration, a legendary story.

आचमनं-**Achamanam**—sipping water before religious ceremonies for Atma tattva, Vidya tattva, Shiva tattva and Sarva tattva being invoked with the sipping of water, at the very start of the recitation of the Sapta Shati.

आत्मन-**Atman**—the self, the embodied soul, the living spirit within the body.

आदि-**Adi**—in the beginning, a commencement. Adi is the starting point of time, known as Serial Time, different from अनादि—Time the Eternal. Mahamaya is the Ādya Shakti, Ganesha is the Ādi Deva, Devi is also known as

अनादिनिधना—beyond beginning or end, Adi karana—the first/primal cause of existence is Mahamaya.

आदित्य-**Aditya**—the son of Aditi. Kashyapa had two wives Diti and Aditi. Daityas are anti-divine forces and Adityas are divine/brilliant forces.

आध्यात्मिक-**Adhyatmika**—the spiritual way of life, relating to Supreme self. Adidaivik—relating to Adhideva-caused by fate (pain, sorrow), Adhibhautik is related to physical.

आनन्द-**Ananda**—bliss, joy, pleasing. Sat-Chit-Ananda is the name/attribute given to Brahman. Devi is Anandamayi, Sarvanandmayi—all blissful Mother.

आपद्-**Apad**—a calamity, misfortune and danger. Devi advises the Devatas to remember Her at the hour of misfortune, that is the Divine declaration.

आरोहणं-**Arohanam**—The act of rising, a yogic term to ascend from Múladhara to the Sahsrara.

आर्त-**Arta**—afflicted with sickness and disease. Artanada is a cry of distress, as was done by the Devas, when they were subjected to humiliation by Mahishasura.

आर्य-**Arya**—worthy, respectable personality, a man of noble birth and character, a preceptor.

Aryavarta is Bharata/India—the region from the eastern ocean to the western ocean, between Himalaya and Vindhya range of mountain (Manu II), abode of Aryans.

आर्ष-**Arsha**—belonging to the Rishi, Vedic in character.

आर्ष साहित्य-**Arsha Sahitya**—Vedic literature, all the four Vedas, Vedangas, the Brahmanas, the Upanishads. The Sutra literature, Brahma sutra, Nyaya sutra, Yoga sutra etc. are covered in the Arsha Sahitya.

आश्रम-**Ashrama**—a hermitage, dwelling place of the Rishis, sages, ascetics, a stage or order of religious life as Brahmacharya, Grihastha, Vanaparastha and Sannyas.

Suratha Raja and Samadhi Vaishya introduced themselve to the Medha Rishi in an Ashrama.

आसनं-**Asanam**—a place for sitting offered to the Guru, preceptor, or to the Deity, a well decorated seat.

आहार-**Ahara**—taking of food, Svalpahara-taking of limited food and Nirahara, taking of no food became a criterion for Suratha and Samadhi, during their hard penances in their Sadhana for attaining the grace of Mahamaya.

इ

इच्छा शक्ति-**Ichcha Shakti**—will to do. It was the Ichcha Shakti of Suratha and Samadhi to be in communion with the Devi, as directed by the Rishi. This type of Shakti is stronger than the physical energy. Ichcha Shakti is the mental attitude to accomplish any work. It is followed by the Kriya shakti—act to do.

इति-**Iti**—then said, told, supposed to be spoken by some one, or used at the end of each Sapta shati chapter. Iti is—it is this, as told.

इन्द्रियं-**Indriyam**—power, force, sense organs and motor organs known as Jnana Indriya i.e. and Karma Indriya eyes, ears, tongue, skin and nose and its power of exhibiting action, to some Manas/mind is also the Indriya.

ई

ईश-**Isha**—the lord, the supreme sovereign, Divine self.

ईश्वर-**Ishvara**—the supreme Lord, feminine Ishvari. Ishvara abides in the heart of every being (Bhagvadgita). Purusha and Prakriti are separate powers, but Ishvara and Shakti contain each other.

उ

उग्र-**Ugra**—fierce, ferocious, frightful, violent. Ugrachanda is name of Durga.

उच्चै-Uchchai—Aloft, high, above, upward.

उतप्त-utapta—burnt, heated.

उत्तर-Uttara—being or produced in the north, following subsequent, Uttara charita is the third episode of the Sapta shati, and covers the chapters from 5th to 13th.

उत्पन्न-Utpanna—born/produced, Raktabija would create Asuras of his own prowess-refer shloka 55. II chap.

उदान-Udana—breathing upwards in the Yoga system.

उन्मद-Unmada—intoxicated, drunk.

उद्भव-Udbhava—birth of things in Time the Eternal.

उपदेश-Updesha—instructions given by a preceptor to the disciple.

उत्तम-Uttama—highest, the best among all.

ऋ

ऋच्-Rich—a Vedic hymn, a verse of the Rigveda, the collective body of the Rigveda.

ऋतु-Ritu—A season of two months, commonly reckoned to be six. The Navaratra/Nava Durgas one invoked in the Vasanta Ritu and Sharad Ritu/season.

ऋतं-Ritam—the right and honest thing, sacred custom, A Vedic term associated with Satyam/the Truth.

ऋद्धि-Riddhi—growth, increase, supernatural powers attained through Yoga.

ऋषि-Rishi—An inspired poet or sage, an ascetic. A Vedic Rishi is he, who has visualised the Vedic Mantras, known as Seer. Markandeya Rishi is the Seer of Markandeya Purana. Medha Rishi initiated the Raja Suratha and Samadhi Vaishya with the Namo Devi Mantra.

The Seven Rishis are Kutsa, Atri, Rebha, Agastya, Kushika, Vasishtha and Vyasa.

एक-Eka—one and only one is Devi. She declares that

Ekaivaham, jagatiatra (chap. V, shloka 5). I alone exist in the universe.

ऐ

ऐश्वर्य-**Aishvarya**—sovereignty, supermacy affluence, wealth, the divine faculties of omnipotence, omniscience, omnipresence, as Mahamaya is.

ओ

ओ३म् ॐ ओं-**Aum**—the sacred syllable Om/Aum, uttered as a holy exclamation at the beginning and end of the reading of the Vedas and the Sapta Shati chapters which cover the famous Om Mantra. Shanti Mantra is Aum Shantih Shantih Shantih.

औ

औषधि-**Aushadi**—the herbs which are used in the Sapta Shati Homa, tila-seasame is also medicinal plant the Samidhas used in the Homa are often of mulbery, mango, pipal trees having the medicinal effects.

औष्ठ्य-**Aushthya**—relating to the lip, with it the recitation of the Sapta Shati has been recommended. It should not be mental reciting, hence the movement of the lips are essentially required.

क

कण-**Kana**—a grain, an atom or particle of anything, a very small quantity (Sapta Shati Chap. I, shloka 52).

कबंध-**Kabhanda**—a headless trunk especially, when it retains life.

कमण्डलु-**Kamandalu**—a water pot, used by ascetics. Kamandalu was offered by Brahma to the Devi, as a token of gift to evolve into the Supreme Shakti for the annihilation of Mahishasura (Sapta Shati Chap. II, shloka 23).

कमल-**Kamal**—a lotus, Kamalanayana-Narayana, Vishnu

known as Kamalekshana-having the lotus like eyes (S.S. chap. I, shloka 101), Kamala is also Pankaja-born out of watery mud substance (s.s. 2.29)

कर्ण-**Karna**—the ear, Madhu and Kaitabha sprung out from the karnamala/ear wax of Bhagvan Vishnu (1.68)

कल्प-**Kalpa**—a day of Brahma or 1000 yugas being a period of 430 million years of mortals and measuring the duration of the world, kalpa is one of the Six Vedangas, that which lays down the ritual and prescribes rules for ceremonial and sacrificial acts.

कवच-**Kavacha/kavacham**—the armour, wearing an armour. The Devi/Devatas are at the different parts of the Jiva/embodied soul, the Devi/Devata is invoked in order to protect that particular part of the body. Kavacham affirms the divinity within the human frame.

काननं-**Kananam**—a forest, a grove, bhu/earth planet is filled with Shaila/mounting, Vana/forests and Kanana groves, thus the Kavacham helps a person to maintain his lineage till the earth planet exists (Devi Kavacham 54).

कारणं-**Karanam**—a cause, a reason.

कार्य-**Karya**—what ought to be done, a mode or what is to be performed. The Devi manifests in different forms to help the Devas.

कुंकुमं-**Kumkumam**—Saffron, Kumkum is offered to Devi, Kumkum is cultivated at Pampore area of Kashmir, where Lal Ded/Lalleshvari was brought up. Bilhan has also referred to Kumkum-keshera in his poetic works.

कौमारी-**Kaumari**—the Shakti of Kumara-Karttikeya, reference is available in the Skanda Purana. Kumari Puja/Kanya Puja/Kanjak puja is being done on the 8th/9th tithi of the Navaratra days. The Kumari should be between the age of 2 and 10.

कुशा-**Kusha**—a bridle, Kusha grass is used in every Vedic/

tantrik ritual, the Pavitri grass ring of Kusha is put on the ring finger, and then the rituals are performed.

कृष्ण-**Krishna**—dark, black, dark blue, Name of Bhagavan Krishna the son of Vasudeva and Devaki, the sixteen/ full digital incarnation of Vishnu, the propounder of the Bhagvadgita, the great yogi/Yogiraj Shri Krishna, his chakra/discus is famous, so is his Panchajanya Shakti conch. In the Sapta Shati Krishna, Kali, Yoganidra are the same universal principles.

कौल-**Kaul**—a clan of Kshetriyas as of Kaula Nagari in the south. (1.5)

कौल-**Kaula**—a worshipper of Shakti, according to the Vama Marga, left hand ritual, followers of Kaulachara system of worship.

क्रिया-**Kriya**—the process of action, practices, rites. Kriya Shakti—the motional and intensive form of being at action, power of spirit within the process of performing action.

क्षण-**Kshana**—an instant, moment, measure of time equal to 4/5 of a second i.e. decimal 8 (6.19)

क्षत्रीय-**Kshatriya**—a kshatriya, high caste among the Aryans, also known as Dvijatiya (Manu Smriti 10.4), Suratha was a Kshatriya king, man of power and excellence.

क्षीन-**Kshina**—emaciated, diminished.

कादि विद्या-**Kadi Vidya**—the Tantrik knowledge of the seed. Syllables, starting from the first consonant क k. It is the first guttural letter, there are 3 kutas/section of the Kadividya. Yantra Puja in done through Kadi Vidya and हादि-Hadi vidya, which start from ह-H.

कुञ्जिका स्तोत्रम्-**Kunjika Stotram**—Kunja is a place over run with plants, or overgrown with creepers. It is a fennel-flower seed. Kunjika in Kashmiri language-very close to Sanskrit language is a key, and in pronounced as

KUNZ. Kunjika Stotram in the seed key of the Sapta Shati, therefore no branches/limbs of the Sapta Shati is recited. Kunjika Strotra shlokas is highly mystical in content. No Stuti is offerd to the Devi, through the Kunjika stotram, because the seed is the very self of the Devi. It is potent with supreme perfection.

ख

खट्वाङ्ग-Khatwanga—a bed-stead, a hammock, a club or staff/stick with a skull at the top considered as the weapon of Shiva, the Khatwanga is one of the missiles of Mahamaya.

खड्ग-Khadga—khadga is sword, the Dhyana Shloka of the first episode starts with the word khadgam, Asi, Kripana are the forms, of khadga, Durga is always manifested with Khadga.

खुर-Khura—a hoof, Mahishasura would over turn the earth planet with his hooves, when he would assume the form of a Mahisha/buffalo.

ग

गज-Gaja—an elephant, Gajaraja is Airavata, the vehicle of Indra. Indira Shakti Aindri was mounted on the Gajaraja, with her thousand eyes (8.21)

गायत्री-Gayatri—a Vedic metre of 24 syllables, Gayatri is the Devi with five faces and revered by all the sections of the Hindu community. The Brahma Sutra/Janeu/ Upavita is the symbol of Gayatri, which is put by the three varnas around their necks. In the ancient past, the girls were invested with the Upavita, but the system is not now prevalent. In Kashmir, the yajneopairt sanskara is performed in 24 hours and the boy is initiated into the Vedic Diksha.

गुण-Guna—A quality, virtue, effect, result, excellence. A property in general with respect to Prakriti/Primordial nature. Prakriti is Gunanidhi, which is embodied and treasured in innumerable ways by difficult combinations of Sattva-Rajas-Tamas, Sattva guna in the mode of height, peace and poise, the quality of Sattva is in Brahma, as he creates, Rajas is mode of desire and passion, related to Vishnu and Tamas is the force of unconsciousness of Sattva which is the inherent quality of Shiva as Rudra.

All the three qualities are inherent in Mahamaya.

गुल्फ-Gulpha—the ankle, the Narasimhi/power of Nrisimha is the presiding deity at the ankle of the devotees. (Devi Kavacham 32).

घ

घट-Ghata—a large earthen water jar/pitcher installed at the Puja Kaksha/sanctum santoram. It is known as the Ghata Sthapana or Kalash Sthapana. The walnuts are put in the Ghata for nine days and all the Pancha Devas are invoked with the Vedic Mantras, Gayatri mantra, stutis, later, on the concluding day the Bahurupa garbha is recited and the water of the Kalasha is sprinked over the assembly, who come for offering Homa to Devi. The Shakti Mantras are also recited. Each one is offered a walnut, as a symbol of the four Vedas.

घंटा-Ghanta—a bell, a missile of the Devi, the third and the last episode of the Sapta Shati, starts with the word घंटा शूल हलानि etc. (Dhyana shloka)

च

चक्र-Chakra—the wheel of a carriage. Chakra of Vishnu, a discus used by Shri Bhagavan Vishnu in cutting off the head of two demons—Madhu and Kaitabha, so that Brahma the creater could be released from the grip of those great Asuras. It is also the missile of Shakti.

चरित्र-Charitra—the episodes, three episodes are in the Saptashati.

चण्ड-Chanda—fierce, violent, wrathful, passionate, Chanda is killed by the Devi, as Mahasaraswati. He was the personification of violence. Chanda and Munda were ready to fight with Devi with their chaturangini force.

चण्डी-Chandi—an epithet of Durga, Chandi is attributed with Chanda parakrama-having the wrathful force of Her innate nature to subdue Chanda and Munda, hence became revered as Chamunda Devi (7.27) the Ishtadevi of some of the Kshetriyas.

चण्डिका-Chandika—is an epithet of Durga. Chandika is always commissioned to save the whole universe (4.4) It is the fierce and deadful incarnation of Shakti, for the purpose of destroying the Asuras/Rakshasas/Daityas/ Danavas.

चित्-Chit—thought, perception, intellect, understanding.

चिति-Chitih, the truth perceiving conscious vision and knowledge.

चित्त-Chitta, the essential consciousness of the spirit.

चित् शक्ति-divine power of being, creative self-consciousness.

चेतस्-Chetas—consciousness, chetna is consciousness (5.17)

चैतन्य-Chaitanyam—the supreme spirit considered as the essence of all beings and sentinent things.

छत्रेश्वरी-Chhatreshwari—Devi with Umbrella, who protects chhaya.

छाया-Chhaya—Shadow, reflection, a reflected image.

छिद्र-Chhidra—Pierced, containing holes, a crack, left, the Homa should always be without any defect, so the process undertaken is known as अच्छिद्र, uninterruptedly from beginning to the end उपयाम/upayama made of kushagrass is put on the left ear, to make the Homa complete in every respect, without any obstacle.

छिन्न-Chhinna—cut, chopped. Devi's lion chopped off the head of various Daityas and sucked their blood (6.18)

जगत्-**Jagat**—moving, movable, the whole world was filled with water, when the fight was going on between Bhagavan Hari and Madhu-Kaitabha (1:10 d-101)

जंगम्-**Jangam**—moving, living, movable. The poison referred to in the Devi Kavacham is both स्थावरं, जंगमं, कृत्रिम, Poison got from botanical world, from the reptiles, snakes, scorpions etc, and chemicals. Devi wards off/protects the devotee from all the poison, he who puts on the Kavcham, as told by Brahma (Devi Kavacham 48).

जागृत-**Jagrit**—wakeful, four stages of mind :—wakeful, sleeping, in dream state and transcendent.

जीव-**Jiva**—the embodied soul, existing entity, the individual/personal soul, jivatman–individual soul enshrined in the body.

जुहूं-**Juhum**–a crescent shaped wooden/copper/brass ladle used for pouring the sacrificial ghee into the Homa/Agni/(Vaikritikam Rahasyam 34).

ज्ञान-**Supreme knowledge**—direct knowledge, without the use of any medium, direct perception. ज्ञानी, blessed with the divine knowledge, but Mahamaya puts them in delusion, this axiom is the basis of dialogue between Medha Rishi and Surath-Samadhi (1:55, 56).

ज्वल ज्वल, प्रज्वल-प्रज्वल-**Jwala Jwala, Prajwala Prajwala**—to blaze, to burn, to glow, to shine, in all the direction, to burn up, a few syllables of the Siddha Kunjika Stotram Mantra.

तत्त्वं-**Tattvam**—true state of condition, true or essential nature, the nature of human soul or the material world as being identical with the supreme spirit. Agni, Vayu, Surya are the triple Tattva/elements, as being the integrated form of the three episodes of the Sapta Shati, respectively.

तंत्र-**Tantra**—a loom, a thread, principal doctrine, a theory of Yantra and Mantra. Also known as the Agama Shastras.

तांत्रिक रात्रि सूक्तम-**Tantrik Ratri Suktam**—is the part of the first episode of the Sapta Shati. It consists of 15 shlokas and one utterance as ब्रह्मोवाच-so said Brahma, Tantrika is a follower of Tantra doctines, also known on as Shaktas.

तापस-**Tapasa**—relating to the religious penances of an ascestic.

तामस-**Tamasa**—quality of inertia, ignorance, darkness, viciousness, a guna of the Prakriti.

तामसी-**Tamasi**—an epithet of Durga.

तिलः-**Tilah**—the seasamum plant, it is mixed with the rice, barley, properly cleaned and offered in the Ahuti. The tila is of two kinds viz, white and black, white sesame is used in the Deva Homa and the black in the Shrādha ceremony of the manes–the deceased persons. It is also mixed with ghee at the time of oblations. After the recitation of every shloka, the Ahuti is to be offered with milk, sesame and ghee. (Vaikritikam 34)

तेजस्-**Tejas**—sharpness, top of the flame, lustre, brilliance, effulgence, prowess, the essence. The fingers of Devi came forth from the effulgence of Arka/Surya/the sun. (2:15)

त्रयी-**Trayi**—the three Vedas taken respectively in the first, second and third episodes of the Sapta Shati. Trayi is triadic understanding of the Rig, Yajur and Samaveda.

त्रैलोक्यं-**Trailokyam**—the three worlds viz. Bhu, Bhuvah, Svah taken collectively for earth, ether and the heaven. (4:23) It is synonym of जगत्त्रय/Jagattraya.

दान-**Dana**—giving gifts

दानव-**Danava,** a titan.

दंष्ट्रा-**Damashtrā**–a large tusk of boar. Devi manifested as Varaharupini with a fierce discus and lifting the earth planet on Her tusk, as being the Shakti of Varaha (11:17).

दीप-Dipa—light, earthen ware in which ghee is put, along with wick and is offered to Devi, by waving light before it.

देव-Deva—gods, these are the personalities and powers of the dynamic divine, देवता is the subject matter of Deva.

देवि-Devi—is the power of the Devas.

द्वीपः-Dvipah—an island, a place of refuge, a division of the terrestrial world.

Bharatvarsha is the portion of Jambudvipa. The number of 'dvips' vary according to different sources, Jambu dvipa in the central one. (see Patha viddih)

ध

धन-Dhana—property, wealth and riches.

धी-Dhi—intellect, understanding, thought.

धूम्र-Dhumra—smoke coloured, smoky, grey, dark, Dhumra lochana Rakshasa was killed by Mahamaya also Chandi killed Shumbha-Nishumbha (6:3)

ध्यानं-Dhyanam—meditation, contemplation. It is said that Jnanam leads to Dhyanam (Bhagvadgita 12.12)

Thirteen Dhyana shlokas are documented in the Sapta Shati. The three Dhyanas are recited at the beginning and concluding of the Sapta Shati Patham/Homa. Every deity has its own dhyana mantra, as visualized by the Rishis. These are the mental representations of the personal attributes of Devi.

न

नमस्-Namas—a bow, salutation, obeisance.

नव-Nava—nine in number, Chandi is Nava Durga in manifestation of Shri Mahakali, Mahalakshmi, Mahasaraswati. Namaskar is bowing and pranama is kneeling down like a staff known as दण्डवत् प्रणाम्. The fifth chapter is the नमस् Namas mantras from shloka number 14 to 80. This is also known as the Devi Suktam (Tantrik), and was taught by Medha Rishi to Suratha-Samadhi.

नाडि /डी-**Nadi**—the tubular stalk of any plant, a tubular organ of the body, a nerve and a vein. Ida, Pingala and Sushumna are said to be the three Nadis Ida–a tubular vessel, one of the principal channels of the vital spirit, which exist in the right side of the body.

Pingala–the eight of 3 tubular vessels, a chief passage of breath and air.

Sushumna–a cord, lying between Ida and Pingala.

नाभि-**Nabhi**—navel, any navel-like cavity, Padmanabha is the epithet of Brahma. Brahma was existent at the Nabhikamal/navel lotus of Vishnu and two great Asuras Madhu-Kaitabha sprang out from the ears of Shri Vishnu/Janardana, and were ready to kill Brahma–the lord of creation (1:68).

निराहार-**Nirahara**—without taking any food, cereals etc.

निष्कला-**Nishkala**—without any digit, supreme existent, abstract, Devi is both Nishkala and Sakala.

निवृत्तिः-**Nivrittih**—ceased, abstaining from worldly acts, dedicated to the supreme way of Nivritti marga, as was the case with Samadhi Vaishya.

नैर्ऋती-**Nairriti**—an epithet of Durga, the south-western direction.

न्यास-**Nyasa**—Placing, putting down, planting, feeling the pulsation through different kinds of Nyasas in the Durga Puja.

न्यूनाधिक-**Nyanadhik**—shortened or made longer less or more, unequal, therefore, Kshma Prarthana is prescribed to please the Devi for any lapse done willingly or unwillingly.

प

पद्मं-Padma—a lotus, the form/figure of a lotus. Arivnda is also lotus.

Devi is seated on the lotus/Arvinda in the Dhyana shloka of the 3rd chapter.

पद्मावती-Padmavati—an epithet of Durga in the 6th chapter Dhyana shloka of the Sapta Shati. Padmavati is Lakshmi.

पयस-Payas—water, milk, पायसं is sweetened rice with milk.

परम-Parma—the highest, the exalted one.

परमात्मन्-Supreme self—the lord of all the souls.

परमेश्वरी-Supreme Sovereign Mother Durga, Mahamaya.

पाठ-Patha—recitation.

पातालं-Patalam—nether worlds, the last of the seven worlds, under the earth planet, said to be inhabited by the Nagas. The seven regions are Atala, Vitala, Sutala, Rasatala, Talatala, Mahatala and Rasatala.

पाद-Pada—the poetic line of a verse.

पाद्य-Padya—water for washing the feet.

पितामह-Pitamaha—a paternal grand father, grand sire, an epithet of Brahma. Markandeya Rishi makes a request to Brahma to disclose the most secret episode, which would be all helping to the humanity and at the same time the spiritual in nature. He addresses him as Pitamaha, thus the Brahma gives him the description of Nava Durgas.

पीठं-Pitham—a seat.

पुराण-Purana—ancient, old, belonging to the olden times ancient or legendary episodes. A Purana treats of five topics known as पञ्चलक्षणानि viz. Sarga, Pratisarga, Vamsha, Manvantara, Vamshanucharitam.

पुरुष-**Purusha**—a male being, the tattva in the Samkhya philosophy, according to Samkhya, it is neither a production nor productive. Kashmiri Shaiva Darshana also enumerates Purusha below Shiva.

पुष्पं-**Pushpam**—flowers, red flowers are prescribed in the Devi Puja, including पाटल, कमल, बन्धूक (rose, lotus and terminalia tomentosa in latin) (12.41)

प्रसाद-**Prasada**—favour, kindness.

प्राण-**Prana**—vital breath, respiration the five Prana, Apana, Vyana, Udana and Samana type of breaths are protected by the Kalyana shobhana (Devi Kavacham 37).

प्राणायाम-**Pranayama**—regulated direction and holding of breath or vital forces, yogic exercise of the Hatha yoga.

प्रत्यक्षं-**Pratyaksha**—real and evident, direct perception through eyes.

प्रवृत्ति-**Pravriti**—the souls evolution into the action, involvement, impetus towards doing actions both mundane and spiritual.

प्रीति-**Priti**—delight of love, with pleasure, pleasantness, "whosoever please me with dedication, and listens to my charitas–the episodes of Saving the Devatas, I do bless them with good health and make them free of all the sins"–says Devi (12:22).

फ

फण-**Phana**—the expanded hood of a cobra or any serpent.

फणि-**Phani**—a hooded serpent. 'Devi is seated on the cobra.

फलं-**Phalam**—fruit, Devi explains herself the glory of the Devi charitam, and the merits thus acquired by the devotees in the 12th chapter of the Sapta Shati.

ब

बंध-**Bandha**—a bond, Durga is the All Supreme Shakti for

keeping this worldly bondage and also she is in transcendental power to librate the devotees and then with Mukti–final release.

बलि-Bali—a sacrifice, oblation coconut is offered as Bali/ sacrifice at the time of Purana Ahuti in the Homa. Brahmans/Vipras, are not allowed to sacrifice an animal (बलि मांसादिपूजेयं विप्रवर्ज्या मयेरिता) Vaikriti Rahasya shloka 28).

ब्रह्मन्-Brahman—the supreme being an impersonal and divested of all qualities and actions, the all pervading soul.

ब्रह्माणी-Brahmani—is the power of Brahma (11:13).

ब्राह्मण-Brahmana—belonging to the Brahmana caste, the first of the four original castes.

ब्राह्मी-Brahmi—is the personified female energy of Brahma, an epithet of Durga. (Pradhanika Rahasya 16).

बीज-Bija—the seeds, Bija mantra is the seed syllables. Nava Durga/Devi is with names and seed syllables. Bija is the source of all creation.

भर्तृ/भर्त्ता-Bhartri—husband, a leader, a supporter. Devi says to Duta/Ambassador of Shumba-Nishumba. "Who would show me down in the battle field, verily, he would be my husband." She did say these words purely to delude Shumba-Nishumbha, so that they would come themselves, to fight with the Devi.

भ

भाग-Bhaga—portion, a quarter.

भुवनेश्वरी-Bhuvaneshwari—the Master Sovereign of the universe.

भू-Bhu—the earth planet, with mountains, rivers, forests, minerals etc.

भोग-Bhoga—passion, desires and enjoyment. King Suratha invoked Mahamaya for Bhoga.

भूत-Bhuta—an epithet of Shiva, as Shiva is known as the Bhutanatha.

भूषित-Bhushita—decorated with, ornamented.

भैरव-Bhairava—terrible, frightful, formidable, relating to Shiva. Shiva is Bhairavanatha, the presiding Ishwara of eight Bhairvas. The Ashta Bhairavas according to the Kashmir Padadati is Anandeshvara, Vaitala, Mangleshvara, Puranraja, Bahukhatakeshvara, Tushka raja, Hatkeshvara and Nandkeshvara all of them are in attendance of Mahalakshmi, at the Sharika Parvat, where Shri Chakra is adored by Hatkeshwara.

Mahasamhara, Astianga, Puru, Kala, Krodha, Tamrachuda, Chandrachuda, Rudranatha, Sometimes other names of Bhairavas are Vidyaraja, Kamaraja, Nagaraja, Svachhandaraja, Lambitaraja, Devaraja, Ugraraja Vignaraja. Shitalanatha is said to be the half Bhairava and Nandakeshvara is said to be the Chief of the Bhairavas. Durga is meditated upon as Sarvajneshwar-Bhairavanknilaya, as she is in the lap of omniscient Lord, who is Bhairava himself (Dhyana Ist chap.).

म

मणि-Maṇi—a jewel, a gem, precious stone.

मद-Mada—intoxication, madness, insanity.

मधु-Madhu—sweet and pleasant, elixer of life, scared wine.

Devi takes Madhu for intoxicating herself for annihilating the Daityas (3:38)

मंत्र-Mantra—A Vedic hymn, addressed to any deity. Mantras are of 3 types–Rik, Yajus and Saman. Rik is recited loudly and is metrical, Yajus is recited slowly, if it is in prose, Saman is meant for chanting, as being metrical, Mantra Siddhi is seaking perfection in the Mantra.

मयूख-Mayukha—a ray of light, lustre, effulgence.

मषी-Mashi—ink, Devi turned black as Ink is.

महामाया-Mahamaya—an epithet of Durga. Medha Rishi introduces Durga as Mahamaya to Suratha-Samadhi. Mahamaya is the Mother-Creatrix of all the Devas. She is the Master architect of the universe. Tridevas Brahma, Vishnu and Shiva can not fathom her fully (chap. iv. 4)

महिष-Mahisha—a buffalo. Devi is popularly known and revered as Mahisha Sura-Mardini Durga. Mahishasura is also worshipped during Navaratra, as he got Sayujya (identity) with Devi.

मातृ रूपा-Matri Rupa—Devi is Matrix-the Mother Spirit of the Universe. She is the universal Mother. She is adored as Mahirupa in chapter 5.

माहात्म्यं-Mahatmyam—Majesty, dignity, glory, Devi Mahatmyam is the glory of Divine Mother which forms a section of the Markandeya Purana. It consists of 13 chapters in 700 shlokas.

मुक्ति-Mukti—liberation through Bhakti/devotion Jnana/ spiritual knowledge and through Karma or right action.

मोह-Moha—loss of consciousness, delusion. Devi puts Moha even to those, who are virtually the Jnanis/men of pure knowledge, who can discriminate between the real and unreal. (1:55-56)

य

यज/यज्ञ-Yaj—Yajna sacrifice, any pious or devotional act. The five yajnas enumerated are : भूत यज्ञ, मनुष्य यज्ञ, पितृ यज्ञ, देवयज्ञ and ब्रह्म यज्ञ, collectively are called the Mahayajnas. Asuras would partake all the share of the Devas in the yajnas, and they would trouble them, and remove them from svarga/their abode. They would get defeat always. Here they pleaded to Mahamaya for their protection, so that they would get the portion of the Yajnas. The battle between the Devas and Rakshasha is on the yajnas as well.

Yajna is performed in Agnikunda, in which Ahutis-sacrifices are offered with ghee, sesame, barley, rice, dry fruits, coconut, betel leaves, etc. as prescribed in the Havana vidhi.

यंत्र-Yantra–that which restrains. Chandi yantra in the abode of Shri Chandi and is written or drawn with the mixture of :

गोरोचनालक्तककुङ्कुमेन, सिन्दूरकर्पूरमधुत्रयेण।

विलिख्य यन्त्रं विधिनां विधिज्ञो भवेत् सदा धारयते पुरारिः।।

Gorochana, Lāksha, Kumkum, Sindur, Karpura and the sweetned things as Ghee, Sugar and honey. Whosoever puts on/wears this Yantra as prescribed becomes identical with Shiva, who has killed Tripurasura. The Yantra must be written, at the midnight of Amavasya tuesday, when the moon would be on the Shatbhisha constelation.

राजन्-Raja—any king, Suratha is the king discussed in the Markandeya Purana, who lost kingdom to his enemies. He was born of the Chaitra Vamsha. Kaulavidhvansinis of Kula dynasty were his enemies.

राष्ट्र-Rashtra—a kingdom, an empire, a reference of Rashtra is in the Vedic Devi Suktam. राष्ट्री सगमनी refers to the whole world, united together. Kashmir scriptures speak of इह राष्ट्राधिपतिः अमुक भैरवः, which means that a particular Bhairava is the presiding deity of that region.

रुद्र-Rudra—Dreadful, terrific, frightful, an epithet of Shiva.

ल

लक्ष्मी-Lakshmi—Goddess of fortune, prosperity, wealth auspiciousness, Mahalakshmi is the presiding Deity of all the Devas/Devis. She is verily, Mahamaya–the Supreme Mother.

ललिता-Lalita—is the benign Mother. She is adored on the

fifth day in the bright fortnight of Ashvina month/ September. Lalita abides in the heart (Devi Kavachm).

व

वज्रं-Vajra—a thunderbolt, a missile of Indra. Indra presented thunderbolt to Devi.

वनं-Vana—a forest, wood, jungle, thicket of trees, Medha Rishi was in his Ashrama/dwelling place in the jungle, and the King Suratha and Samadhi Vaishya approached him to tell their tales of their sufferings and misfortunes. Tapovana is a place for austerities under the sun, in a jungle.

वह्नि-Vahni—fire, igniting.

वासंती पूजा-Vasanti Puja—starts from 1st Navaratra in Chaitra.

वैश्य-Vaishya—the third caste among Hindus. Samadhi Vaishya attained Mukti, after great penances. He prayed along with Surath Raja, with the bijamantra of Devi suktam.

व्रत/व्रतं-Vrata—a vow, vowed observance or austerity. A devotee of Durga is to act according to the Vratas as prescribed in the Puja.

श

शक्ति-Shakti—power, energy, force. Shakti is the innate power of Shaktiman, the possessor of Shakti.

एकैव शक्तिः परमेश्वरस्य भिन्ना चतुर्धा व्यवहार काले।

पुरुषेषु विष्णुः भोगे भवानी समरेच दुर्गा प्रलये च कालीः।।

One unified Shakti is of the sovereign supreme Lord, but in executing the activities, She becomes four fold. She is Vishnu/Vaishnavi Shakti in the Purusha the male principle of the universe, She is Bhavani, when to be enjoyed in the mundane world, She is Durga in a war, and assumes the role of Kali, when there is complete annihilation. Shakti is verily, Durga. Shakti is one of the missiles of Devi Durga. Every Devata has his own Shakti. A fine description is given in the triple Rahasyas.

शक्र-**Shakra**—Indra, who lauded Devi, as described in the 4th chapter of the Sapta Shati.

शंख-**Shankha**—conch-shell, making of the sound through a conch is considered auspicious during Navaratra days.

शास्त्र-**Shastra**—a precept, scripture, sacred treatise the Durga Sapta Shati is the Shastra of the Shakti worshippers known as Shaktas.

शैल-**Shaila**—A mountain, the daughter of the king Himavan is Shailaputri, the first Nava Durga, told by Brahma. श्री-Shri is auspiciousness, affluence. Shri in the prefix of the sacred text Durga Sapta Shati.

ष

षष्ठं-**Shashtam**—the number sixth, the sixth Nava Durga is Katyayani, the daughter of Rishi Katyayana. Shadkona is also the abode of Mahalakshmi, where the Bindu/dot represent the Shakti–all pervading energy.

स

संवाद-**Samvada**—a dialogue. All the Puranas are based on the Samvada between the disciple and the Rishi. Medha is he Rishi and Suratha-Samadhi are the disciples and the Samvada is on Mahamaya, the existence of Mahamaya, the nature of Mahamaya.

सगुण-**Saguna**—with qualities of Sattva, Rajas and Tamas. All the incarnations of Durga are with attributes names and forms.

सत्त्व-**Sattva**–Being, existence, substance, a natural property or quality, a characteristics.

समिधा-**Samidha**—wood used as fuel in the Homa.

सरस्वती-**Saraswati**—the goddess of speech revered as Sharada in Kashmir, the residing deity of Kashmir. She in the Shakti of Brahma. Saraswati is the ocean of knowledge. All the shastras/scriptures are manifested in Saraswati. She is Arya, Bharati, Bhasha as well (Rahasya of the Saptashati).

सिद्धि-Siddhi—perfection, accomplishment, Siddhidhatri is the 9th in the line of Nava Durga.

सिंदूर-Sindoor—red lead applied on the forehead of Devi.

सृष्टि-Srishti—creation, the creation of the world, the existence of properties.

स्फटिक Sphatik—a crystal, quarts. Three dimensional Yantras are carved/embossed on the crystals.

ह

होम-Homa—offering oblations to Devi, by throwing ghee into the consecrated fire. For Sapta Shati Homa, the recitation is done ten times. 1/10th of the recitation is done at the time of Homa.

ह्रीं-Hrim—is the lajja bija of Devi. Hrim is modesty. In the Navarna Mantra, Hrim is followed by क्लीं, which is the emotive force of the Shakti of Life urge. Hrim is the Primal triangle of the Chandi Yantra. Hrim is the Bija Mantra of Bala Tripurasudari. Shri Bala is adored at the Balahama at Kashmir, where Devi's abode is in the four Devadaru trees. Hrim is one of the phonemes of the हादि विद्या, which start from ह H alphabet.